Beyond Fundraising

New Strategies for Nonprofit Innovation and Investment

SECOND EDITION

For Lisa —

KAY SPRINKEL GRACE

With appreciation and respect —

Kay Sprinkel Grace
11/14/07

WILEY

John Wiley & Sons, Inc.

The AFP Fund Development Series

The AFP Fund Development Series is intended to provide fund development professionals and volunteers, including board members (and others interested in the nonprofit sector), with top-quality publications that help advance philanthropy as voluntary action for the public good. Our goal is to provide practical, timely guidance and information on fundraising, charitable giving, and related subjects. The Association of Fundraising Professionals (AFP) and Wiley each bring to this innovative collaboration unique and important resources that result in a whole greater than the sum of its parts. For information on other books in the series, please visit:

http://www.afpnet.org

THE ASSOCIATION OF FUNDRAISING PROFESSIONALS

The Association of Fundraising Professionals (AFP) represents 26,000 members in more than 170 chapters throughout the world, working to advance philanthropy through advocacy, research, education, and certification programs. The association fosters development and growth of fundraising professionals and promotes high ethical standards in the fundraising profession. For more information or to join the world's largest association of fundraising professionals, visit *www.afpnet.org.*

2004–2005 AFP PUBLISHING ADVISORY COUNCIL

Linda L. Chew, CFRE, Chair
Associate Director, Alta Bates Summit Foundation

Nina P. Berkheiser, CFRE
Director of Development, SPCA of Pinellas County

D. C. Dreger, ACFRE
Senior Campaign Director, Custom Development Systems (CDS)

Samuel N. Gough, CFRE
Principal, The AFRAM Group

Audrey P. Kintzi, ACFRE
Chief Advancement Officer, Girl Scout Council St. Croix Valley

Robert Mueller, CFRE
Vice President, Hospice Foundation of Louisville

Maria Elena Noriega
Director, Noriega Malo & Associates

John Wiley & Sons:

Susan McDermott
Editor (Professional / Trade Division), John Wiley & Sons

AFP Staff:

Jan Alfieri
Manager, New Product Development, AFP

Walter Sczudlo
Executive Vice President & General Counsel

Dedication

This second edition of *Beyond Fundraising* is dedicated to my ever-expanding belief in the power, potential, and importance of philanthropy. If anything is to change the world so it is a better place for the next generations—for my beloved grandchildren and those who follow them—it will be the philanthropic acts, unwavering dedication, and generous investments of visionary people. May this book be an inspiration to those who will make those investments and to those who will guide and steward them.

In that spirit, this book is also dedicated to the memory of my friend and colleague Phillip Desbrow, a creative and visionary pioneer for philanthropy in Australia, whose courage, joy, and tenacity embraced the true spirit of giving and characterized his creation of the Leukaemia Foundation of Australia. His legacy is far more than a single organization.

Contents

Preface to the Second Edition

Going "beyond fundraising" is no longer the startling idea it was when I prepared the first edition of this book. I remember receiving calls from perplexed colleagues across America who questioned my use of the word "investment" in the subtitle—particularly in the same breath with my rhapsodic approach to philanthropy. Then, and now, I see no contradiction. And, over the last eight years, the idea of "investment" has been the take-fire trend in philanthropy. Social investment is understood, sought, and welcomed. Volunteer "tool kits" for campaigns list "investment opportunities." The idea is no longer dissonant with the values premise of giving. Indeed, we have seen how the investment approach to community building through philanthropy has been the formula for increasing success.

The other principle I advanced in 1997 was the need for innovation. I stand today even more firmly behind that notion. Where I see success both in the United States and abroad, it is because of innovation and creativity. Where I see failure, it is from the opposite behavior: unwillingness to change, the creation of internal and external silos within organizations and the sector, the resistance to taking the best ideas from the business sector and applying them to our organizations. The absence of shared vision in communities and organizations continues to inhibit the realization of our sector's power.

We are in many ways the most powerful sector. Not the largest, but the most powerful. Rooted in community trust and meeting clear and pressing needs, we make a profound difference and, in the words of Robert Payton, "ease human suffering and enhance human potential" as no other community resources can. Our universities, schools, hospitals, arts and cultural centers, human and social services organizations, environmental services and other organizations help determine the quality of society and life and advance the ideas of personal and community fulfillment. Unhampered (we hope!) by government's layered bureaucracy and freed from the pressure of purely bottom line accountability of corporations, we can be nimble as we assess, respond, reach out, accomplish, evaluate, grow, and have an ever-expanding impact.

Revising *Beyond Fundraising* has given me the gift of time to step back and reflect on our sector today, at the beginning of the twenty-first century. I remain bullish. Recent economic twists and turns and global events caused some small setbacks in fundraising but strengthened our sense of mission. And that, after all, is what we are about.

BEYOND FUNDRAISING: WHAT IT MEANS

Because this book is written for volunteers and staff people working in a sector that is based on the measurable success of its fundraising, the title may seem odd. The principle is simple: To go beyond fundraising, organizations must do *more* than fund raise. They must also:

- Believe and practice the principle that development is a comprehensive process of which fundraising is a pivotal part.
- Understand that development is the series of deliberate activities by which we involve and retain funders in a donor–investor relationship with our organizations.
- Give up the idea that "development" is synonymous with fundraising, the series of approaches to prospects and donors (direct mail, phone appeals, fundraising events, fall campaigns, winter campaigns) that yield revenues and donors from year to year. Development is much bigger than fundraising. And fundraising alone is not enough.

THE NEED CONTINUES TO GROW

The need for the nonprofit sector to go "beyond fundraising" and to understand and apply development principles continues to grow. Increased competition among funders and a higher level of sophistication among donors have changed the nature of philanthropy, development, and fundraising.

Once viewed as needy institutions to which people gave out of a sense of obligation, nonprofits now find they are being evaluated against different and tougher criteria based on their own financial and community performance and their capacity to meet donor needs. This shift in expectations requires organizations to practice the longer term process of *development;* to go *beyond fundraising.*

THE ORIGIN OF *BEYOND FUNDRAISING* AND THE BASIS FOR ITS REVISION

Although I have written several other books since *Beyond Fundraising* was first published, this book embodies my core beliefs and has been a continuous writing project for nearly a decade. Many of its principles and strategies formed the basis of my first workshop when I began my consulting career. "Putting Away the Tin Cup" was, starting in 1987, my "signature seminar" and was given for more than a decade to boards of trustees, other volunteers, and staff members of hundreds of not-for-profit organizations in the United States, Canada, Australia, the United Kingdom, and western Europe.

The primary purpose of "Putting Away the Tin Cup" workshops was to raise the comfort level of board and staff members as they raised money for nonprofit organizations. It challenged old notions about fundraising. The workshop introduced new concepts and new ideas that allowed organizations to position themselves more positively in their communities. These same ideas have also guided my consultation with scores of organizations, have grown out of and informed my more than 20 years of teaching with The Fund Raising School and other organizations, and they are the basis of this book. Importantly, I was a good listener at those sessions. I heard what volunteers and professionals were saying about the obstacles and challenges they faced, and I was heartened by their successes. I still am. And in my own volunteer work with Stanford University and serving on boards of other organizations, I saw things from the perspective of the busy volunteer who wants time, tools, and training and to be a partner for change.

Over the years, my insights have sharpened to reflect the experience and needs of the thousands of volunteer and staff leaders with whom I have worked. These leaders have represented many places and institutions: public television across America, a national domestic violence policy and education organization headquartered in San Francisco, a university in England, a library in Paris, a leukemia foundation in Australia, a land trust in California, a technical institute in New Zealand, a preparatory school in Seattle, a medical center near Los Angeles, a children's hospital in Canada, a church organization in Sweden, opera companies in New York and San Francisco, orchestras from across America, and museums in New Mexico, Colorado, and France. Although these organizations differ, and the volunteer and staff roles vary, the concerns expressed by clients and workshop attendees have many common threads:

- Fear of rejection and a reluctance to be viewed as beggars as their principal reasons for feeling uncomfortable with fundraising
- Worry about asking too often, and wanting strategies for asking more effectively
- Weariness of the relentless cycle of fundraising activities that they must pursue to generate revenues for their programs, and wanting to know how to cultivate and retain donors by building relationships with them
- Enthusiasm about their organizations and their own capacity to make a difference in their communities
- An eagerness to learn how to position their organizations in their communities as the constructive, vital, and important organizations they are

PRINCIPAL CONCEPTS

The principal concepts in this book are the "aha" ideas that have been formed from these common needs and tested in these workshops and consultations. To go beyond fundraising, nonprofits need to:

- Position themselves as organizations that *meet* needs, not as organizations that *have* needs

- Know that a gift *to* them is really a gift *through* them into the community

- Focus on program *results,* not just on financial *goals*

- Remember that the process of asking and giving is based in shared values

- View our organizations, and encourage others to perceive them, as vital additions to communities whose services and enhancements must be balanced and strong

- Engage nonprofit leaders and donors at all levels in a process that will convert them to donor-investors, committed to a long-term relationship based on shared values and vision

- Position all contributions to nonprofit organizations as social investments and all contributors as donor-investors

- See the process of revenue generation and constituency involvement as a much larger, inclusive, and energizing process called development.

THE BREAKTHROUGH INNOVATION

Organizations try new fundraising tactics but do not see they still lack the development framework that will create a lasting base of donor-investors. They seek innovative strategies for increasing revenues: the event no one has tried, the cleverly (or emotionally) crafted mailing that will survive the 15-second initial exposure test and result in a first-time gift, or hiring the best possible "fundraiser" (as they persist in inappropriately calling development professionals). None of these strategies is enough to bring a consistent and stable base of funding to an organization without the principal innovation that goes beyond fundraising and inspires development.

The innovation that has the most singular impact on all organizations with which I have worked during my years as a consultant and teacher to the philanthropic sector is this: an innovation in attitude about the entire *fundraising* process, one that properly puts it into the larger context of *development* and *philanthropy.* Only then does true innovation occur. Attitudes shift. One person wrote, after a particularly rigorous workshop, "I will now feel proud to ask for money for our college."

Innovation requires a willingness to set aside old ideas. A certain entrepreneurial spirit must prevail; there must be a willingness to risk. Courage is fundamental and confidence is critical. The enviable mystique that surrounds those who are successful at fundraising is nothing more, in my experience, than the attitude those individuals have about the process:

- They know it is hard work, but it is worth it.

- They are passionate about the causes for which they are raising money.

- They come not as beggars, but as individuals offering others opportunities to invest in the future of their communities.

- They are the catalyst for converting citizens to donor-investors in the organizations whose values they share.

- They find the process to be satisfying and gratifying.
- They see it as a way of involving people known and unknown to them in organizations that are making a difference in their communities.

For those who have made the attitudinal breakthrough, an invitation to provide or ask for funds for an organization is an invitation to invest or ask others to invest. Each act of giving and asking is an honor, a privilege, and a trust. We can measure the impact of gifts by the results the organization achieves.

I have watched as board members, other volunteers, staff members, and the curious who are not yet involved with philanthropy realize that asking for money is an invitation to invest. I have heard their stories of the transforming nature of both asking and giving, and I have listened as they relate their increased stakeholder role. I have seen what happens to attitudes about fundraising when people realize that the investment goes beyond the organization: that an investment made in a not-for-profit organization is an investment in the community. And I have seen donors transformed through their investments and their sense of involvement and belonging.

These are powerful realizations. We have been helped in the last five or more years by an increased awareness in the media of our power and impact. No longer relegated to page 16 of local and national newspapers and magazines (or to the local or social section), news of philanthropic investments is front page. Magazines understand us now as a vital social force. We can hope that the old days of disparaging and ignorant coverage of our sector are gone. When I reflect on the way things were, I remember how one of the high-circulation magazines wrote about major university capital campaigns that were under way a decade ago. The article was titled "America's Top Universities Go Begging in Style." I hope we have gone beyond that image. We do not come from weakness. We have no need to beg. We come from the strength of our visible impact, convictions, and values. The perception of our sector is changing, and with it the demands for accountability and disclosure are rising. We are meeting those demands, but still have a distance to go. We need to promote ourselves more vigorously as the "public benefit sector" and as public benefit organizations—leaving the label of "charity" to the more appropriate description of the purpose for which we have been created and the reasons that people give (charitable intent, charitable purpose). "Charity" connotes to far too many people organizations that are needy. We are not needy: we meet needs. Even "nonprofit" has its drawbacks—what other sector of the economy describes itself by what it is not? (Peter Hero, CEO, Community Foundation Silicon Valley)

As we go ever more deliberately beyond fundraising into systemic development practices that focus on the donor, the community, social investment, and innovation, we will ensure that the new perception of our sector holds.

A Book of Tested Ideas

In 1997, with the first edition, I drew on my experience for the observations, strategies, and tips in this book. As I reviewed them in 2005, the vast majority remained true.

Clients and audiences change, the marketplace has definitely changed, donors are vastly different, and yet the core principles set forth in this book have lasted. Perhaps it was ahead of its time.

My passions about the not-for-profit sector are many. These passions include ethics, values, creativity, innovation, professionalism, board participation, pride in the sector, partnerships at all levels of an organization and in the community, and a keen sense of mission and vision. My passions are characterized by an absence of cynicism and an abundance of enthusiasm. Recently a colleague asked me if I am always "so optimistic." My answer was yes. I remain optimistic about the power and potential of philanthropy and the great gains we are making in America and around the globe. The late John W. Gardner, both mentor and friend to me, instructed us that as leaders we must offer hope. That has always been my goal.

A Book for Volunteers and Staff Throughout the World

This book is for both paid and unpaid leaders and servants of the not-for-profit sector throughout the world. Its principles are universal. Many philanthropic practices and strategies, long a part of the American tradition, have been implemented with vision and success in countries throughout the world. Cross-cultural adaptations will of course be made by those in other countries implementing American ideas—even by our close neighbors and colleagues in Latin America and Canada—but the kernel of each strategy is sound.

As my work has expanded globally in recent years, so has my perspective and understanding of both common and divergent practices.

Certain ideas and issues have distilled with force and clarity. Although the primary focus of the sector will always be on ways to generate more revenue, it is a growing reality that fundraising is not enough. Experienced organizations know this is so. In practice, unfortunately, they too often ignore this crucial truth. They do not take the time to do the kind of relationship building that is indispensable for long-term development. Even if they cultivate their prospects well—building relationships as a prelude to asking for the gift—they often fail repeatedly at donor stewardship. In a recent survey done to assess factors that would lure lapsed members back to public television, one woman responded: "They would have to show me that they know me."

Stewardship is not just diligent monitoring of the way in which a person's gift is invested or used. Stewardship is the process of involving and appreciating donor-investors and bringing them into a deeper relationship with the organization after the gift is made. Stewardship is the most critical development practice. It encourages long-term investment in our sector. The importance of stewardship threads its way through this book, and there is an entire chapter dedicated to it as well.

With business and government unable, unwilling, or ill-equipped to do what we do, we play an increasingly vital role. In a healthy society, nonprofits must provide both initiative and response. We need only reflect on the outpouring of sympathy and support following the 9/11 terrorist attack in the United States and the Tsunami that devastated South Asian and African communities on the Indian Ocean in December, 2004, to see the capacity of people to care. Organizations quickly positioned themselves to meet the desperate human needs of these communities and people responded.

Going forward into the twenty-first century, the philanthropic sector has an opportunity to build stronger communities through boldness, innovation, and new models for action that are based on results, not needs; investment opportunities, not institutional financial urgency. As observer, counselor, teacher, constructive critic, and confidante, I have been privileged beyond expression to work with staff and volunteer leaders who are truly making a difference in the health and stability of our society. This book is for you, and for all those who wish to bring innovation and investment to their communities.

KAY SPRINKEL GRACE
March 2005

Introduction to the Second Edition

The changes that have occurred in philanthropy since I began writing *Beyond Fundraising* in 1995 and since it was published in 1997 are substantial. We have seen the American economic bubble swell and burst and begin to grow again. With the unprecedented growth in wealth came an extraordinary and generation-spanning awareness of the power of philanthropic investment.

Cover stories during 1999–2001 in *Business Week, Forbes, Success, Fortune* and comprehensive articles in publications as far-reaching as *The New York Times* and *The Economist* focused on the awakening of widespread interest in ways for individual social investors, through philanthropic gifts, to help meet the needs of their communities. The "golden age" of philanthropy came upon us: Vast wealth was created, and the "new philanthropists" (whether in their 20s or their 70s) recognized the satisfying return of this new kind of investment. But that satisfaction was based on new demands on the sector. Accountability and transparency became the requirement for philanthropic investment, and public benefit corporations (nonprofits) not only began providing more information but began offering more opportunities for donor involvement in their organizations.

Astride this fast-paced movement toward greater and deeper investment, which was influenced in tempo and leadership by young entrepreneurs impatient to change the world, our sector rode a roller coaster. Eager for the investment, some organizations agreed to conditions that placed undue strain on their management and boards, and often led to disappointed investors. "Venture philanthropy" became a hotly debated topic, and standards for performance by organizations in our sector were scrutinized.

Parallel with these changes in the United States, our active exportation of philanthropy to far-flung corners of the world flourished. Many of our great social entrepreneurs and investors—Bill and Melinda Gates, George Soros—saw with keen vision that globalization was not just about economics. It was about our interconnectedness with people and our common quest to improve education, eradicate poverty, and eliminate both chronic and catastrophic diseases. Our greatest social export, philanthropy, found new markets—driven by new freedom in eastern Europe, a rising epidemic of AIDS in

Africa, a persistent need for social services and change in western Europe and Asia, and a growing recognition in all parts of the world that governments were never again going to fund community organizations at the level many countries had experienced in previous centuries.

As social investors demanded more oversight of their investment and wanted more control over their wealth while considering to what philanthropic purpose it would be put, another change occurred. Community foundations in the United States burgeoned, swelled by donor-advised funds and supporting organizations that provided investors with advice from experienced philanthropic managers while offering them the desired control over their money and their investments. This movement, too, resonated with resourceful people outside the United States and the community foundation movement took fire. WINGS (Worldwide Initiatives for Grantmaker Support), in its May 2004 "2004 Community Foundation Global Status Report," highlighted these developments among others:

- 42 countries have community foundations, up from 36 in 2003, and 8 more countries are seriously considering forming foundations.

- 1,120 community foundations exist worldwide with another 142 in active formation.

- 37.5 percent of these exist outside the United States, up from 34 percent in 2003; Canada and the United States together represent 47 percent of the foundations, down from 52 percent in 2003.

- Between 1999 and 2004, the number of community foundations outside North America grew by 176 percent.

- The first ever global meeting of community foundation practitioners from around the world gathered at the Community Foundation Symposium in Berlin in December 2004 — a "recognition of how far the global movement has progressed in just ten years."

The truly remarkable aspect of all of this is that the core philanthropic interest, curiosity, and energy of the late twentieth and early twenty-first centuries persists in spite of the fact that we have, since September 11, 2001, been coming to grips with enormous changes in our economy, our sense of personal safety, and the overall stability of the world. The War on Terrorism will most likely be the long war that politicians and scholars predict, and no country is immune. From the United States to Indonesia to Spain to parts of the former Soviet Union, the threat of terrorism spawns fear and distracts people from the dreams and vision they once had.

The influence on philanthropy of the focus on global safety has been visible in measurable ways (giving was down in the United States in 2002 as philanthropy did not respond with its usual safety net to the economic downturn and loss of public funding) and in the most subtle ways (people feel a sense of "psychic poverty" that causes even those who maintained or have now restored their wealth to feel less inclined to give it away). In the hierarchy of human needs that Abraham Maslow listed so many decades ago, we slipped down from the lofty perch of focusing on self-actualization and began to worry about food, shelter, and other basic needs as the economy continued to remain volatile even late into 2004. Philanthropy is recovering, and we need only reflect on the overwhelming response from individuals around the world to the plight of those who endured and survived the Indian Ocean Tsunami of December 2004 to see that once again, when confronted with extreme human tragedy, people give as much as they can to help others.

So what is philanthropy's role today? And how does this book—whose ideas seem remarkably resilient even 10 years later—become your travel guide for the uncertain and sure to be surprising road ahead?

Philanthropy's role today is, for me, more important than ever. When kept free of politics and based on a mission-secured vision of meeting community needs and enhancing the quality of life, what greater safety line can we grasp in these uncertain times? Community problems do not recede in times of international crisis, they grow. And while our sense of helplessness or powerlessness may rise during times of threats to health, security, or social conditions, what better way to restore our sense of being able to have an impact than by investing in organizations that are making a difference in lives nearby or those far away? And there is no more effective way to bridge both of these worlds: last year for Christmas I "gave" my grandchildren goats, chickens, and rabbits through Heifer International, animals that are now providing food and industry for families in Asia. Even the smallest children in the family understood the message of philanthropic outreach.

Beyond Fundraising has sold more than 12,000 copies in its first edition and is still selling well. This new edition incorporates the new context for philanthropy, but the solid principles that have led to this book's success have not been altered. The values basis for philanthropy is still the only basis; mission is still a reflection of why an organization exists, not just what it does; the importance of regarding donors as donor-investors (or just as investors) has grown; vision is still the star to hitch your wagon to; and the basic strategies for annual and capital fundraising are little altered. There is one entirely new chapter, the two chapters on planning in the first edition have been combined into one, and the remainder have been revised, edited, and updated.

In the near decade since I began the first writing of this book, my insights and career have changed along with the philanthropic environment. The variety of clients has not changed (arts and culture, public broadcasting, secondary and higher education, health and human services, environment, and religion), but I now spend more time speaking and writing. Annual exposure to hundreds and hundreds of people who work or volunteer in philanthropy has spiked my passion for what our sector accomplishes. Increased work with boards of directors has increased my respect for the changes we may have to make in governance policies and procedures to accelerate access by investors. My work with public broadcasting, now an all-consuming role that will continue for the next several years, is a microcosm of each of our communities here in the United States, integrating arts, education, health, public affairs, and other programming with community partnerships that are based on the reality that broadcasting is not *what* public broadcastings does, it is *how* it does what it does. It has provided me a window into all of your worlds, and the view is one of potential realized and potential that remains. My work internationally has likewise given me a new filter—to see the life cycle of philanthropy reflected in its entirety in a classroom at the International Fundraising Congress is a rare gift—and I become less a teacher than a facilitator; less a pedant than a midwife. When I hear how an African gentlemen who administers a trust has the responsibility to spend $1 million a year on children orphaned by AIDS—and he then tells me there are 1 million children in his country already orphaned—I am humbled by the wisdom he must use to make his decisions. And when I see how philanthropy is soaring in Australia and New Zealand, I am thrilled by the changes I have seen since I first went there 11 years ago to speak at a fundraising conference.

We work and volunteer in a remarkable sector. Our capacity to build long-term relationships will be critical to its further impact. These relationships must be based on an understanding between organizations and their donor-investors of their mutual responsibilities. It needs to be a relationship based on partnership, respect, and vision.

This book is about building those relationships. It is about strengthening the platform from which you operate so that you can truly soar. Filled with concrete examples and tips, it is also abundantly stocked with philosophical and strategic morsels that will satisfy your appetite for something more meaningful than what is in your in-box—but something that will help you deal better with the pile of daily duties.

Your role is great and important. Our sector represents hope for the future.

CHAPTER 1

Values: The Context for Philanthropy, Development, and Fundraising

Philanthropic behavior is motivated by values. Board member commitment to serve and ask, volunteer enthusiasm, and a donor–investor's sense of satisfaction in giving are based on an implicit search for ways to act on their values. Matching volunteer, funder, and institutional values is a critical practice of successful nonprofit organizations.

PHILANTHROPY DEFINED

Historically, philanthropy was "love of mankind" or (later) "love of humankind." Its manifestation, particularly in the United States where philanthropy has been practiced consistently since the earliest years of its founding, has included voluntary offerings of time, money, and goods to meet the needs of communities. The popular perception of philanthropy that grew during the nineteenth and twentieth centuries focused on major financial support of wealthy individuals like Andrew Carnegie, John D. Rockefeller, and in more recent times, David and Lucile Packard, and Bill and Melinda Gates. Recognizing that philanthropy is historically and in practice much more than giving money, a newer definition of philanthropy was developed decades ago by Robert Payton in his book *Philanthropy: Voluntary Action for the Public Good* (1988): all voluntary action for the public good. Based in values, voluntary action includes giving, asking, joining, and serving.

We know by observation and experience that people do not engage in philanthropic activities on behalf of organizations[1] whose values they do not share. The match between the values of our organizations and the values of our constituencies predicts the level and intensity of the response a donor or volunteer will have to a cause.

To be innovative and attract long-term donor investment, organizations in the nonprofit sector must define and apply their values. They should organize their internal systems, marketing and communications programs, and community outreach to maximize the understanding of, response to, and impact of those values. Only then can organizations attract supporters for the right reasons and engage them in a lasting and mutually satisfying relationship.

THE ROLE OF VALUES IN THE NONPROFIT SECTOR

Complex and passionate values are often present at the creation of nonprofit organizations. Wishing to act meaningfully on those values, people create and help sustain organizations that meet a variety of community needs. They do this through their philanthropic gifts of time and money.

- Parents whose son or daughter dies of a drug overdose channel their grief into constructive options for other young people by creating a counseling program at the local high school.
- Because she values independent living and the dignity deserved by all individuals, the grandmother of a developmentally disabled young adult helps create a center for her grandchild and for others with similar disabilities.
- The American Library in Paris is founded by the father of an American poet-soldier killed in World War I.
- The families of leukemia patients in Queensland, Australia, help create an apartment building where they can stay while loved ones receive hospital treatment.

Other motivations may be less personal but are no less value-driven.

- In the United States, the movement to keep local and regional symphonies strong and accessible is based in values: Community leaders realize that live music performances enhance the attractiveness of their communities, that children and adults need opportunities to appreciate and learn about music, and that local musicians need to play together as an orchestra.
- Public school districts in California and other parts of the United States, constrained by cuts in tax revenues, create private foundations to raise money to support jeopardized school programs. They are the invention of parents motivated by values of quality and opportunity in education.
- In Slovenia, citizens ensure the creation of a children's services agency to replace vital healthcare programs previously provided by government.
- In countless public broadcasting stations across America, staff and volunteers wishing to sustain the independent and local media voice in their communities create and implement new ways for their members to invest at higher levels in support of programs that advance classroom education, children's programming, arts and culture, civil discourse, lifelong learning, and other basic needs of their communities.

Global philanthropy is growing exponentially. Throughout the world, communities are responding to changes in traditional sources of services and revenue by creating and sustaining support for museums, schools, social and human service agencies, and other vital institutions. Motivated by their own values and the values of their communities, leaders are taking on new roles as community builders.

While inspired by America's globally unique nonprofit leadership, international philanthropic organizations are developing their own unique character, reflecting the values and needs of the communities they serve. The growth of the ResourceAlliance, a global philanthropic organization headquartered in the United Kingdom that provides conferences and training to professionals throughout the world, is a stunning sign of this growth. From a single, modestly attended annual International Fundraising Congress held 25 years ago in The Netherlands, the organization has grown to sponsor not only its annual conference with capacity attendance but regular regional conferences throughout the world (Africa, South Asia, Latin America) that are dedicated to increasing the capacity of organizations in these countries to meet pressing community needs through appropriate and effective philanthropy. The rapid spread of philanthropy is an unexpected benefit of globalization, accelerating needed change by drawing on resources and ideas that are readily shared among caring people and organizations.

DEVELOPING A VALUES-BASED APPROACH

Systems and structures that successfully attract volunteers and funding rely on the identification of common values. These values become the foundation of all outreach and operations. Board members, other volunteers, and staff know intuitively why they are committed to an organization or to the voluntary sector, but most have not articulated the values that attract them. Nonprofit leaders, who may be stymied in their ability to convey a fresh or convincing message asking for community support, benefit from revisiting the core values of their organizations as a first step in addressing their mission and marketing. The results of such an exercise are heartening. Renewed motivation is often immediate, and there is reaffirmation of founding or sustaining principles. They take the first step toward values-directed outreach to the community that can result in revitalized support. One venerable organization, preparing for a campaign to coincide with its 150th anniversary, engaged board and senior staff in a "deep-dive" session that identified their core values. Two outcomes were important: (1) the sense of unity that came from the realization of the extent of their shared values and (2) the ease with which these identified values formed the basis for an entirely new marketing program.

Whether an organization is long-established and looking for a current perspective or new and looking for a solid basis on which to construct its outreach, the identification of values is a significant first step.

Identifying Values

Values orientation is outward. It requires organizations to replace their windows with mirrors and identify those aspects of their beliefs and practices that will link with the needs of the community and the values of their existing and potential constituencies. In organizations that are evolving from a focus on the needs they have to an emphasis on the needs they are meeting, this can be a difficult step. Used to conducting community outreach and fundraising based on internal financial needs, they require some coaching to transcend old habits and focus on the core values that can attract and retain like-minded people.

Values vary among organizations and donors. Here are some examples of core values expressed by staff and volunteers in organizations during sessions conducted to discuss the values that motivate people to give to and serve their organizations:

- A YMCA: youth, leadership, families, community, health
- An arts education organization: creativity, expression, learning, opportunity, family involvement
- A children's services organization: safety, health, care, concern, families, healing, opportunities
- A medical center: healing, continuum of care, excellence, compassion

Some will argue that the values which drive some people to support highly visible arts, cultural, and educational organizations are self-serving: recognition, opportunity to mingle with the rich and famous, or prestige. These motivations should be viewed without criticism and as opportunities for exploration of other values. A person's motivation for giving an annual or capital gift, as long as it is within the ethical and values framework of the recipient organization, should be the starting point of a relationship. Over time, the initial WIIFM (What's in it for me?) motivation can be converted to a desire to work together with an organization to make a difference in an area of mutually perceived importance.

The identification and nurturing of the values that people bring to their initial interaction with an organization are the first steps toward going beyond fundraising.

Organizations that position themselves as facilitators rather than judges create opportunities that bring people into a larger understanding of the impact of their involvement. Many initial gifts, given in response to peer pressure during an annual or capital campaign, can, with patience and the application of good listening skills, be not only renewed but grown when the donor's values are uncovered and matched with the values of the organization. While some gifts should not be accepted, and your organization should have policies that indicate sources or purposes that are inappropriate, most volunteers and professionals are wise enough to know when donor motivation is inconsistent with the mission of the organization and could lead to a compromise of the institution's values. Such instances are quite rare, and these gifts are almost always rejected. Many years ago, Yale University returned a $20 million gift to the donors. The gift had come with a string attached: The donors wished to influence the curriculum in the academic area for which the gift was designated. Yale's commitment to the integrity of its curriculum development process prevailed. In another instance, an environmental organization rejected the offer of a gift from a corporation whose purpose was counter-value to the mission of the nonprofit.

EXHIBIT I.I   INTERRELATIONSHIP OF VALUES-BASED PHILANTHROPY, DEVELOPMENT, AND FUNDRAISING

Philanthropy

Based in values

Development

Uncovers shared values

Fundraising

*Provides people
opportunities to
act on their values*

A Model of Values-Based Philanthropy, Development, and Fundraising

Mastery of the interrelationship of values-based philanthropy, development, and fundraising is a critical achievement for organizations seeking innovative and powerful ways to position themselves in their communities. Exhibit 1.1 shows how these three functions operate as one seamless context for donor development. The integration of these functions is the primary catalyst for going beyond fundraising.

Understanding the Model

The largest element of this model is philanthropy, as redefined by Payton and others. It is the context in which development and fundraising must be set.

Most nonprofit volunteer and staff leaders, introduced to the bigger idea that philanthropy is all voluntary action for the public good, not just gift-gathering, immediately grasp its role as a larger and more exciting framework in which to plan and set priorities. The challenge to old ways of thinking comes even more forcefully in understanding the difference between *development* and *fundraising*. In a survey administered as part of a video teaching guide by the BoardSource (formerly the National Center for Nonprofit

Boards), the majority of participants indicated that "development" was just a "nicer way" of saying fundraising. This model illustrates why that is not true.

This three-part model distinguishes between development and fundraising and places these functions as embedded in philanthropy. It separates the process of development from the activities of fundraising and assigns each a different function within the values-framed structure.

The model has three elements: philanthropy, development, and fundraising.

Philanthropy: Based in Values

Philanthropy is the largest part of the model. It is based on the belief that philanthropy is directed by values. The research of Payton and others has verified this conclusion. We do not give to, ask for, join, or serve those organizations whose values are inconsistent with our own. At the most altruistic, this motivation draws people into a rewarding involvement with organizations that are advancing and strengthening basic community and individual values. At the other end of the continuum, there will be those whose initial motivation is WIIFM (What's in it for me?). These initial motivations (recognition, enhanced community position), as discussed previously, can be grown over time into a deeper understanding of *mutual* benefits for donor and organization.

Because core values are broad (e.g., dignity, independence, excellence, compassion, quality of life), they permit access to organizations by a wide range of donors with differing needs and perceptions. Messages can encompass all or one of these values. Values also cross boundaries from one organization to another. Those who value families or health or safety will find several organizations in a community in whose work they can invest. This reduces the sense of competition among organizations and focuses instead on the importance of fulfilling a values-centered community mission that may be acted on by several institutions.

Two Institutions: Common Mission, Common Values

In one community, two organizations working with women and their children who had experienced domestic violence combined their efforts in one community campaign. An emergency shelter and a transition housing/job training program conducted a joint fundraising campaign one year under the mutual banner of "breaking the cycle of violence." An advertising agency provided high-quality pro bono print and electronic public service promotional materials, and a well-respected county supervisor was the keynoter at the campaign kickoff. The two organizations shared more than $75,000 in contributions from the joint campaign. Each organization also conducted its own fundraising activities that year, separate from the joint campaign but reflecting the common mission. Community awareness of the issue of domestic violence was heightened by the joint campaign, and response to the individual agency campaigns reflected this as well. The public service announcements were timeless in their production and appeal, and still are seen occasionally on the local television station. The two organizations attracted new donors who identified with their shared values and renewed existing donors who saw with fresh clarity the importance of breaking the cycle of violence.

Translating Philanthropy: In Conveying Values, the Mission Is the Message

The invitation to participate as a donor-investor or volunteer in values-based philanthropy is best offered through a mission statement that reflects those values. Many nonprofit organizations have succumbed to the pressure of people who are uncomfortable with statements that incorporate values or emotions and have created mission statements that are "corporate," describing *what* the organization does, rather than *why*.

To embark on successful values-based philanthropy, development, and fundraising, it is very important to have a mission statement that states *why* the organization exists. It may also say *what* the organization does, but the function (what) should be secondary to the purpose (why). One major donor to a midwestern public broadcasting licensee parsed a model mission statement and observed that a good one combines the "users' emotions with the station's (or organization's) functionality." An astute observation with application far beyond public broadcasting.

What Mission Statements Should Say and Do

Nonprofit organizations exist to fulfill community needs. People do not give time and money to organizations because organizations *have* needs; they give because organizations *meet* needs. In that spirit, we know that a gift *to* an organization is really a gift *through* the organization: It is an investment in the community. These are the two key premises for going beyond fundraising.

Mission statements that describe only the *function* of an organization need to frame that function with the *purpose: Why* does an organization exist? What need is being met? Although some values are present in a statement of what an organization does, the core values that will ignite interest are more boldly expressed in a statement of why the organization exists. The Fundraising School, a program of Indiana University's Center on Philanthropy, has generated the seminal work in values-based mission statements. Its basic course materials include numerous examples of statements that answer the question "Why do you exist?"

Two Examples of Values-Based Mission Statements

Over the years, certain organizations have framed and used mission statements that are powerful invitations to invest. Vector Health Programs of Eureka, California, which specializes in procedures for repairing severe injuries to hands, developed one nearly 15 years ago that, although no longer in use, remains a stunning model. Its executive director at that time, Karen Angel, prepared the statement as part of a workshop exercise. Her initial mission statement, which was a description of Vector's services, was challenged as not answering the "why" question and lacking an expression of core values. In response to the question "Why do you exist?" she wrote:

> *Next to the human face, hands are our most expressive feature. We talk with them. We work with them. We play with them. We comfort and love with them. An injury to the hand affects people personally and professionally. At Vector Health Programs, we give people back the use of their hands.*

The statement went on to describe *how* Vector restores the use of people's hands. The board chair, hearing this statement the first time, was moved to tears. She said she had not realized, until then, just why she was involved. The mission statement had intersected with, and revealed, her values of full participation in life, love, work, and play.

In another example, Yale University School of Medicine positioned this values-based mission statement as the lead to its case materials for a capital campaign conducted nearly three decades ago, when the scientific world was in the beginning of the explosion of knowledge about genetics. Like Vector's mission statement, time has not tarnished the luster of this strong example of an excellent mission statement:

> *We are in the midst of one of the most profound intellectual revolutions of all time, the revolution in the biological sciences. Its implications for understanding life processes and for combating disease are boundless. Yale is in the forefront of this revolution.*

Succinct and potent, this brief statement reflects values of excellence, innovation, and involvement, and invites those who share those values to participate in the campaign.

A recent example (October 2004) comes from public broadcasting. WVIA in Pittston, Pennsylvania (western Pennsylvania) has drafted this new mission expression:

> *People change and lives improve when powerful ideas confront us. WVIA is a regional catalyst, convener and educator, using media, partnership, ideas and programs to advance the best attributes of an enlightened society.*

Getting Comfortable with Expressing Values

It is not enough to have values. To attract those who share them, values must be expressed. If organizations are reluctant to present a values-based mission statement to an increasingly critical and pragmatic public, they still should go through the exercise of identifying their core values and incorporating them into a written expression. The statement they develop may be for internal use only, but its presence will serve to inspire and motivate those who must engage others in institutional advancement.

Organizational reluctance to create and publish a values-based mission statement is puzzling. A look at most American and international advertising shows how emotions and values are used for commercial gain. Makers of automobiles, soft drinks, food products, cleaning goods, ice cream, insurance, health plans, and other consumer goods are not at all reluctant to use values language and benefits in their marketing. A nonprofit's mission statement is not an advertisement, but it is used to attract potential donors and volunteers in the way an advertisement is used to convince the consumer to purchase a product or service. As reflected in the three mission statements just quoted, there is room for modest expression of emotion in nonprofit mission statements. This emotion is anchored by values and is never excessive or offensive. Most nonprofit organizations have an emotional basis to their origin and impact: To deny this in a mission statement or other materials seems oddly contradictory to purpose.

An advertising executive offered himself as a constructive critic of his alma mater's series of fundraising mailings. He cited an overintellectualism that did not ignite any memories or emotions for him. He admonished the university's development staff to evoke the images that stirred nostalgia, a key value among alumni: the smell of a campus grove after a rain, the sound of the stadium at a football game's halftime, the taste of coffee hastily drunk between classes and with friends. His ideas were incorporated into the next year's mailings, with positive results.

Creating a Values-Based Mission Statement

Creating a values-based mission statement is not easy, but it is important to do. The embodiment of values in a mission statement can inspire other materials including mailings and proposals. It can be a talking point when recruiting volunteers and the core of speeches and presentations. A mission statement cannot be written by a committee, but it will benefit from an initial idea-generating session that involves key constituents. Identifying core values is the first step.

In the previously mentioned session at the 150-year-old institution, each person wrote down what he or she believed to be the three core values of the organization. The facilitator then asked each person to state one value from their list. After the first round, participants were asked to repeat the process, stating any values on their lists that were not yet on the master list. Duplications arose by the second round, which is why it is important to request just one value from each person at the outset. A side benefit of this process is participant awareness of the degree to which they recognize and share the organization's values.

Organizations will find this exercise very helpful in focusing board and staff on common values. Once these values have been identified, the same participants are asked to complete this sentence: "(Our organization) exists because. . . ." They should be coached that the statements are not to be written using the infinitive form of the verb (to inform, to educate, etc.), but rather as a statement incorporating the values just identified and expressing the reasons why the organization exists. This instruction was the inspiration for the mission statement about hands from Vector Health Programs. Examples help get people started on this new approach to mission statement creation.

These "why" expressions, and the lists of core values, provide the raw material for shaping the first draft of a mission statement. Assign the writing task to an individual with writing skills and a command of institutional history and priorities. Establish agreements regarding the review process and the extent to which the statement will be edited before the writing begins. Many fine, nimble, evocative, and inspiring statements turn into clumsy, inclusive, meaningless, and rambling paragraphs because too many people are given opportunities to whittle and alter the first or subsequent drafts. In one organization, a whole board meeting was devoted to the subtle yet substantial difference between "social *injustice*" and "social *injustices*" as contained in the draft mission statement. The group was divided irreconcilably over the nuance of these phrases, and the mission writing process was blocked.

Once a draft has been approved internally, organizations can benefit from circulating the statement to a select group of donor-investors. This group may include former board members, major donors, and others who will respond to and appreciate being included in this "insider" communication. One organization, testing concepts derived from its mission for use in a capital campaign, received valuable feedback that led it to shape the campaign materials in a slightly different way. The modification created a more broadly appealing message and resulted in participation by a constituency that otherwise might have not been involved.

Accepting and Using Values-Based Mission Statements

Some mission statements, reflecting organizational values and the need the organization is meeting, may never receive endorsement by boards or staff. Instead, leaders may approve and publish a more expository statement of the organization's functions. Although almost always uninspiring, these statements satisfy the need people have within and outside an organization for a mission statement that more closely matches those written for corporations or law firms. It is still prudent, however, to have an expression of the institution's values on hand.

Sometimes a values-based mission statement will be adopted later or integrated into materials not as a mission statement, but as a framework for expressing the organization's purpose. On numerous occasions, organizations have turned to values-driven expressions of their mission when making tough decisions about their future. An organization that operated summer camps for a large religious organization found itself turning toward a statement of values and purpose at a decisive moment in its history. The development director had participated in a workshop in which he was asked to create a mission statement. On his return to his organization, the statement was received negatively. The director kept what he had written, feeling there might be use for it some day. There was. A year later, at a board-staff retreat, the participants were at loggerheads about the direction in which the organization should be heading. Hours of debate created acrimony and dissent. A proposed action was outside the mission according to some; to others, it was the next logical step. The development director saw this as the moment to reintroduce his values-based mission statement to the group. When he finished reading his statement, there was no longer any question about what direction they should take. He had affirmed for each person the basic purpose of the organization and had redirected their focus onto the need they were committed to meet.

Another key aspect of writing a values-based mission statement is to position the values or the need being met as the primary or opening phrase. (This was the case with the Vector, Yale, and WVIA statements discussed earlier.) In this way, people of like values are attracted prior to being introduced to the name or function of an organization. By starting with a description of the need that exists and continuing with succinct and powerful words that tell what the need is and why meeting the need is critical, people who share similar concerns and values are alerted to a deeper purpose. When organizations begin their mission statements with the name of the organization or its principal function, some listeners or readers may tune out before the values or purposes are revealed. When that happens, the opportunity to draw people into the organization's mission may be delayed or lost. The perceived need must be identified first.

It is perhaps apocryphal, but there is a story from Black and Decker that sums up this approach. It concerns the Black and Decker drill and the way in which sales associates are trained to sell it. They are asked, "Why do people buy a Black and Decker drill?" The answer most immediately given is "Because they want a drill." But that is not the right answer. The reason people buy a Black and Decker drill, the trainees learn, is "Because they want a hole." It is the same with nonprofit organizations. People need to see what need the organization fulfills before they will invest in what the organizations does. Just as people only buy a drill if they want a hole, they only invest in organizations if what the organizations provide is something they see as important to themselves and/or the community.

The philosophical mission statement, expressing institutional values, is a fundamental tool for creating a solid constituency and donor development program. It can convey a message that moves people to action and communicates the impact the organization has in the community. It is the context for philanthropy and a fundamental building block for *development*.

Development: The Process of Uncovering Shared Values

The second element of the model is *development,* which functions in the larger context of *philanthropy.* Development embraces, but is not synonymous with, *fundraising.* Often considered a euphemism for fundraising, development is much more. Philanthropy is based in values, and development is the *process of uncovering shared values*—a process that includes their identification, nurturing, and reinforcement through publications, actions, and community impact. It is a process driven by the importance of providing potential and current funders with opportunities to explore and apply these values on behalf of organizations.

Organizations seldom realize the full potential of the development process. Here are some important insights that can be gained with a more inclusive view of development.

- Development is a series of deliberate activities through which organizations involve and retain funders in a donor-investor relationship.

- Organizations that realize the power of the development process regard their new knowledge as the basis for the revitalization of their development and fundraising practices.

- Development is understood as a much larger and deliberate process, characterized by patience and focused on initializing, nurturing, and maintaining relationships.

- Development is the way nonprofits bring their potential and existing donors into an understanding of the impact of their investment on the organization and on the community.

- Development creates *donor-investors,* individual and institutional funders who seek and receive a lasting and dynamic relationship with an organization.

- Development is based on the premise that all giving is a form of community investment, the return on which is the knowledge that those values which the organization, the community, and the donor-investor share are being acted on.

Why Development Must Be a Priority

To be successful at fundraising, it is important to spend a lot of time on the development process. When development is crafted and pursued as the sensitive and systematic process it can be, organizations increase their funding stability.

Those organizations that implement long-term strategies for identifying and developing the match between donor and institutional values, and then focus on developing relationships based on those shared values, are better able to withstand change. They survive, and can even benefit from, shifts in the economy, evolutionary funding patterns, pendulum political changes, and other forces that mar the capacity of some organizations to retain donors. We saw this with the economic downturn of the late twentieth and early twenty-first centuries and in the aftermath of the terrorist attacks on America on September 11, 2001. The pressures on organizations were huge; The environment for raising funds was softer than it had been in decades. Arts organizations in particular suffered as people turned their philanthropy toward what they felt were more "basic" human needs. The institutions that suffered but still attracted investment were those universities, cultural organizations, schools, and others that had a solid base of good relationship-retaining development practices. Unwavering, even in dire times and with an economy turned on its head, these organizations continued their outreach, stewardship, and communication. Finally, the recovery began, and these organizations were the beneficiaries. Donors embraced their constancy.

But for every organization that meets this description and is admired as a pacesetter locally, nationally, or internationally, there are too many others whose annual campaigns flounder and whose capital campaigns, when attempted, are either extended repeatedly to ensure financial success or wither into obscurity without reaching their goal.

The problem is simply this: When development is not a firm and deliberate practice in an organization, when human and financial resources are not deployed toward this vital function, then fundraising ultimately fails.

Defining Development

So what is "development"? Development consists of those often subtle, frequently intangible, and not immediately measurable acts that draw donors and volunteers closer to the organization and more deeply into an understanding of shared values. These acts include:

- A prospect identification and qualification process that engages board, other volunteers, and staff in the regular and willing generation and screening of lists of potential donors and volunteers
- Development of strategies for approaching potential and existing donor-investors utilizing a plan of action based on volunteer-staff resources and donor interests
- Cultivation of prospects and donors through a well-articulated series of activities, mailings, and opportunities based on a strategic cultivation plan to heighten interest and build relationships

- Solicitation of gifts using a donor-centered process that results in the transformation of prospects into donor-investors
- Stewardship practices that engage the donor in a way that is desired and appreciated by the donor and that strengthen the donor's understanding of the extent to which there are shared values with the organization
- Promotion of overall community visibility of the values-based impact the organization is making in the community

Strategic implementation of development practices is the critical prelude to successful fundraising and is the key to growing the relationship after the gift has been solicited.

The exposition and application of these practices is a principal focus of this book.

Fundraising: The Process of Giving People Opportunities to Act on Their Values

Fundraising, within the model presented here, is the vital resource-leveraging function that depends on development and philanthropy for its success. The three elements that have been discussed are interdependent and somewhat circular: Successful fundraising is an outcome of philanthropy and development. Philanthropy and development, which require healthy nonprofit institutions in order to thrive, are dependent on the success of fundraising.

Fundraising, in this model, is *the process of giving people opportunities to act on their values.* If all that we do in development, and all that we understand about philanthropy, is values based, then fundraising is a values-related process as well. Viewed this way, fundraising becomes less formidable and frustrating. It is viewed with less apprehension by volunteers and staff, and its potential as a transforming act for asker and donor-investor is clear.

With this new definition of fundraising, we can put away the tin cup. If asking for a gift is seen as a way to let potential donors act on the things they value, then asking no longer feels like begging.

Asking as Release, Not Pressure

Instead of a process implying *pressure* on the potential donor, asking is understood as a process that implies *release.* If a prospect has been developed appropriately and brought into a relationship with the organization based on shared values and an emphasis on results, not needs, then asking becomes a positive experience for both asker and prospect.

Asking is a values-based transaction and is transforming for the donor. The values of the asker and the prospect are fulfilled when an organization receives a gift that advances, preserves, and protects those programs and results that the asker and the donor value. This is a relatively simple realization, but one that is new for many volunteers and staff who perceive fundraising as an uncomfortable process. It is also a reaffirming realization for those who have not minded the task of asking for money. They will have a broader understanding and sense of pride about the impact of their action.

Fundraising, as presented in this book, is based on these key ideas and on the integration of fundraising with philanthropy and development.

A PARADIGM SHIFT: INTEGRATING PHILANTHROPY, DEVELOPMENT, AND FUNDRAISING

Successful implementation of the three-part model occurs when its elements are integrated into a unified and seamless program. Values-based relationship-building in an organization is based on a belief that prospective funders move from a basic belief in philanthropy to engagement with organizations through development to a need to act on their shared values through fundraising.

This belief has some variations in practice. Most organizations have donor-investors who initially self-identified through fundraising (direct mail, special appeal, memorial/in honor, special event, phone appeal) and then were brought into a relationship that explored and grew their shared values (development) and their passions and concerns for the community (philanthropy). This determination of values and interest that comes after the initial gift inspires future gifts. This is one reason why early and personalized stewardship is critical to the development process (see Chapter 8).

It is important to see the model as flexible and as applicable to relationship-building practices whether donors are traditional or nontraditional in their initial and subsequent involvement with the organization.

Lasting integration of the three parts of the model requires two basic institutional decisions, both of which initiate a major paradigm shift for most organizations:

1. To market the values-based model internally to board members and other volunteers and to program, administrative, and development staff

2. To allocate human and financial resources within the organization to *development* as well as to *fundraising* and to make a commitment to supporting the development process in the institutional plan

Internal Marketing

Internal marketing of the values-based development function is a strategic management practice. Well-advised internal communication regarding the importance and impact of development can make a major difference in the level of institutional support for development. This support is critical to getting broader involvement in development by volunteers and all staff.

Internal marketing is always important, but never more so than when an organization is repositioning itself with a newly integrated and inclusive model for development and fundraising. One key way to accomplish this is through the involvement of the entire team of staff and volunteers in promoting development. An emphasis on values-based development and on results, not needs, instills pride. Program staff and volunteers, encouraged to convey these results to those with whom they interact, become willing advocates for the organization and champions of the development process.

Another important technique is to promote internally the impact of development on the organization: the increase in volunteer and funder involvement and the implications of new or increased financial support for programs. Decades ago one organization, determined to market the importance of development among staff who were skeptical and critical of a process that seemed cost-intensive, was persuaded of the importance of development by a "Good Newsletter" that appeared weekly in employee mailboxes. The "Good Newsletter" summarized community outreach activities, site visits by potential funders, board activities on behalf of the organization, successful foundation and corporate proposals, and regular reporting of revenues from direct and planned gifts. Staff members began to see that positive changes were the direct result of development activities. The same can be done today using intranet applications and by making reports and presentations at staff meetings. One of the key outcomes anticipated for the newly-implemented Major Giving Initiative (MGI), funded by the Corporation for Public Broadcasting and involving 117 public television licensees in the United States, is the creation of a "culture of philanthropy" and an understanding by all staff (from programming to technical support to financial systems) that they are part of the full development team and that every interaction with the public contributes to the eventual success of the MGI. To achieve this outcome, participating stations are conducting full station staff meetings to give everyone an overview of the way in which the licensees are using a new mission, vision, and values platform to increase donor involvement and ensure long-term relationships.

Budget Allocations for Development

Budget allocations for development, not just for fundraising, are critical to implementation of the philanthropy/development/fundraising model. The activation of consistent cultivation and stewardship practices requires allocation of funding for staff, materials, outreach, and analysis. At first, advocates for development may find that these budget allowances are difficult to gain. Fundraising costs, which are measurable and easily understood because of their short-term return, must be complemented with expenses allocated for development. Otherwise, fundraising costs will spiral. Without donor retention and growth of donor-investors, the only recourse is increased activities designed for donor acquisition (direct mail and special events). These are the most costly of the fundraising functions and, although they always will be necessary in a balanced fundraising program, they can be offset only by the growth in larger donor-investors and the involvement of volunteers who will be partners in the development process.

SUMMARY

This three-part model of the interrelationship of philanthropy, development, and fundraising is powerful. And, it works. Since it was introduced in 1997, it has weathered countless applications in hundreds of organizations with the same results: greater clarity around the importance of development, greater understanding of philanthropy, and better results in fundraising. The immediate and lasting impact of this model lies in its implementation. The elements are interdependent and are strongest when integrated with the others.

The chapters that follow are designed to encourage and instruct nonprofit leaders—volunteers and staff—in the implementation of the model and in how to build institutional capacity to go beyond fundraising.

Note

1. Robert Payton, *Philanthropy: Voluntary Action for the Public Good* (Oryx Press, 1988).

CHAPTER 2

Putting Away the Tin Cup:
Changed Attitude, Changed Practices

As a sector, we have gotten better about how we approach people to ask them to invest in our organizations. Seldom, in a personal meeting or phone solicitation, do people fall back on the desperation appeals of the past. However, many of our direct mail appeals and other public communications still rely on presenting ourselves as needy organizations rather than as organizations that meet needs. Adoption of the three-part model of values-based philanthropy, development, and fundraising described in Chapter 1 can move organizations away from the short-term begging syndrome into a much deeper process of donor and institutional development.

Such movement requires volunteers and staff to let go of the idea that fundraising is a *begging* process based on the needs of the organization and view it as an *investment* process based on the needs the organization is meeting. Organizations must believe that asking for funds is not begging for money, but an invitation to invest; not holding out a tin cup, but offering opportunities to work together to meet community needs.

Even those who view philanthropy and development as values-related processes in which they can participate with comfort and pride may balk when asked to fundraise. Whether it is the engagement of a prospective donor in a one-on-one ask, participation in a phone appeal, selling tickets to an event, or writing a letter, volunteers and staff still confess to an uneasiness and a feeling they are carrying a tin cup. It is fundamental to going *beyond* fundraising that organizations first get comfortable *with* fundraising.

WHY THE TIN CUP ATTITUDE PERSISTS:
ASKER, FUNDER, AND INSTITUTIONAL REASONS

Why the Attitude Persists for Askers

The tin cup attitude is tightly bound into the fear of rejection. This fear is the root of most discomfort with the asking process. Volunteers and staff slip into apologetic and begging asking patterns because they fear they will be rejected and they want to cushion themselves for the inevitable response. Subconsciously, they frame their request in a hesitant or apologetic way that conveys their lack of confidence that this is a good investment. ("You probably don't want to give, but I have been assigned. . . . ") After being rejected once or twice, askers feel as if the entire effort is a frustrating foray into an arena where they will be refused. They procrastinate when they receive their assignments. Their resistance to getting involved in fundraising mounts.

This fear of rejection is, without exception, the most voiced impediment to comfort in fundraising. Skilled lawyers, accountants, community volunteers, media specialists, or bankers—all of whom bring talent and experience to boards and committees —readily confess that, when it comes to fundraising, they fear rejection. The signature cartoon for my early "Putting Away the Tin Cup" workshops showed a teddy bear sitting on a sidewalk with a tin cup by his side and a sign that read: "Dumped by a six-year-old for a computer. Please help." Most participants identified strongly with that bear, confessing that is the way they felt when asking for money. They admitted that they lacked confidence that people would want to give and ended up positioning the ask (see Chapter 5) in such a way that it was easy for those being asked to say no. This process reinforced the reality of rejection and confirmed people's fears.

Six Keys to Overcoming the Fear of Rejection

Very few people say they look forward to asking for money. Some say they steel themselves for the process but actually end up enjoying it. They are a curiosity to others.

When probed, people who enjoy success as askers said they:

1. Understand the importance of the need the organization is meeting and the impact a gift will have

2. Feel passion for the organization or project

3. Have adequate information about the organization to feel capable of handling objections

4. Have been given enough information about the prospect to feel knowledgeable about interests and concerns

5. Received effective training or coaching in how to ask

6. Were supported by staff or volunteer leadership with tools including appropriate materials, research, and resources

These six essentials help overcome the fear of rejection and enable volunteers and staff to ask from a position of strength, not weakness. Focus is placed on the need that is being met by the organization, not the organization's needs; it is also on the donor's need to see his or her values acted on by a successful organization. Asking becomes a conversation based on shared values as well as an exploration of how the donor and the organization can combine their efforts to accomplish goals that are important to both.

Training Volunteers and Staff to Feel Comfortable with Fundraising

All six of these strategies for overcoming rejection can be addressed to a major extent through effective training and reinforced by one-on-one coaching. Even if a board members says, "I know how to do this. Just give me my assignments" or a new staff member says, "I've been doing this for years. Just let me get started," it is important that everyone receives the same messages. This is particularly true when an organization is shifting to a values-based development process. Some very experienced volunteers are heavy-handed with the tin cup or other less effective methods of asking. Whether a staff member, board member, or outside facilitator is used for the session, there should be enough new information each year about the organization and the constituency to make the training valuable. A training session of several hours is usually enough time: Some organizations conduct an extended board meeting for this purpose. Sessions should focus on

- The community needs the organization has met (results) and will continue to meet (impact projected for current fundraising goals)
- Organizational priorities (vision and goals)
- The profiles and motivations of key prospects while treating such information with discretion and confidentiality
- Objections that will arise and the appropriate responses (both general and specific to the organization)
- Specific techniques for making the ask (detailed in Chapter 5)

Training sessions should be fast-paced and challenging, energizing and informative. And they should be fun. People should leave a training session feeling like they want to go right out and make their calls. Good training can curb procrastination. The session should be timed so that prospect assignments are ready. People forget the strategies and lose the excitement if there is too much lag time between training and asking.

Why Training Is Essential

Reluctance to participate in development and fundraising often is based on the ignorance a person feels about the process itself. Insecurity about saying the right words, asking for the right amount, closing effectively, following up appropriately, or dealing nobly with defeat can prevent volunteer involvement and effective staff support. No matter how talented professionally in their own fields, board members (with few exceptions) need to be educated in the fundraising process. This is as true for annual campaigns as it is for capital drives.

A training session need not always be called a training session. Experienced volunteers and staff may consider themselves beyond the point of needing a skills session. Training sessions can be called refresher sessions, kickoffs, campaign orientation, leadership orientation, retreats. One organization where training sessions are exceptionally well attended by staff and board members each year refers to the weekend program as their "roundup." People come from all over the United States and internationally for a true refresher course that reconnects them with the mission and each other, reignites their enthusiasm, and sharpens their skills.

Whatever it is called, the training session should have three basic ingredients:

1. Inspiration

2. Information

3. Motivation

Inspiration is provided by bringing board, other volunteers, and staff closer to the mission. This "product demonstration" at training sessions is a key factor in helping askers feel passionate about the cause. A report from a program staff person is not enough. To inspire volunteers and staff, they must be connected directly with the process and impact of the programs. This can be done through:

- A facilities tour to observe the program (if appropriate and possible)

- Personal witness or testimony from someone who has benefited from the program.

Inspiring through Firsthand Presentations

Many organizations structure their training sessions or retreats around presentations by those who have been involved as clients or recipients. One organization had particularly powerful results from using this technique. A community organization, whose primary purpose and activity had been the awarding of scholarships from funds provided by another foundation, found itself challenged by that foundation to raise $3 million in matching funds for child care scholarships. The community organization was very apprehensive about its ability to raise that amount of money, and most of the board members felt very uncomfortable about asking. The energy for development and fundraising increased only slightly over time as new board members were recruited who had experience in fundraising.

The turning point came at a board retreat. Three parents who were recipients of the kind of scholarships to which the matching funds would be directed were invited to share their stories and their gratitude. As the board, other volunteers, and staff watched and listened to these parents, the true mission became apparent. A young mother with two children explained how the assistance for child care had enabled her to finish school and start her own business. A young man who had left south-central Los Angeles with his son in search of new opportunities was able to go to college because he had after-school care for his son. His nine-year-old son told of his pride in his father, adding that he and his dad were both "getting As in school." An older immigrant woman, formerly a domestic worker and now a bank teller, described how the scholarship funds had also provided care for her children so she could return to school. The inspiration provided by these stories exceeded anything the staff could have provided with mere descriptions of success. Suddenly the impact of the child care scholarship program was apparent: not only on these individuals, but on the community. The campaign stepped up its pace with new commitment.

Information

Information also builds confidence in volunteers and staff. Inspiration ignites, but information sustains. Although it is important to engage the heart, it is just as important to satisfy the left-brain needs of those who will ask, or be asked, for support. Information should be clearly presented, documented with statistics, and include financial as well as program material. The use of visual aids to understand budgets, income sources, program demographics, community involvement, program impact, and other key "talking points" is important. Some people, when confronted with budgets, annual reports of income and expenses, campaign reports, or other financial data, respond with the "MEGO" syndrome: "Mine eyes glazeth over." Help these people internalize this information by providing visual aids that explain. Pie charts and bar graphs can explain a great deal. For some, a narrative is also helpful: "Last year, boosted by the gift from the community foundation, we increased our service units by 27 percent and were able to attract 42 percent more funding from other community funders."

Types of Information

Information is more than financial. Program information gives people something to talk about with their prospects. Be sure it is accurate, easy to understand, free of jargon, and accessible. Fact sheets are good tools. Print them in 14-point type so askers can glance at them easily during a presentation in person or on the telephone. When preparing the information for a training or orientation session, the organizer should be familiar with the prospect base and anticipate what information will be requested. There is nothing more discouraging for a volunteer than receiving a series of questions from a potential donor for which no answers have been provided. One eager solicitor, calling on a prospect for the renovation of a community cultural center, was stumped with his very first question: "Tell me, just how many square feet is the current center, and how large will it be after the expansion?" Because the prospect was a developer, that question was very important. His curiosity should have been anticipated. Remember, it is also helpful to equip askers with a list of possible objections and the appropriate responses. Everything should be done to build the confidence of askers.

During the information session, the steps in the actual solicitation process are introduced, reinforced, and either demonstrated by several willing volunteers or practiced by everyone at the session. These steps are presented in Chapter 5.

Motivation

Motivation is the third element of training. What motivates people to be an advocate for an organization is a feeling of confidence that their efforts will be valued and appreciated, and will make a difference. This part of the training is locked in when program or administrative staff convey to the development staff and volunteers how critical their efforts are to the capacity of the organization to meet community needs. For example, with hospital foundations, chief executive officers (CEOs) can have a tremendous impact on volunteers by just being at the training session. If they also provide a state-of-the-medical-center presentation and show the impact of contributed income on certain programs, it is particularly effective. Hearing that news from the CEO reinforces the sense of worth that staff and volunteers feel they have to the organization and is highly motivational. The same is true for all organizations: Those responsible for development and fundraising are motivated by hearing from leaders about the impact of their efforts.

Each of these three aspects of effective training sessions is important. They can be blended, alternated, and fashioned into a smoothly sequenced program that is appropriate to the organization, the time frame, and the skills and expertise of those attending.

Although training will not entirely cure the tin cup tendencies of those who are asked to ask, it will contribute substantially to their understanding of the value and importance of their role. They will begin to develop a new attitude toward the process (see Chapter 5).

Why the Tin Cup Attitude Persists for Funders and Institutions

In spite of work with volunteers and staff to help overcome their concerns about asking, tin cup fundraising is still practiced regularly by organizations around the world, most frequently in donor acquisition. Here is the paradox: Organizations attract people with messages of obligation and desperation, and then try to convert them into donor-investors. Why not use the same message from the beginning: that an investment in the organization is an investment in a community that the donor cares about; that the organization embraces key community values; and that it is a robust financially sound institution?

The lingering tin cup attitude within organizations is based in the belief that organizations have needs that individual and institutional funders must meet if the organizations are to survive. Although this is true in the strictest sense, the attitude has a dangerous implication: that nonprofit organizations are dependent on these funders in a more or less *one-sided relationship* and that fundraising therefore requires a supplicant posture. This attitude leads to language that insults the integrity of philanthropy (begging, arm twisting, messages of desperation) and has two problematic implications:

1. It can lead funders to believe that nonprofit organizations always should appear "needy" rather than successful: inadequate facilities, inferior office equipment, budgets that do not permit donor development activities, and other visible or subtle symbols of continuing institutional needs as the basis for giving.

2. It can lead nonprofits to believe that giving is an "obligation," and there is no need to develop dialogue or relationship with donors. It is an attitude of "you owe it to us because we are in this community." That approach may work for a while, but it does not build a long-term sense of loyalty or involvement and is the antithesis of the concept of voluntary investment. Public television in the United States currently is grappling with this issue, and successful repositioning has begun.

These outcomes block the necessary synergy between nonprofit organizations and community investors that is required for them to continually grow and address changing needs. The benevolence of funders, if conveyed as a one-sided relationship in which the funders are strong and the organization is dependent, becomes a block to the natural maturing of the nonprofit and its potential for being perceived as an agent of change in the community. This eventually impedes the ability of the organization to attract long-term donor-investors capable of making transforming gifts.

A Paradox

Ironically, one-sided donor relationships are encouraged by one of philanthropy's kindest motivations, the desire for people to help those who are in need. The need to put away the tin cup is often challenged by this paradox: *Can* we put away the tin cup, or do funders want the nonprofit sector to continue to present itself as an array of needy organizations dependent on community support? Much donor education is required if the nonprofit sector, particularly human services organizations, is to be perceived differently.

As mentioned in the previous chapter, a connotation of the word "charity" tends to perpetuate this problem. Rooted in biblical heritage, as a concept applied to the nonprofit sector, charity often implies a "handout" and an image of the wealthy helping weak organizations survive. Although "charitable giving" and "charitable intent" are the legal and historic framework for philanthropic gifts, being called a "charity" connotes something quite different. In the United States, Peter D. Hero, president of the Community Foundation Silicon Valley in San Jose, California, has led a movement to shift the way nonprofits identify themselves. He and others advocate "public benefit sector" as a more appropriate description than "charity." Hero's principal argument is that the nonprofit sector is the only one that describes itself by what it is not. Think about it. Nonprofits need to get away from identifying ourselves as charities if they are to be viewed as equal players in the increasingly difficult game of keeping communities strong.

Funders increasingly view nonprofit organizations as *vehicles* for accomplishing efforts of mutual purpose. They recognize that investments in nonprofit/public benefit corporations are really investments in the community: Such corporations are the vehicles through which they accomplish change. The new philanthropists have to see nonprofits as successful, sturdy, and progressive institutions that act on their behalf before they will invest. They want to see institutions as good *investments* for the stability of the community. Their influence is spreading as philanthropy finds itself needing to be more accountable about "returns on investment (or ROI)." Companies have been created on the shirttails of heightened interest in community investment whose business plans are based on quantifying a donor-investor's return on philanthropic investments. One such company, Capital Strategists Group from Smyrna, Georgia, is based on what it calls an Organizational Value Proposition, a compilation of many distinct community impacts, integrated into a comprehensive demonstration of an organization's value as a business entity, an assessment of negative social outcomes avoided, and service delivery savings. Today's business climate has been cited as the driver for donor-investors wanting nonprofits to position themselves in a different way.

WHY INDIVIDUALS AND INSTITUTIONS MUST CHANGE

The evidence is clear. When fundraising is positioned as begging, both the asker and the organization lose credibility in the eyes of the potential donor. Desperation replaces dreams as the focus of the transaction, and the excitement of investing in an organization whose services are fundamental to the quality of the community is lost.

To go beyond fundraising, nonprofits have to assume a posture of pride regarding themselves as worthy investments. Then, if requests for funds are turned down, it is not the rejection of the *asker,* or even necessarily the organization: it is the rejection of the *need* the organization is meeting. It is simply not a priority for the person being asked. This leaves the door open for repositioning the need as a priority for the prospect or identifying another interest or motivation of the prospect that will provide better access for presenting the funding opportunities.

A NEW VIEW OF FUNDERS: DONOR-INVESTORS

The idea of the donor–investor has already been introduced. Another description that has caught on in the early twenty-first century is "social investor." Whatever designation is chosen, there are reasons for getting away from the more traditional idea of "donors" or "contributors." Exhibit 2.1 conveys the difference between the ideas inherent in "donation" "contribution," and the power of "investment." Although organizations will continue to use the words "gift," "donation," and "contribution" to describe donor support, all three have implications that can lead to a passive relationship. Only "investment" conveys the dynamism that organizations should seek in donor relationships.

Organizations that are strategic innovators know the importance of putting away the tin cup attitude and embracing fundraising as the logical outgrowth of solid philanthropic and development practices. The key to this change is found in the way these organizations view their prospects and donors and their responsibility to them. They bring their donors into a dynamic relationship beginning with their initial gift. It is a relationship based on values and characterized by continual communication of the return on their investment. Their practices are based on the implicit belief that donors are really *donor-investors,* and that there are two "bottom lines" in the nonprofit sector by which we measure the return on investment:

1. The *financial return,* which reflects solid administrative, program, and fundraising performance and sound management of earned and contributed revenues
2. The *values or social return,* which conveys the impact the organization is making in solving problems, providing services, improving quality-of-life opportunities in the community and acting on its stated values

As nonprofits, we have the opportunity to work with people as they consider the best way to turn their two "portfolios" into community impact: We alone can counsel effectively regarding both their *financial investment* and *social investment* portfolios. We can offer

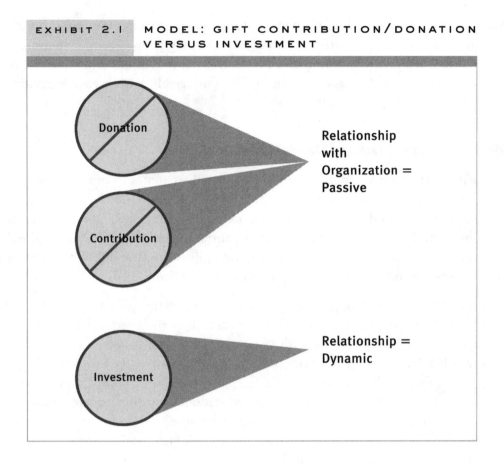

EXHIBIT 2.1   MODEL: GIFT CONTRIBUTION/DONATION VERSUS INVESTMENT

excellent returns for both. Conveying these two bottom-line returns to potential and current donor-investors is one of the best ways to cure the lingering tin cup attitude. Pride grows from a review of the organization's accomplishments and frames the message. Initial or increased investments are sought based on the acknowledged impact the programs are having or will have on those served. Focus is shifted away from the internal fundraising goal and on to the impact of each investment and the value of the programs in the community. Donor-investors are invited to be participants, not just part of the donor base. Their role is dynamic, not passive, as Exhibit 2.1 reveals.

THE INVESTOR RELATIONSHIP

In seeking and engaging donor-investors, organizations are making a commitment to communicate regularly regarding the return on the investment: the impact of the gift, the stability of the organization, and the continuing importance of the need the organization is meeting in the community. They also are making an implicit commitment to continue to find out about the values, interests, and needs of their donors. They are making a commitment to stewardship (see Chapter 8).

Some organizations are reluctant to move from a passive to a dynamic relationship with their donors. They cite inadequate resources (time, money, people) for maintaining donor relationships. They perceive donor-investors as the result of fundraising, not the reason for development. And they also may be more comfortable with a passive relationship because it seems to be what their donors want.

Understanding Prospect and Donor Motivation

Nonprofits must identify and develop three principal attributes in our constituents: *connection, concern,* and *capacity.* It is important to uncover these attributes during the initial development process and to continue to explore them as the relationship matures. When a gift is made as the result of a relationship, organizations are already aware of the depth and direction of these attributes. When a person's gift is the first link with an organization, the meaning and intensity of each of these motivations needs to be verified.

1. *Connection* is the strongest factor in determining the potential for the donor-investor's involvement. Also called "linkage," it is the emotional connection an individual or institution has with an organization, and comes from the person or institution's own experience or connection to a board or staff member. A grateful patient gives to a hospital; an appreciative surviving spouse contributes to a hospice; a symphony receives support because its educational outreach was appreciated by the donor's children; a university receives a gift because of the impact of reconnecting with old friends at a reunion; a patient or student feels gratitude toward those who helped; a close friend serves on the board. It is fundamental to values-based development and fundraising that these connections be identified, cultivated, and nourished. Emotional connections cannot be taken for granted; neither should they be treated with any but the highest regard. The *values return* for donor-investors is closely tied to their connection with the organization. Organizations must be very diligent in their efforts to keep the connections strong and vibrant. In *connection,* the inherent motivations are usually inspired by closely held and strong values.

2. *Concern* is intellectual or thoughtful. A person can be concerned about an organization's mission without being emotionally linked to it. Concern about the hungry or homeless in communities is evidenced among those who have never experienced those conditions. A corporation or individual invests in the local arts programs not out of passion for that particular art form, but in recognition of the importance of having a balanced arts program for its employees. Citizens of Iowa will fund HIV/AIDS programs in Africa because they are concerned about the decimation caused by the epidemic. People from all over the world poured their hearts and their gifts into New York following the terrorist attacks in 2001. They were concerned for the well-being of the survivors and for the economic impact of the attacks on the lives of citizens even though most did not know any of the victims or their families. Values inherent in concern may be more intellectual in their root (availability of a

balanced arts program for employees, programs for the hungry and homeless) than the values embedded in *connection,* but they are no less strong. These values are based in issues, and studies of the motivation of new philanthropists[1] revealed issues as a very high motivator for giving. People focus their giving in one or a few areas that are of concern to them: education, literacy, global health. They want to solve problems. One young philanthropist, when asked to identify what his primary social investment focus was, just said, "change."

3. *Capacity* is the most obvious, but weakest, indicator when assessing a funder's inclination to give. Too often, it is the only focus when preparing a list of prospects. It is the origin of the worked and reworked "A list"—those known in the community to have wealth but who have no connection to your organization and no interest in your issues. Every organization tries to draw from that list. If capacity were the strongest motivator for giving, then organizations could simply take the Forbes 400 or the Fortune 500 listings and write each person or corporation a letter saying "You've got it, we need it, let's make a deal!" Capacity is a difficult attribute to measure. Very visible wealth may not be stable enough to warrant major investment in an organization. Often great wealth is very quiet, manifesting itself occasionally and dramatically with gifts that have a huge impact on the community. Organizations need to be cautious in balancing the capacity factor against connection and concern. Capacity predictably informs some very strong values regarding an organization's financial performance bottom line. For many donors whose capacity is great and for whom the requests are many, it also influences the kind of values return they seek overall from an organization: quality, excellence, pride, and satisfaction. Another note regarding capacity: As planned giving grows as a source of major support for organizations, a source pattern has emerged. Many planned gifts come from people whose wealth was virtually unknown and whose gifts (if any) may have been modest. However, most of these legacy investors have had a strong connection (patient, student, docent, member) or intense values-based interest (animal welfare, children's services) in the organization(s) they benefit.

Volunteers and staff who are increasingly comfortable with values-based donor development will find that both connection and concern intensify as relationships develop. And although nonprofits can do little to increase a potential donor's absolute capacity (e.g., income, net worth), they do have a opportunity to increase *relative capacity:* the share of wealth a donor will consider giving to an organization.

Understanding donor motivation is essential to fundraising and development, because motivation is bound so tightly to values. It is also a helpful tool for raising confidence in asking and putting away the tin cup. A knowledge of donor motivation, when coupled with increasing comprehension of the organization's value and performance, can take volunteers and staff a long way in becoming more comfortable about asking for money.

The two factors combine to develop a new attitude, one that enables institutions to go beyond fundraising.

CONVEYING A NEW ATTITUDE: WHOSE NEEDS ARE YOU PRESENTING?

It is imperative that nonprofit organizations transfer the focus of philanthropy from organizational needs to community needs. They must position fundraising as a process of investing in successful institutions that are solving societal problems or providing fundamental enhancements to the quality of community life. Donors then perceive the importance of their gifts not from the standpoint of annually rescuing organizations in need, but of continually providing support for those in the community who benefit from programs and services.

Messages, from mission statements to newsletters, can convey this new positioning. People can be overwhelmed by needs; they become excited about results (especially when those results are attributed to the impact of their investment in an organization or program).

Analyze the content of your newsletter and other messages. What do they convey? Do they focus on community impact (how many were helped, or are doing something they could not do before) or only on the organization (fundraising events, capital needs campaign, management changes)? Is there an overemphasis on the social side of the organization's volunteer activities, with too many photographs of people holding wineglasses and too much gossipy insider news? It is far better to keep that kind of reporting for internal volunteer or staff communications and focus instead on photographs of volunteers doing program-related work and on patrons or clients benefiting from services.

Choosing Words That Work

An extremely successful human services organization reflects just the right balance in its newsletter. The lead article is always an in-depth piece about the impact of one of its programs on a family or individual. Information is always presented (statistics, statements from leading spokespeople) about the need the organization is addressing in the local community and how it relates to national trends and programs. Donor listings are provided quarterly; news about volunteers and staff are kept to an interesting minimum, and the information is usually mission or client related; and there is a visible emphasis on spotlighting the ways in which the programs are making an impact while keeping costs contained. The newsletter itself is appropriately designed and produced for the organization: Never glossy or burdened by excessive or inappropriate photographs, its writing conveys just the right tone of substance and authority. Over time, this newsletter has done a great deal to position this organization as a prudently managed community asset. A capital campaign for a new program and administrative center was hugely successful, exceeding even the most optimistic projections. Part of its success was due to the image of stability, strength, and service promoted over the years through the newsletter and by the portrayal of its overall outreach to the community.

A community arts education organization increased its return from a year-end mailing by 70 percent over all previous results when it removed the negative tin cup language from the letter and substituted a lively description of its many accomplishments of the previous year. The letter invited the community to participate in its continuing music education programs and conveyed the good news of a foundation challenge grant that community giving would help the organization meet. In its first draft, the focus had been entirely different: The overwhelming sense was desperation to meet the challenge. The second and final draft repositioned the focus from simply needing the money to why this was a great investment in the future of music education in the city.

Changed Attitude, Changed Practices: The True Innovation

It takes encouragement and training to help volunteers and staff put away the tin cup and to bring an organization's development team to the point where it considers gifts as investments and the asking process not one of pressure but of release. It also requires education of funders so they will let organizations retire the tin cup. However, even the best encouragement and training will fail, and fundraising will persist in being an exhausting, unfulfilling, and only moderately successful activity, if:

- The attitude persists internally and is conveyed externally that fundraising is driven primarily by the organization's need for money instead of by the needs it is meeting in the community through its programs and services (that the organization is the end point instead of the conduit).
- Fundraising is conducted without the benefit of the strategic acts of development and the philosophical framework of philanthropy.

The foundation for successful repositioning can be built by taking certain key management and organization steps.

Getting Organized for Values-Based Development and Fundraising

Systems liberate. Part of the attitudinal shift comes from getting organized for values-based development practices. The creation of internal systems for managing the development process is driven by a vision for institutional and development achievement. Borrowing a phrase from athletics, it is vital to "keep your eye on the prize." The prize, in the nonprofit sector, is a stronger community, people who are better served through the sector, and the fulfillment donors feel when their values are acted on through their investments. Organizational disarray and a failure to secure the entire management structure to a foundation of broadly involving development activities erodes the nonprofit's capacity to achieve these results. If there is chaos within the organization, it will be difficult to focus on a community-based mission. Likewise, if there is no sense of a values-based mission, the organization will quickly deteriorate. Chapter 3 discusses how to prevent mission drift.

SUMMARY

How Development Practices Help Organizations Put Away the Tin Cup

Chapter 1 presented the relationship between development and fundraising and explained the need for internal marketing of the development process to implement the three-part model. This chapter looked at how those principles can move an organization away from tin cup fundraising. Once an organization adopts an attitude toward development that positions its needs as opportunities for community investment, change occurs. Fundraising and volunteer recruitment materials reflect results and success, and people want to buy in. Volunteers, drawn into a process of development, find there is a way for them to be involved that is both comfortable and constructive.

People who participate in donor development and relationship building grow in their willingness to play a role in fundraising. They see how potential donors, and current donors with greater potential, derive pleasure from involvement with the organization. As the relationship grows, staff and volunteers move seamlessly to the next step: inviting potential funders to make an initial or increased gift. This transition from reluctance to confidence in asking is the principal result of a changed attitude. It requires board and staff members to exhibit four attributes:

1. *Pride in the achievement of the organization.* Communicate accomplishments, and surround them with information about what resources are required (human and financial) to further strengthen the programs and services.

2. *Involvement and communication.* Inform board members, other volunteers, and program staff about accomplishments and concerns, and invite them to participate in celebrations and problem-solving.

3. *A belief that the donor-investor, not the organization, is the center of the marketplace.* Guide board members and staff into a better understanding that donor-investors and the community's needs are paramount, not the organization's. Their interests, enthusiasm, attachments, and concerns must be the focus in determining the potential relationship.

4. *An overriding conviction about the value and impact of services.* Build ever-higher confidence in the organization and in the process of development and fundraising. It is the key to innovation and changed practices.

The tin cup attitude can and will disappear as organizations are increasingly positioned as investments that reflect donor and community values. A passive donor-institution relationship will not provide the dynamic partnership needed within nonprofit institutions. The dynamic donor-investor relationship must be created.

NOTE

1. Kay Sprinkel Grace and Alan L. Wendroff, *High Impact Philanthropy: How Donors, Boards, and Nonprofit Organizations Can Transform Communities* (John Wiley & Sons, 2000).

CHAPTER 3

Preventing Mission Drift:
The Leadership Imperative

A nonprofit's mission, as described in Chapter 1, is its compass and rudder. It helps the organization stay on course and guides and stabilizes it through change.

Commitment to the mission is the core of good management and is the heart of effective development and fundraising. It is what attracts leaders and maintains donor-investors. As the expression of the organization's most basic values, it must be continually validated and carefully protected. The leadership imperative for nonprofit volunteers and staff is to prevent mission drift: to adhere to the mission and keep the organization on course.

MAINTAINING A STRONG ORGANIZATION AND A STRONG MISSION

Nonprofit leadership is a juggling act for boards and staff. Complex organizations require extraordinary leadership. Leading and managing any organization is difficult; the engagement of many constituencies and the community-entrusted mission of nonprofits produce even more challenging situations. To ensure dynamic values-driven support, administrative, development, and fundraising leaders must focus in all community outreach on external impact and lessen the emphasis on the organization's internal needs. The mission must be the message.

The simple principles and practices of leadership given in this chapter are expanded throughout the book. This chapter focuses on the ways in which effective leadership prevents mission drift.

DEFINING MISSION DRIFT

Mission drift is a condition, either long term or temporary, in which an organization becomes so consumed with its institutional issues that it loses sight of its mission. A popular cartoon several decades ago showed a man with only his head visible, being sucked into quicksand and surrounded by alligators. The caption read: "When you are up to your neck in alligators, it's hard to remember that the original mission was to drain the swamp."

The most common source of mission drift is deterioration of leadership. Systems within the organization start to crumble. The organizational focus shifts from strategies for meeting community needs to tactics for controlling internal problems. Symptoms that indicate mild to severe mission drift include:

- Board meetings in which there is little or no mention of the programs or services except in the financial report
- Board members who refuse to get involved with the organization except at board meetings and make little or no financial commitment
- Leaders who fail to encourage leadership growth and succession
- Battles for control between board and staff and among staff and board members
- An approach to organizational priorities that ignores the needs of constituencies and changes in the marketplace
- A shift from the passionate commitment that characterizes board membership in an organization at its founding or early stages to an overly pragmatic view that can jeopardize mission-based decision making

Any of these symptoms is dangerous and can damage an organization's capacity to enroll others in its mission and stay financially stable. Each should be addressed as it arises and dealt with decisively. All detract from an emphasis on mission and can unsettle the requisite balanced focus on both organizational issues and program accomplishments. Uncontrolled, these problems can become so consuming that the organization ends up getting in the way of the mission.

Avoiding Mission Drift

Leadership is the primary anchor against nonprofit mission drift. Without strong and consistent leadership, an organization falters in times of difficulty and cannot move ahead smoothly in times of calm.

Leadership in the nonprofit sector has a dual structure: It is the responsibility of both board and staff. Board or staff members in organizations that manifest one or more symptom of mission drift too often begin blaming each other for the problem. This is not only counterproductive, it is inappropriate. In no other sector is the responsibility for leadership as interwoven between an internal leadership/management team and an externally elected or appointed board. Peter Drucker refers to this unique relationship as a "team of equals." The nonprofit sector is disciplined by partnerships within organizations and with constituencies. The power of partnerships, explored in Chapter 4, begins with leadership that is perceived as a shared responsibility. The fundamental partnership in nonprofits is that between board and staff. Strategies for building effective boards are detailed in Chapter 9.

PRACTICES OF ABLE NONPROFIT LEADERS

Able and respected staff and volunteer leaders demonstrate their strengths in numerous ways, stabilizing their organizations and keeping them tough and resilient. They provide or encourage nine attributes:

1. An emphasis on mission and purpose at all board and/or committee meetings and in all institutional decisions.

The tone and tempo of meetings convey a great deal about an organization, particularly to a new or prospective board member. Leaders ensure that agendas are well drawn and adhered to, time is provided at each meeting for a testimonial or presentation by a program participant or recipient, time frames are respected but meetings are not "railroaded," discussions are well guided, and tough decisions are made using a process that includes exploration of issue(s) as they relate to the mission and purpose of the organization.

2. A commitment to passionate pragmatism throughout the life cycle of the organization.

Those involved in the leadership of nonprofit organizations are aware of the ways in which the board's role changes as an organization matures. From hands-on involvement during the early stages to functioning as a corporate oversight board as the organization approaches and achieves maturity, these changing roles require board members to keep their passion and pragmatism balanced.

In the beginning, when the ideas that have inspired the organization's founding are fresh, there is no lack of passion among board members. They are living the mission. This passion, which arises out of common vision and shared values, characterizes board behavior. Board members move swiftly to decisions, act boldly on opportunities, and take appropriate risks based on their dedication to the mission. Board members extend themselves into the community as ambassadors, askers, and advocates. The communication of the leader's vision and the organization's mission is steady and intense. Pragmatism is sometimes in short supply.

As organizations grow, they rightfully begin to focus on systems and structure. Passion can wane. Board members are recruited who were not present at the creation and who may not even know the founding members. These new board members must be given the big picture: They should not be recruited only for their professional expertise (legal, financial, marketing). Otherwise, they may view the organization narrowly and have little passion, and the mission can drift as they focus on issues in the absence of a larger context. Passion must be sustained to frame the pragmatism. Throughout the life of an organization, it is essential to keep these two dynamics in balance.

3. Leadership succession planning, including enforcement of board member evaluation and limits to years of board service.

No matter how effective or valuable a board member or officer may be, wise leaders will enforce bylaws that limit terms of service or office. Terms should not be automatically renewable if board member attendance or participation has been poor. Healthy boards provide space for new people who bring a fresh balance to the governance tasks.

Most bylaws have provisions for allowing board members to be reelected after a year or more off the board. A person with expertise that is vital to the organization can always be placed on a committee during the off year(s). Leaders who are good succession planners are constantly looking at the other board members and nonboard volunteers and thinking how people might be engaged more effectively within the organization. They also provide opportunities for people who are new to the organization to get involved. Board succession planning is covered in greater detail in Chapter 9.

4. Regular evaluation of the executive director/chief executive officer.

A function related to board self-evaluation and leadership succession is regular evaluation of the executive director. Although this step is a requirement for all boards, this duty is often neglected. Executive directors can go for years without receiving an evaluation. Leaders encourage leadership: The board's executive committee should provide an annual evaluation for the executive director, one that provides motivation, validation, and feedback for growth.

5. One hundred percent financial participation by the board in all fundraising campaigns.

Leaders do not accept the response: "I give my time; I do not have to give money." By their own example, they inspire others to give at an appropriate level, and they also convey the importance outside funders place on 100 percent board giving. Board participation in annual and capital campaigns is requisite for inviting the participation of others.

6. One hundred percent participation by the board in donor and fund development activities.

Because development is the process of uncovering shared values in potential donors, and involves much more than fundraising, all board members can and should be involved. Strong organizational leaders create opportunities that motivate all board members, even the most reluctant, to get involved in development. Not everyone has to participate in face-to-face solicitations, but everyone should be involved with one or more of the other steps in the development process (identifying, cultivating, being a steward) or with other kinds of solicitations (letters, telephones, special events).

7. Early and thorough attention to budding program or people problems (board, other volunteers, or staff) that could grow and overwhelm the focus on mission.

Strong leaders are problem solvers. They know at what level a problem should be solved within the board or staff or between board and staff. They bring only the most critical problems to the board, preferring to solve others within the structure of personnel, executive, or another committee. They have mastered and use techniques for problem-solving that are fair and objective, and they try to hear all sides of an issue during the process. Decisions, and the reasons behind them, are communicated openly and in a timely fashion. Conflict is not allowed to escalate. If the leaders cannot solve the problem, they bring in outside professional help before the problem overwhelms the organization.

8. A focus on solutions, not problems.

Hand-wringing consumes energy and accomplishes little. Leaders see beyond problems to how they can be resolved. In the problem-solving process, they identify and examine the problem but emphasize solutions. Leaders get people involved in the implementation of solutions and use their delegation skills in ways that tap into the creativity and interests of board, volunteers, and staff. Leaders welcome evaluation of ideas and implementation and are willing to make changes if an original course of action is not working.

9. Respect for staff, board, and nonboard volunteers as partners who share a mutual dedication to the organization and the mission.

Leaders trust and respect those with whom they work. They understand the unique contribution each person can make, and they encourage and respect, through their words and practices, a mutual focus on mission.

These practices are not unique to nonprofits, but they are basic requirements for effective leadership of the nonprofit sector.

SPECIAL CHALLENGES TO NONPROFIT LEADERS: BALANCING THE DEMANDS OF MISSION FULFILLMENT AND ORGANIZATIONAL REQUIREMENTS

Balancing a strong organization and a strong mission provides unusual challenges:

- Nonprofits are accountable to donor-investors for two bottom lines: financial performance and values-based program results;

- Overlap and confusion exist about the roles of board and staff.

- Turnover among development staff is inevitable.

- Volunteer leaders must balance the nonprofit's demands against their full-time jobs or other commitments.

Two Bottom Lines

Managing two "bottom lines" is the greatest challenge, and the greatest opportunity, for leaders who want to prevent mission drift. It is a challenge because the importance of the financial bottom line, examined without benefit of the values bottom line, may result in decisions that curtail the organization's capacity to act on its mission. Reduction in staff or programs that may seem prudent relative to the financial bottom line can diminish the availability of vital programs and services in the community and result in reduced opportunities for investment by those who share the organization's values.

The opportunity presented by the two bottom lines is the capacity to develop donor relations and fundraising practices based not just on financial information but on values-based results. This opportunity can be the countervailing force against harsh reductions in staff or services. It can be turned into a strong motivation for potential funders to make increasingly larger investments to ensure the continuation of programs that are needed in the community. Donors carry two portfolios: financial investment and social investment. When they are persuaded that an investment will enrich their social investment portfolio, they are willing to draw down on their financial portfolio. It is imperative that a balance be maintained between the two bottom lines so that the strength of one supports the results of the other.

Overlap and Confusion about Board and Staff Roles

Defining board and staff roles is a nonprofit leadership challenge of the first order because of the unique dual leadership structure of all nonprofits. Failure to define these roles is one of the principal contributors to mission drift. The challenge can be met by determining and conveying expectations. Executive directors, boards, committees, and volunteers with other assignments benefit from having expectations conveyed to them either individually in special sessions or in an annual discussion or retreat. People are evaluated daily by the expectations others have of them. Most often these expectations are not revealed until problems arise. Clarity regarding board, committee, other volunteer, and staff roles helps maintain organizational strength and prevents mission drift. When roles are understood and carried out, internal communication improves. An increasing number of organizations are placing a priority on expectation-setting as part of their annual retreat. This process, which should be guided by a facilitator, has three required exchanges:

1. Executive director (and staff) convey their expectations to board members and other volunteers.
2. Board members convey to executive director (and staff) what their expectations are of staff leadership.
3. Board and staff convey to each other what they expect of themselves.

The value of this process is significant. Following one such session, a former executive director, who was filling in as business manager while the new executive director hired other staff, said to the board: "If I had known this was what you expected of the executive director, I might still be here." We cannot lead by expectations if we do not convey them. When we fail to let people know what we expect, we continue to evaluate them against standards they may not know about. Tensions arise, communication crumbles, and energy that should be given to tasks is diverted to worry or quarreling about relationships and responsibilities. Some board or staff members may feel threatened by the thought of exchanging expectations, but the process encourages organizations to be fair and frank in their definition of board and staff roles. The result is a stronger organization that can focus more fully on its mission.

Inevitable Turnover among Development Staff

Although there has been considerable improvement, particularly at the higher levels of management, the tenure of mid- and entry-level development officers is still averaging about two years. As compensation for development staff has improved, thanks to efforts by the various professional societies serving the profession, there will be further improvement in job stability. Management and compensation is a continuing area of study and action for leaders of the Association of Fundraising Professionals (AFP) and other similar professional organizations, such as the Association for Healthcare Philanthropy (AHP) and the Council for the Advancement and Study of Education (CASE).

Efforts made to retain good development staff have a high payoff. Development staff turnover has a considerable effect on nonprofit organizations. Everything that is known about development indicates that it is a process that takes time and requires continuity in communication and stewardship. Turnover on the development staff disrupts this continuity. Leadership among board members and other volunteers, especially those on the development committee, must see that development managers and staff are compensated adequately and given regular evaluation and appropriate feedback for their accomplishments, and that the development director is included as part of the management team in budgeting and other policy matters. At the same time, to keep the organization stable when changes do occur, board and executive leadership must ensure that development systems are so well established that changes in development staff do not substantially disrupt the development program.

The executive director and board chair, faced with the resignation or necessary removal of the development director, must make sure that the transition is managed as smoothly as possible. Likewise, capable development directors need to handle turnover on their staffs smoothly and quickly, exercising personnel management skills and networking capabilities to find the best person possible in the shortest amount of time. In the case of the removal or resignation of the person in charge of development (development director or vice president for development), the executive director and board or development committee chair should:

- Communicate the decision openly and promptly to all key leaders and constituents, including major donors and fundraising volunteers

- Prepare and implement a plan for transition: search strategy, interim workload distribution, anticipated timeline

- Convey confidence that work will continue uninterrupted and be handled with skill and professionalism

- Keep important constituencies informed regarding the progress of the search and the continued progress of development activities

- Involve key board and development committee members, and select major donors, in the search process

- Create an opportunity, shortly after the person is hired, for the new development officer to share vision and expectations with the board and development committee

- Support the new development officer in every way possible, including regular evaluations with constructive feedback and ample reinforcement to maintain energy and enthusiasm

Turnover among development officers is often attributable to the pace, intensity, and complexity of managing the development function. Burnout is common, and there are those who leave the profession temporarily or permanently. Prevention of burnout is critical: Key maintenance factors for keeping development officers include support from board and other volunteers, clarity of expectations, direct and honest feedback, and appreciation. Strong development officers are dedicated to making volunteers look and feel good. Development staff do the majority of the background work and position volunteers to be successful and visible. A successful solicitation for a major gift, or the production of an outstanding special event, is usually a partnership between volunteers and staff in which the volunteers receive the community recognition. It is very important for executive directors and board leaders to remember the role that development officers have played in such successes. A handwritten note, a bouquet of flowers, special recognition at a board meeting: These techniques keep volunteers involved and keep development officer burnout to a manageable minimum.

Volunteer Leaders Must Balance the Nonprofit's Demands with Other Commitments

Volunteer involvement is a strategic contributor to the nonprofit sector's capacity to respond to community needs. Because volunteers represent the community, they provide the insights and perspective that nonprofits must have to shape their programs and outreach appropriately. Volunteering is a highly important form of philanthropy.[1] Although gifts of time must be balanced by gifts of money for philanthropy to be complete, the satisfaction of the volunteer experience often intensifies the willingness to make a financial commitment.

Reciprocal appreciation helps volunteers stay involved. Just as board members and other volunteers have a responsibility to provide feedback and support to development staff, staff members who work with volunteers need to ensure the quality of the volunteer experience. Every executive director, development officer, and development or program staff person should find time to volunteer at another organization. By doing this, they never forget the demands on their own volunteers, and they maintain a sensitivity and respect for volunteers' time. Volunteers want to feel their time is valued, makes a difference, and is well spent. Like donors, volunteers are looking for an *exchange* with the nonprofit: skills, values, opportunities, recognition, and opportunities to act on their values.

Appreciation needs to be accompanied by clear standards for volunteers. Nonprofit organizations that succeed in retaining valued board members and other volunteers:

- Provide written job descriptions, including time and service expectations, for all board, committee and other assignments.
- Set high standards for volunteer involvement: attendance at meetings, timely completion of assignments, quality of work.
- Ensure that staff members also adhere to these standards.

- Consult volunteers on key decisions and ask them to review drafts of materials they will be using (case statements, brochures, letters for community mailings).
- Develop and follow enlistment (and deenlistment) policies and procedures for all volunteer positions, including board membership.
- Value volunteers' time by making sure that all meetings and assignments are necessary and important.
- Offer appropriate appreciation and recognition.
- Communicate regularly regarding the progress or results of projects in which volunteers are involved.
- Provide special opportunities for volunteers to be involved with the mission of the organization through interaction with program staff and/or clients (as possible and appropriate).
- Make assignments that fit the motivation and needs of each volunteer.
- Provide all support necessary for the volunteer experience to be successful and rewarding.

THE ROLE OF LEADERS IN MAINTAINING EFFECTIVE SYSTEMS

Highly productive nonprofit organizations rely on effective management, development, and fundraising systems. Systems provide a framework that helps leaders stay focused on the achievement of the mission. Good systems are among the primary preventers of mission drift.

Systems provide structure. Systems are the policies and procedures that have been developed by the organizational leadership to guide its principal activities: bylaws, articles of incorporation, board policies, personnel policies, institutional and development plans, and other written or understood rules. Systems guide; systems liberate.[2] When well designed and agreed on within an organization, systems contribute to continuity and stability. Effective systems ensure that routine and predictable activities can be handled with relative ease, allowing organizations to spend time on program and donor development and on other creative or strategic activities.

Basic nonprofit systems include:

- Development and institutional plans
- Internal communication system
- Board recruitment and development procedures
- Values-based development and fundraising
- Acknowledgment, recognition, and stewardship practices
- Appropriate computer systems to support donor and financial development

LEADERSHIP IN TIMES OF CHANGE

The last several years have been times of great change for philanthropy. Accountability and transparency demands by communities and funders, increasing competition, and the impact of global violence and economic uncertainty have all had an effect on the sector. As small comfort, change has always been the most consistent aspect of the nonprofit sector's environment. The sector is about change; we who work in it are change agents. Successful nonprofits anticipate and initiate change through sound institutional planning. When hit with unanticipated changes, they retain their stability. The most admired organizations are those that are able to implement and constantly adjust their practices to meet the challenges of change.

Because they exist to meet community needs, nonprofits are constantly challenged by the unexpected. A natural disaster such as the December 2004 Tsunami or the December 2003 earthquake in Iran calls organizations into action. A previously undiscovered illness, such as HIV/AIDS, becomes an epidemic. Voters curb tax spending for schools, as they have in countless states in the United States, and citizens rally. A nationally funded European museum, undertaking a major capital renovation, finds itself needing private endowment funding to help support the enlarged and more highly attended institution. In this climate of change, organizations are continually asked to adapt their internal practices and programs to meet emerging external challenges. A suicide prevention organization fails financially, and a family counseling organization is asked to absorb its services. Two hospitals merge, along with their foundations, creating new opportunities but eliminating others. A library responds to needs for after-school programming for middle school youngsters by increasing its young adult collections and supervisory staff.

How leadership responds to change is pivotal in an organization's acceptance of that change. Change perceived as opportunity and responded to creatively leads to growth. Change perceived as a threat and responded to with fear leads to decay. Leaders make choices when they react to change. They can implement responses that harm the organization's initiative and impair its growth; or they can rebound with options that will position the organization more strongly than before.

Four Leadership Attributes That Can Help Prevent Mission Drift

Organizations cannot go beyond fundraising into values-based development if their missions drift. The mission is the message, and leaders are in place to convey and explain it. Board and staff leadership must reflect qualities that will help ensure the organization's continued role as a sound community investment.

Four qualities of nonprofit leaders contribute to the strength and stability of the organizations they serve: courage, confidence, creativity, and commitment.

Courage

Leaders, especially those in the nonprofit sector, must have courage, and they must *en*courage. To have courage is a more commonly acknowledged attribute of leaders, but to *encourage* is equally important. Jim Kouzes and Barry Posner tell us that a task of leaders is "to encourage the heart."[3] To prevent mission drift, leaders must maintain their own courage, and that of others, by encouraging the heart, the mind, the passions, the willingness to serve. They must encourage others to grow, excel, produce, and become leaders themselves.

Courage manifests itself in calculated risk taking that produces change and makes a difference in our communities. It also is demonstrated internally by the direction board and staff leaders set for the institution and the way in which they implement planning. In the various studies of corporate culture and its impact on organizations, one of the common threads among all researchers or observers is that "heroes" comprise a very strong part of organizational culture. These are people who were courageous in advocating for the organization, standing by their own beliefs in board or community meetings, taking an unpopular but ethical position on an internal or external issue, making a tough ask and doing it well, and/or having the courage to inspire others through their own perseverance and success. There is not much talk about courage among leaders, perhaps because so little of it is seen. But when it occurs, we know and respect it. Leaders become more courageous when they master another quality of leadership—confidence.

Confidence

Confidence is derived from an understanding of the importance of an organization, the mission it is fulfilling, and the sector the nonprofit serves. Confidence grows for board and staff in an environment where there is pride, rather than apology, for the development and fundraising process. Likewise, that atmosphere of pride and shared success promotes confidence. Confidence in the organization and confidence in the sector are important in the encouragement of leadership.

Just as confidence is built by understanding the organization's impact and successes, and by a focus on results, that confidence is extended when viewing the accomplishments of the entire philanthropic sector. A story that embodies both courage and confidence is illustrative. It was part of an article published in the December 19, 1991, issue of the *Wall Street Journal*. Its points are as well made today as they were then. In the article Peter Drucker spoke admiringly of the nonprofit sector's capability to accomplish much with little and cited the activities of several organizations. But one story conveyed the message of courage and confidence most powerfully. At that time, in Royal Oak, Michigan, the "tiny Judson Center" had created a program to move single mothers and their families off welfare while simultaneously getting severely handicapped children out of institutions and back into society. The program replaced two government-funded programs that had shown little success: one for welfare mothers and the other for children institutionalized with disabilities. The center trained carefully selected welfare mothers to raise in their homes, for a modest salary, two or three developmentally disabled or emotionally disturbed children. The success rate for the mothers was close to 100 percent, with many of them moving into employment as rehabilitation workers. The impact on the developmentally disabled children was equally dramatic. Institutional confinement was reduced to 50 percent and, Drucker added, "every one of these kids had been given up as hopeless." He summarized his viewpoint in this way: "The nonprofits spend far less for results than governments spend for failure." Such statements elevate the philanthropic sector in the eyes of the general public and make those who work and volunteer in the sector feel good. The proliferation of newspaper and magazine articles about the impact of philanthropy, and increasing focus by public radio and television on the stories of individuals whose philanthropy has had an impact, all serve to elevate confidence in our sector as a whole.

Confidence in the sector, and in its organizations, leads to self-confidence — the basis of courage. Self-confidence grows as the felt need for apology fades. When nonprofit support is approached from a position of service or strength, rather than weakness, self-confidence flourishes. People can speak with confidence about the organization's accomplishments and the pleasure of their involvement and advocacy. It is this self-confidence that rescues a difficult solicitation or saves a cultivation activity that is veering off course. Self-confidence is a strong quality of those who successfully generate and maintain values-based relationships within and for nonprofit organizations.

Creativity

Creative solutions, creative approaches, creative results: Communities expect this of non-profit leaders and their organizations. Creativity is a quality often overlooked when defining leadership. It manifests itself in effective problem-solving and containment of conflict and in new approaches or perspectives. It is most obvious in the materials and programs of organizations, particularly those that are produced on small budgets and have high impact. A dance company, once broadly supported in the community, had an artistic director who honestly told donor-investors that he made "one dollar do the work of five." His creativity, both on stage with his choreography and administratively with community investments, was a source of pride and satisfaction to staff, volunteers, and donor-investors. After his retirement, the company lost that creative connection, and with it a great deal of funding. Hard times ensued, and the future is in doubt. For board members, creativity includes bringing new ideas to the boardroom table and new volunteers to events or meetings. Creativity requires a keen sense of opportunity and a willingness to be a leader in advancing new ideas.

Creativity and change are strongly linked. An organizational environment that endorses and rewards creativity usually responds more positively to change. Resilient organizations are those in which change, while not always welcomed, is accepted or initiated when required. Creative approaches to changes in internal or external conditions contribute considerably to the avoidance of mission drift: When organizations become consumed with the imagined impact of change, they lose sight of the positive alternatives the change may imply.

Commitment

Some would argue that commitment is the strongest quality of leaders. It certainly is essential and, when combined with courage, confidence, and creativity, it can result in

dauntless and innovative leadership. Commitment is seen in acts that nourish and support the organization: loyalty in time of crisis, willingness to give and ask, and enthusiastic advocacy for the organization that invites others to enroll in the mission.

Commitment is sustained passion. It manifests deeply felt and understood beliefs.
It exemplifies values. Commitment is encouraged and sustained by effective leadership.
It is kept healthy and fresh through constant reconnection to the values and mission
of the organization. Commitment is reinforced when trustees grasp solidly not only
what the organization does, but *why* it exists. Commitment grows from a respect for
and a dedication to the values of the organization and to the needs it is meeting in the
community.

When trustees and other volunteers connect with the values the organization has as
its basis for existence, and the value of the work it is doing in the community, commitment grows. Joy and energy override apathy. Volunteers become the asker-advocates who
will leverage the resources organizations need to deliver their services effectively. Commitment is seen and felt in long hours volunteering in a child care center or cancer ward,
involvement in the board-building process in an organization that is reengineering itself,
pro bono legal or financial service to nonprofits, and countless other ways.

Commitment is an elusive yet visible quality. In the development and fundraising
process, it is the aspect of the asker that is most convincing to the potential donor-
investor. Commitment is shown through gifts of time and money, but also through willingness to participate in the full range of philanthropic activities: giving, asking, joining,
and serving.

Strong leadership, exemplified in these and other qualities, can prevent mission drift.
The importance of avoiding mission drift cannot be overstated: When organizations veer
away from their mission and become consumed with organizational issues, they endanger
their ability to sustain development practices that will move them beyond fundraising.

Organizations whose missions drift can get back on course by reconnecting their boards,
other volunteers, and staff members with the mission. They can do this in a number of
ways, including:

- Presentations and testimonials at board meetings
- Facilities' tours
- Meetings with constituents and clients
- Occasional opportunities to immerse those closest to the organization in positive
  feedback about the impact of the services or programs on the community

Messages to board members and other volunteers need to be balanced: They should
include the good news as well as that which will create concern; focus on solutions, not
just on problems; maintain optimism even in times of crisis; and let people know how
valued their involvement is.

Organizations need both anchors and sails. They need pragmatism and passion to keep
them on course. Leadership should reflect both.

SUMMARY

Leadership as Passionate Pragmatism

A focus on mission and values, conducted in an environment in which courage, confidence, creativity, and commitment flourish, can result in "passionate pragmatism"—that balance of qualities which ensures that even as an organization matures, the passion of the founding is not forgotten.[4] If passion and pragmatism are kept in balance, then even as the board's role changes, its commitment to mission can be sustained.

Here are 10 tips for maintaining passionate pragmatism. They can help both board members and staff prevent or cure mission drift.

1. *Maintain a balance* on the passion to pragmatism continuum even in the early stages of an organization. Recruit volunteers and staff who evidence both, and let them blend to create and sustain a strong organization.

2. *Infuse the mission* constantly: Believe it, live it, examine it, value it. Words are not enough. The creed behind the receptionist's desk is believable only if it is practiced.

3. *Be sure board members give* first and as frequently as they can. Giving is a transforming act, in which the donor-investor becomes a participant. When there is appropriate and sustained stewardship of the board member as an important donor of both time and money, a sense of belonging and involvement grows. This feeling of belonging translates to loyalty that sustains passion while encouraging pragmatic and appropriate solutions to institutional issues.

4. *Enroll board members as asker-advocates* and encourage staff members to participate in solicitations as appropriate. In talking about the organization to others, their own commitment is renewed.

5. *Inspire and reward commitment.* Board membership does not automatically bring deep commitment, particularly if an individual is brought onto the board because of a particular expertise or talent and is given a narrow view of his or her responsibilities. The same is true for staff with highly specialized assignments. Tie all board and staff recognition and rewards into the ways in which their actions or service have advanced the organization's ability to meet critical community needs or improved the quality of life in the community.

6. *Set standards for board participation and staff performance* and maintain them. Passionate pragmatism is the result of commitment to the cause and awareness of what it requires to act on that cause. Passion for an organization is increased, not diminished, when standards are conveyed during enlistment of board members and hiring of staff. Evaluation and reward systems need to be in place. It is a singular truth of organizational behavior that having effective systems in place actually can help prevent mission drift. Because good systems liberate, they permit staff and board to utilize their energies in creative pursuits that support the fulfillment of the mission.

7. *Create a sense of ownership.* Involve board and staff in planning (see Chapter 10). It creates ownership among those who participate and provides greater support for decisions and change.

8. *Keep the "product" on view all the time.* Bulletin boards, newsletters, testimonials at board meetings, DVDs, computer-projected presentations, videos, and people who can tell the story are effective ways to keep a base of passion in pragmatic decisions. They also inspire people to ask for money. At one kick-off of an annual campaign, a presentation by a staff therapist was more effective in inspiring the volunteers to go out and fund raise than the pep talk by the fundraising consultant. The therapist let them know why what they were about to do was so important: She told them a success story about a breakthrough with an extremely troubled youngster. With that story in mind, fundraising became driven by the urgency and importance of meeting the needs of children, not just the goals of the campaign: They could talk *results* with those on whom they were calling.

9. *Encourage board and staff to attend local, regional, or national meetings* of umbrella organizations. By comparing notes with other board or professional staff people, they gain a larger perspective. Their pride increases for what their organization has accomplished, and they learn from others.

10. *Be honest.* Passion turns to anger and pragmatism into resistance and control when boards and staff find out they have not been told the whole or true story about the financial or program status of the organization.

This decalogue of strategies, combined with knowledge of the symptoms of mission drift and the qualities and practices of able leaders, can help chart a course for nonprofits that will keep the mission firmly in place and avoid the kind of organizational mishaps that throw passion and pragmatism, mission and organization out of balance. There is convincing evidence that staff and board connection with the mission stabilizes an organization through both unexpected and inevitable change. Organizations can and must protect and advance their missions through balanced and dynamic leadership.

NOTES

1. Robert Payton, *Philanthropy: Voluntary Action for the Public Good* (Oryx Press, 1988).
2. Kay Sprinkel Grace, "Leadership and Team Building," chapter 24 in Henry A. Rosso & Associates, *Achieving Excellence in Fundraising* (Jossey-Bass, 2003).
3. James Kouzes and Barry Posner, *The Leadership Challenge,* 3rd edition (Jossey-Bass, 2003).
4. Kay Sprinkel Grace, "Towards Passionate Pragmatism: Building and Sustaining Board Commitment," pp. 109–120 in Richard C. Turner, ed., *Taking Trusteeship Seriously* (Indiana University Center on Philanthropy [550 West North Street, Suite 301, Indianapolis, IN 46202], 1995).

CHAPTER 4

Successful Development:
Partnership and Process

The nonprofit sector is built on partnerships. We in the nonprofit sector are partners with the community in solving problems and enhancing the quality of life. We initiate partnerships with funders for the mutual accomplishment of our mission and with volunteers to help us leverage time and money in the most effective way possible. The dual leadership structure of nonprofits, in which board and staff share responsibility for the organization, is itself preeminent nonprofit partnership. Partnerships, and the teamwork implicit in their formation and function, are a distinguishing aspect of excellent organizations.

The most successful development programs and fundraising campaigns are based on partnerships. From the outset, staff and community volunteers need to work together to create goals, materials, and strategies. They must establish the structure and systems that will enable them to work most productively. The end result of these efforts will be the implementation of a development process that will lead to increasing numbers of major gifts and donor investors.

PARTNERSHIPS FOR DEVELOPMENT AND FUNDRAISING

Effective development and fundraising partnerships are based on a shared understanding of the importance of meeting a critical community need. That understanding is enhanced by shared enthusiasm regarding the capability of the organization to address that need. Partnerships are strengthened through regular opportunities for honest and substantive communication and are reinforced by mutual trust based on that communication. Partnerships are powerful alliances of dedicated people working together on behalf of an organization.

To be effective, partnerships need to be understood, encouraged, and rewarded. This is particularly true with the development partnership—one of the most critical in any nonprofit organization. The development partnership is both cooperative and coordinated. In it, staff and board and other volunteers work together in each of the steps in the development process to ensure five vital outcomes:

1. The attainment of shared financial and outreach goals, including the engagement and retention of donors with capacity and willingness to make large gifts

2. Involvement of board and other volunteers in development-related tasks that are appropriate, rewarding, challenging, and purposeful

3. Mutually satisfying results, including enhanced donor relationships and better board-staff communication

4. Strengthening of board and staff respect for each other and the unique roles each can play in the donor and fund development process

5. Realization, by funding partners, of their investment in an organization that is enhancing their community

Building a successful development process takes complete organizational support. The full partnership will include all of these individuals or groups at various times and for various purposes:

- Chief Executive Officer, President, or Executive Director and his or her staff
- Development Officer and his or her professional and support staff
- Development Committee
- Chair of the Board of Directors/Trustees and Members of the Board
- Other volunteers engaged in program, administrative, or development support
- Program staff as expert support for critical proposals and solicitations

Working together, these individuals can help ensure the future of the organization.

CREATING DEVELOPMENT PARTNERSHIPS

Too often, establishing the environment in which partnerships flourish is difficult and discouraging. It requires a great deal of internal marketing of the development process (see Chapter 1): what it is, why everyone benefits when it works well, what is expected of each person relative to the process. Taking the time to do internal marketing requires a leadership commitment to the importance of the eventual result. The creation of a donor and fund development program and a culture of philanthropy (see Chapter 8) is a long-term systemic solution to the chronic and exhausting need to scramble for funds to meet ongoing or special needs. When people understand the value of the development process and of the partnerships that support it, it becomes a true partnership effort and enjoys much greater success.

In theory, few dispute the value of partnerships. In practice, sometimes partnerships are difficult to implement. All partnership building requires shared institutional vision, coordination of human and financial resources, a spirit of cooperation, and a willingness to take the time to delegate tasks and empower leadership. For development, this means that organizations initially must rally board leadership and key staff into a common understanding of three things: (1) what the partnership entails, (2) why it is important, and (3) what impact it can have.

What the Development Partnership Entails

The development partnership is inclusive. At the outset, it involves a core development team: key board, other volunteer, and staff leadership in planning and attainment of agreements regarding the goals and scope of the development and fundraising effort. At its maturity, the partnership will involve the full development team: the entire board, more volunteers, program staff (who will feel as if development is working on their behalf to ensure the funding of critical programs and services), administrative staff, and funders.

Why the Development Partnership Is Important

Partners are mutual stakeholders in an effort or enterprise. In development, this sense of ownership is vital to the commitment required to involve the community deeply and continuously in nonprofit organizations. If fundraising and development are seen only as the responsibility of the development staff and/or the development committee, it may discourage a widened sense of engagement and purpose that allows development to become the powerful function it can and must be.

The gradual involvement of the entire organization in the development process is one of the most powerful processes in all of nonprofit leadership and management. When staff and board come to understand the essential role each member can play in the full development process, there is an elevated sense of pride and involvement. It is a fascinating evolution. In one children's services organization, the program staff, previously not engaged at all in the activities of development and fundraising, became active participants in development. Through a series of brown-bag lunch "funder forums" conducted by the development director, they were provided with information about potential foundation, corporate, and government funding opportunities and were encouraged to share pertinent program information with the development committee members and staff. Eventually program staff were willing to help identify prospects from their program constituencies and be active participants in the preparation of proposals and in meetings and site visits with current and potential funders. A solid partnership had been forged.

Impact of the Development Partnership

A medical center received a major gift for the cancer treatment program from a woman who had undergone radiation therapy following her surgery. The story of that gift underscores how a development partnership can work. The head of the medical center foundation makes outreach to the medical staff a top priority. At the invitation of the hospital

CEO, whose confidence he has gained through his dedication and performance, he goes on rounds with the physicians, attends medical staff meetings, and meets regularly with the various units at the medical center to let them know about the services of the foundation, what the fundraising and "friend-raising" goals are, and how staff members can participate in identifying potential gifts among those with whom they work. He emphasizes that all referrals are handled discreetly and with the confidentiality of the patient's rights and records in mind. Further, the foundation does an excellent job of internally marketing the development function: how it works, who the involved community volunteers are, and what the impact has been over the years (this particular foundation raises in excess of $18 million annually for a wide variety of medical center programs).

The patient whose gift made such an impact on the cancer treatment program was identified to the foundation by a radiation therapist. The patient had told the therapist, during the course of her treatment, that she wished to do something for the hospital in gratitude for her care. The therapist notified the foundation and discussed the particulars of the situation with the chief executive. Foundation staff conducted research to identify whether the patient was a previous donor, was known to others on the foundation staff and board, or had made gifts to other medical centers. The foundation president and a volunteer then called on the woman and found out more about her interests and needs and what size and type of gift she was interested in making. They showed her the plans for a proposed cancer treatment center and arranged for her to meet with other key staff and volunteers over the course of the next several months. One of these subsequent meetings included the radiation therapist who had referred the patient initially. Other medical center and foundation staff participated in the process by attending meetings, preparing information, or supplying financial data. When the gift was made, all those involved experienced a sense of satisfaction: the donor, whose needs had been met with tact, skill, and consideration; and the medical center and foundation, which had put forth its best team in a true spirit of partnership.

STRUCTURING A SUCCESSFUL DEVELOPMENT PARTNERSHIP

The importance and potential impact of development partnerships cannot be overstated. To ensure the implementation of the development partnership, an organization should exhibit five attributes:

1. A solid plan for achieving development and fundraising goals.

Board and staff leadership need to develop a plan based on the reality of the previous year's (or campaign's) actual performance; the number of volunteers available, including board members, to be involved with each aspect of the development process; the conditions influencing fundraising and volunteer enlistment; the vision and goals of the organization; and a current and objective assessment of the "marketplace"—a substantiation of the needs in the community. The plan must be linked to the overall institutional plan and reflect in its funding goals the priorities of program and administrative staff.

2. Adequate paid or volunteer staff to support the development program.

A visionary partnership for development requires an organizational framework to support it. It is far worse to excite volunteers about potential involvement in development and then give them no opportunity to act on the nonprofit's behalf than it is to delay the program until the organization is completely ready. In one major university capital campaign, a group of solicitors was trained prematurely. No prospects for their particular program (gifts in the $10,000 to $100,000 range) had been researched and ready for cultivation, and staff, who were focused on larger gift prospects, were not yet ready to launch the program. The training, which had been historic in its thoroughness, inclusiveness, and impact, was without lasting value: the volunteers, enlisted carefully and trained expertly, had no immediate role to play. When the prospects were ready to be assigned, some of the volunteers no longer had the time available for the campaign or, if they were still available, had to take a refresher course in solicitation techniques.

Lack of staffing keeps many organizations from forming development teams or partnerships. An alternative management strategy for start-up or transitioning organizations, in which there may be no paid development staff except the executive director, is to enlist, train, and give responsibility and authority to volunteer "staff" to manage the development process. These volunteer staffers may be one or more individuals from the board or development committee willing to coordinate the various development tasks under the executive director's leadership until paid staff is available. This process can work well. When the organization matures to the point where it can afford to have paid staff, the phaseout of volunteer staff needs to be handled with sensitivity and appreciation for the hours and energy they have given to the organization. The development officer should learn as much as possible from these volunteers and keep them involved in a way that is newly defined and appropriate, such as on a development committee or advisory board or as solicitors. Otherwise, this can be a painful transition during which feelings are hurt, momentum is lost, and volunteer enthusiasm is squashed.

3. Specific job descriptions for staff and volunteer development workers.

This step is essential. The development officer's job description should be part of a complete set of job descriptions for staff, all of which are related to the institutional plan and are revised annually to reflect changes in priorities or performance. Related to the development officer's job description are the job descriptions for the volunteers who will be required if the plan is to succeed. These jobs, for which volunteers will be recruited, include: chair(s) of the annual campaign; chair(s) of the capital or endowment campaign; volunteer solicitors for individuals, foundations, or corporations; team captains or other "administrative" volunteer jobs; phone volunteers; annual mailing volunteers (signers, stuffers, labelers, baggers, etc.).

By having these job descriptions always ready, an organization can go about the important task of matching the right volunteer to the right job. Most critically, however, volunteers know from the outset what the job entails. Some organizations take this a step further and enter into an actual contract based on the job description with volunteers. For every enthusiast of volunteer contracts, there is a critic. Those dedicated to the volunteer contract say it provides a solid businesslike basis for evaluation and enlistment/reenlistment of volunteers. Those opposed to the formal contract say it is off-putting and violates the charitable and voluntary nature of volunteer participation. Organizations must decide for themselves what is appropriate for their culture, their needs, and their volunteers. If no formal contract is drawn, it is still extremely important to have a volunteer job description so the mutual expectations are clear. Likewise, it is often appropriate to share the scope of staff job(s) with volunteers as well. Volunteer expectations of staff sometimes exceed the staff person's job description, leading to unwarranted volunteer frustration and disappointment and undue pressure on staff. Exhibit 4.1 presents a sample volunteer contract.

EXHIBIT 4.1   SAMPLE VOLUNTEER CONTRACT

[Name of organization] and [name of volunteer] enter into the following agreement based on the attached job description for [name of volunteer job].

[Name of volunteer] agrees to provide the following volunteer services for [name of organization]. [List comes from the job description.]

In support of these services, [name of organization] agrees to provide the following for [name of volunteer] in the fulfillment of the agreed-on tasks:

1. Requested information within mutually agreed time frame
2. Regular reports of progress and results
3. Staff support as required for carrying out volunteer responsibilities
4. Access to staff members or other volunteers whose participation or information is required for successful completion of assignments
5. Prompt return of phone calls or response to faxes/materials
6. (Others added as desired)

The completion/expiration date of this [task] [term of office] is [date]. It is anticipated that the successful achievement of these responsibilities will require [number of days per month, hours per week, weeks per year]. The volunteer agrees to commit this amount of time or to notify the organization if such time commitment is not possible.

Periodic review of [service] [progress toward completion of task] will be provided by [name of staff person(s) or volunteer leader(s) who will also serve as supervisor(s) for this volunteer job]. If at any time during the period of this contact either party wishes to terminate the contract, a face-to-face meeting will be provided to review the reasons. At that time, all unfinished assignments or materials will be returned to [organization or person] for reassignment.

[Name of organization] looks forward to working with [name of volunteer] in the productive fulfillment of this important volunteer assignment.

Signed and dated.

One copy retained by volunteer; second copy for organization's files.

The sample letter of understanding may be used in place of a contract. It is sent following a face-to-face or phone meeting in which responsibilities have been reviewed and the volunteer has committed to undertake the task or office. Exhibit 4.2 presents a sample letter of understanding.

EXHIBIT 4.2   SAMPLE LETTER OF UNDERSTANDING

This may be used in place of a contract. It is sent following a face-to-face or phone meeting in which responsibilities have been reviewed and the volunteer has committed to undertake the task or office.

[Inside address]

Dear [first name, in most cases],

Thank you for agreeing to [name of task or office] for the [time period, completion date or duration of office]. We are looking forward to working with you on this important assignment. As discussed, we anticipate that this assignment will take approximately [number of hours] each [month or week or year].

The job description is enclosed. You will find that it reflects the points we reviewed in our conversation. If there are any listed responsibilities that do not match your understanding of our agreement, please let us know as soon as possible.

It is our understanding that you have the time and the willingness to provide this volunteer service to us, and we are very pleased. If, during our work together, problems arise that will prevent you from completing your assignment, please let us know as soon as possible so we can make other arrangements. [Name of staff person(s) or board leader(s)] will be your primary contact person during this assignment. Please contact him/her if you have questions or concerns.

Thank you for working together with us. Your volunteer service is essential to the successful delivery of our programs into the community.

---

4. A development plan that provides funding for both direct and indirect costs of donor development.

It costs money to raise money. Fundraising budgets tend to focus almost entirely on the *direct* costs of fundraising (stationery, postage, development salaries, telephones, printing of brochures), forgetting two *indirect* costs that are key aspects of going beyond fundraising: cultivation and stewardship. If board members and other volunteers are to be involved with the full development process, there must be budget for refreshments for prospect review sessions, cultivation and stewardship events, extra postage for nonrevenue-producing mailings (thanks yous, special mailings with "white papers" or newspaper clippings), special stationery for annual or capital campaign chairs who wish to write personal thank-you letters, requested reimbursement of out-of-pocket volunteer or staff expense for cultivation lunches or dinners. These are critical costs that organizations should not necessarily expect volunteers to absorb. In many organizations, volunteers are more than willing to contribute these costs. However, they should not be expected to do so unless it is communicated at the time of enlistment and reaffirmed before each event or activity. Also, an organization should consider its own program budgeting and how these costs are reflected even if they are covered by volunteers. It is important to keep realistic figures about the cost of fundraising—for purposes of accounting records and also for future planning. Be cautious about understating the costs of fundraising and development if, in fact, volunteers are funding certain activities that should be included in a total cost analysis. It is unwise to attempt to build development partnerships without clear communication of the financial implications of development and fundraising or an understanding of who is responsible for those costs.

5. A willingness on the part of staff and volunteers to approach development and fundraising at three levels: philosophical, strategic, and tactical (see Chapter 10).
   The philosophical, or "soft," side of the development process is the base from which staff and key board leaders set the tone that will inspire the structure, commitment, retention, and success of the development partnership. A commitment to the philosophical basis of philanthropy in general and the organization's mission in particular will be reflected in the quality and dedication of both staff and volunteers. The nonprofit sector has a serious and important purpose: to provide, in partnership with public and other private institutions, those programs and services that will meet the health, human services, cultural, artistic, educational, social, environmental, religious, and other needs of our communities. Those who keep their eye on this broader mission are more successful at keeping their own organization's mission in focus and in "putting away the tin cup."
   In recruiting volunteers, nonprofit organizations tend to be shy about the philosophical side of the sector. It is our philosophy or mission that distinguishes our sector from the corporate or business sector and it is uniquely appealing to prospective volunteers and donors. Nonprofits are an alternative. Nonprofits provide meaning and hope and social change, offering people an opportunity to become involved with something that is purposeful and powerful.
   In nonprofits, we must also convey, as volunteers and staff, a sense of the strategic. We must show our development partners that we have a clear strategy for the future. Within this strategy is a commitment to consistent evaluation and modification of plans and practices. We should conduct an annual evaluation of our long-range plan, quarterly evaluation of annual objectives, and monthly evaluation of the budget. Such strategic practice and intent, paired with a solid philosophical commitment to the sector and the organization, create an attractive opportunity for involvement by those whose thoughtfulness will be an asset to the organization.
   However, no amount of philosophy or strategy can keep an organization moving forward if the people involved do little or nothing. This is particularly true with development and fundraising. Organizations with perfect mission statements and textbook institutional

and/or development plans still fail at fundraising. The chief reason is an inability to perform at the tactical level. Inertia is a terrible organizational disease, easy to diagnose and difficult to cure. Tactical execution of the steps in development requires a workable framework.

THE DEVELOPMENT PROCESS: A PARTNERSHIP FOR DONOR AND RESOURCE DEVELOPMENT

The development process is a logical, seamless, and fluid sequence of steps that can be internalized over time by the participants in the development team. The following process, a uniting of several processes observed, taught, and implemented over the years, is intentionally detailed. Organizations need to know at the outset the intricacies of building relationships that will ensure their ability to go beyond fundraising. As the framework is used and tested, certain steps may be combined or omitted, depending on the needs of a particular prospect or organization. The goal with this process, as with any other with which the reader may be familiar, is to implement it in such a way that the prospect is not aware of his or her journey through the steps. The 10 steps in donor development are:

1. Identify/Qualify
2. Develop Initial Strategy
3. Cultivate
4. Involve
5. Evaluate and Determine Final Strategy
6. Assign
7. Solicit
8. Follow-through and Acknowledge
9. Steward
10. Renew

There are two critical ideas to remember when using this framework. First, every step in the process benefits from a partnership between board and staff and provides each with opportunities to be a resource, catalyst, and implementer. Second, only two of the steps require asking directly for funds: solicitation and renewal. Board members who are reluctant or lack confidence about asking—or who, for professional or conflict-of-interest reasons, cannot solicit funds (e.g., judges in certain communities are restricted from fundraising)—are able to play one of eight other key roles in the development process. These other roles are not "make work." They are vital to making the ask successful and retaining the donor as a renewing investor in the organization.

Be sure each step of the process involves the appropriate people in the development partnership. The effectiveness of the process depends on broad involvement.

1. Identify/Qualify

Identifying and qualifying potential prospects for initial or major gifts is an easy aspect of the development partnership. At every board meeting and at every staff meeting, provide a regular opportunity and system for identification. At board and staff meetings, on the top of the agenda and materials, include a half or full sheet of paper headed: "Since our last meeting, I have met the following individuals or heard about the following corporations and foundations who share our values and might be interested in our work." Provide space for the name(s) and addresses (if available) and for the person filling out the form to indicate the next steps (please add to the mailing list, please see me, another contact person is _____, etc.). Encourage people to write down names even if they do not have the address or phone; those numbers can be obtained after the lists are submitted. The person filling out the list should sign his or her name so the staff person (or volunteer leader in charge of prospect identification) can follow-up.

Then check these names against the existing database and add new names to the prospect files for further research. Those identified as appropriate to receive the newsletter (do not include a solicitation envelope for this initial mailing) are placed on the mailing list. When mailing out the first newsletter, it is very important to send it in an envelope with a cover note. If the recommending person has given permission to use his or her name, add a personal note: "At the suggestion of Roger Duncan, we are sending you a copy of our latest newsletter. He felt you would be interested in the work we are doing." Also state what follow-up the prospect may expect: receiving the newsletter for six months, a call from the recommending person, a call from the board chair, and so on. If the recommending person's name cannot be used, include a note that says: "It has come to our attention that you might be interested in learning more about our organization. . . ."

Qualification of prospective donors is now done in two primary ways: electronic database screening and personal review of prospect lists. The best approach is to do both: Perform the electronic screening to quickly identify who in the existing database has potential to make a larger gift, and perform the personal review to get those all-important insights and comments from people who know the prospects. The data screening information will not tell you the person's passions, values, linkages, issues, or relationship to others in the organization. Board members, staff, and nonboard volunteers can reveal those things.

Electronic Database Screening

Once used only by universities, major medical centers, large arts organizations, and other institutions with research budgets, today electronic database screening has become quite affordable. Many donor database management software programs offer screening for batches of names; and numerous fundraising consulting companies have added this service to their practice. When considering whether to go ahead with an electronic database screening:

- Be sure you have cleaned up your database before you screen it; otherwise you will waste time and money.

- Plan the screening close enough to whatever major fundraising you are planning so it is fresh—this information ages rapidly.

- Screen only the number of prospects you think you can review and prioritize within a reasonable time period—too often these lists grow stale in a box on the floor because there is not the time or personnel to use them appropriately.

- Be judicial in how the information received is used and shared: A researcher at a major university once said that his hardest job was getting his researchers to distinguish between what was interesting (but not relevant) and what was important.

Organizations that are large enough to have their own research staffs or organizations that use off-site researchers probably are aware of these resources. Most nonprofits do not have full- or even part-time research staff. In the increasingly competitive marketplace, getting this kind of information has become a necessity for developing strategic outreach to prospective donors. Pricing and strategies vary among the many screening organizations. Professional and electronic screening services for qualifying donors and prospects can be further researched by consulting with the American Prospect Research Association (APRA).

Silent Prospecting

As names are researched by a screening program or submitted by staff and board and added to the database, be sure to begin reviewing them regularly. Once a quarter, or more often if an electronic screening has just been done, pull lists of newly screened prospects (and other strong prospects who have not yet been run through a screening process) from the database for silent review by various staff and board groups.

"Silent review or prospecting" is a discreet and thorough approach to qualifying or "rating" prospects. Each participant at a silent prospecting session is provided with an identical list of 100 to 200 names to review. The names are presented as they are produced by the computer or on a form, and instructions are provided (see Exhibit 4.3). Each participant is asked to review the list silently, writing down comments regarding capacity to give, concern for the organization's issues and programs, and connection with the organization or with people associated with it. Questions can be open-ended or in a checklist. At the end of the session, lists are turned in to the staff or board person overseeing the session. Reviewers should write their names on each page of the list. Silent prospecting can be done as part of a board meeting or as a special session. It may also be done one-on-one with people who are unable to attend a meeting.

Silent prospecting is another opportunity for partnership. When reviewing a list that has been built over a period of months—a list that also may include some noncurrent donors and/or some names from published lists of donors to other similar organizations (other organization's annual reports are a good source for new names)—care and confidentiality are essential. Those reviewing the list learn a great deal about the ethics and integrity of an organization from observing this process.

Silent prospecting involves one or more sessions to which board members, staff members, key community volunteers involved with the program, former board members, and others who have knowledge of the community are invited. Be sure the sessions are arranged

EXHIBIT 4.3 SAMPLE INSTRUCTION SHEET FOR SILENT PROSPECTING

Thank you for agreeing to participate in our "silent prospecting" program. This is a vital step in our ability to identify those individuals in the community who will have the greatest interest in our organization and be most willing to contribute through our giving program. **The process is silent and confidential.**

The enclosed lists were drawn from existing and new lists put together for fundraising purposes. They include current donors, likely prospects, and others who have shown interest in our organization. In each case, the name and address are noted, and opposite the name are boxes for you to check, and places to comment. **Each person participating in the process has the same list.**

1. We are asking you to evaluate each individual according to **connection** (do you know this individual, and how well [primary link]; or does someone else [secondary link] know them who might be willing to contact them). Also, please indicate whether you are willing to contact the individual.

2. We would also like to know (of course) your estimate of their **capacity** to give. We have set this up to make it easy for you—just circle a number opposite each name. (These will vary according to goal.)

   A — $10,000 or more

   B — $5,000 – $9,999

   C — $1,000 – $4,999

   D — less than $1,000

3. **Concern** or interest is a big factor: choose from this checklist (suggestions for various organizations, e.g., arts education, historical societies, human services).

Dance	Piano	Vocal
Preservation	Special collection	Archives
Family service	Respite program	Childcare

A sample entry looks like this:

Mr. and Mrs. John Doe
2222 Jackson Street
Hillsborough, CA Zip
Phone

Primary link?   yes/no
Secondary link?   yes/no
Name of best contact: _____

Known or suspected interest: _____
Ability: A   B   C   D

I am _____ am not _____ willing to ask this person.

Comments:

Please work silently. If you have questions, ask a staff or board member for help. Be sure your name is on your envelope before you turn in your lists. Thank you so much. Please keep this process confidential.

at convenient times and places. Insist that people come to the organization; do not mail out lists for review. If people cannot attend a session, offer to take the list to their home or office and go over it with them. Because this list of potential donor-investors represents a great amount of time and involvement, regard it as one of the nonprofit's most valuable assets. This list of potential prospects should be guarded well and ideally should not go outside the organization's offices without an escort.

A computer-generated list can be used, allowing spaces between each entry for comments. Or a more structured approach may be used. An easy way to set up a more formal silent prospecting list is to run labels with the names and addresses of those the organization wishes to qualify. Using the suggested format (see Exhibit 4.4), set up a Master List using the labels. Reproduce a copy of the master list and an instruction sheet for each session participant. Give verbal instructions as well, and let each person proceed through the list at his or her own speed. A brief opportunity for socializing afterward may be provided, or a board or committee meeting. A strategy that improves attendance at silent prospecting sessions is to offer several alternative times and places: breakfast at a centrally located board member's home, afternoon at another board member's home in a different area of the community, and an evening at the agency's offices.

After all group and individual sessions have been held, appoint a board and staff prospect evaluation team to organize and analyze the responses. The silent prospecting form is designed so that each page can be cut or separated into three prospect evaluations. If a participant provided information on only one or two of the three names on the page, retain only the names on which information was provided. Discard the blank forms. Be sure the name or initials of the person providing the information is on each retained section of the form. Each name is handled separately, and multiple evaluations of the same person are grouped together. If a regular computer printout with space for writing has been used, the separation and collation may have to be approached differently. In either case, the aim is to have a system in which the body of information about a potential prospect is accumulated and can be analyzed for consistency and accuracy. This accumulated information becomes the basis for development of preliminary prospect profiles. These profiles are used by the development committee for screening and rating prospects for setting up a Key Prospect List (Exhibit 4.5) in Excel or on the donor database management system. Those names that had been electronically screened before the silent prospecting session should be well enough researched to take priority position on the Key Prospect List. If other names that had not been screened seem well positioned because of shared values, interest in the organization's issues, or capacity can be set aside for the next electronic screening, or the nonprofit may feel it has enough information to move forward with cultivation or solicitation.

Silent prospecting works for organizations of all sizes and should be done regularly to keep the prospect pipeline full. In addition to verifying and enhancing electronic data screening research, it is also useful for:

- Identifying potential capital campaign prospects (in which case silent prospecting may be done more often than quarterly when ramping up for and during the campaign)

EXHIBIT 4.4   SAMPLE MASTER LIST FORMAT FOR SILENT PROSPECTING

By: Initials _____

PROSPECT: Primary Link?   YES   NO

                                 Secondary Link?   YES   NO

                                 Name of Best Contact: _____

                                 Known or Suspected Interest: _____

                                 Ability: A   B   C   D

I am _____ am not _____ willing to ask this person.

COMMENTS:

_____

_____

_____

By: Initials _____

PROSPECT: Primary Link?   YES   NO

                                 Secondary Link?   YES   NO

                                 Name of Best Contact: _____

                                 Known or Suspected Interest: _____

                                 Ability: A   B   C   D

I am _____ am not _____ willing to ask this person.

COMMENTS:

_____

_____

_____

By: Initials _____

PROSPECT: Primary Link?   YES   NO

                                 Secondary Link?   YES   NO

                                 Name of Best Contact: _____

                                 Known or Suspected Interest: _____

                                 Ability: A   B   C   D

I am _____ am not _____ willing to ask this person.

COMMENTS:

_____

_____

_____

EXHIBIT 4.5 KEY PROSPECT LIST

Name	Due Date	Primary Contact	Amount Requested	Past Activity	Current Cultivation	Comments	Amount Committed
STRATEGIC GIFTS—$100,000+	*Tier One*						
	12/1/20___		$250,000	Key major donor			
			$300,000	Special project support		Additional in-kind support—site review, project management and videotape	$300,000
	12/1/20___						
	12/1/20___		$100,000				
	2/1/20___		$100,000	Special project support			
	12/1/20___		$100,000				
	12/1/20___		$250,000	Key major donor			
	open		$300,000	Key major donor			
	To follow corporate ask		$100,000	Key major donor			
	1/15/20___		$300,000				
	11/15/20___		$750,000				
	2/15/20___		$100,000				
	9/1/20___		$300,000	Key major donor		Called on 9/28/20___. She said "everything looks good." Prelim. review 10/20___; decision 12/20___	

(continues)

61

EXHIBIT 4.5 KEY PROSPECT LIST *(Continued)*

Name	Due Date	Primary Contact	Amount Requested	Past Activity	Current Cultivation	Comments	Amount Committed
	11/1/20___		$300,000				
	12/1/20___		$100,000	Special project support in ___			
	12/1/20___		$100,000				
	8/5/20___		$468,358	Key major donor	$150,000 pledged for 20___	Reapply for second year of funding—7/15/20___ deadline for 20___ funds	
	12/1/20___		$100,000	Key major donor			
	2/1/20___		$100,000	Special project support in ___			
	12/1/20___		$100,000				
	12/1/20___		$100,000				
	12/1/20___		$300,000				
	1/15/20___		$200,000	Have asked to invite to site in 1/20___			
MAJOR GIFTS— $10,000+	*Tier Two*						
	11/15/20___		$25,000				
	4/1/20___		$15,000				
	4/15/20___		$50,000				

Tier Three names are usually included at the end of the Key Prospect List, but are not analyzed thoroughly until moved into Tier Two.

- Qualifying existing lists of members, subscribers, donors, parents, students, or other constituencies
- Infusing new names into a stalled annual or capital campaign
- Requalifying donor-investors who are thought to have greater capacity, connection, or concern

One very successful silent prospecting session occurred toward the end of a capital campaign. A performing arts organization, having "plateaued" in its fundraising for a new building, realized it had not been moving prospects into the pipeline. In an all-out effort to infuse the prospect base with new names, the organization set up a meeting to which were invited a wide range of potentially helpful constituents: parents of students (and former students) in the training program, people who had participated in travel/study trips, current and former board members, staff people, and current funders. At moments the effort seemed chaotic: Lists circulated, the "silence" was often broken, people moved in and out as they completed their evaluations. However, it was fruitful and provided some new high-potential prospects as well as a somewhat daunting list of individuals and organizations needing more cultivation and/or research—all of whom had been previously overlooked. The eventual success of the campaign was partially derived from the results of that session.

In silent prospecting, success of the process is directly related to the comprehensiveness of the constituencies represented by those participating in the process. Organizations that cast their nets broadly are rewarded by excellent information.

2. Develop Initial Strategy

Based on the results of the electronic data screening and silent prospecting sessions, certain prospects will emerge as those most likely to make a gift within the shortest period of time. They are the ones who have a clear connection to the organization, a known concern about the programs or services and those they serve, and capacity to make a gift at whatever level has been identified in the qualifying process. Others with known concern or capacity and/or connection will be identified, but may not have all three vital qualifications. Still others will be seen as great potential prospects, but too little information will have been generated during silent prospecting to make informed judgments about the next step in the relationship building process.

Creating a Key Prospect List

Priority prospects, and the strategies for their cultivation and solicitation, are organized into a Key Prospect List (see Exhibit 4.5). Many database management software programs have the capacity to generate such a list. Organizations can also maintain these lists on Excel or a similar spreadsheet software or set up their own format in another preferred software program. Whatever option chosen, the list should be organized into three parts:

1. **Tier One** includes prospects about whom a great deal is known and with whom there is already a relationship. For these individuals or institutions, the strategy will

be to move them toward solicitation in the most appropriate and timely way. Preliminary volunteer assignments can be made for initiating the cultivation and solicitation steps and a tentative figure and target date set for the ask. All strategy at this point is preliminary. The strategy may change several times depending on the actual readiness of the prospect to make a gift. In the process, the development partnership members may decide that another solicitor is more appropriate or that they have incorrectly estimated the capacity or concern of the individual. For purposes of getting the process rolling, however, the Tier One list should reflect preliminary solicitor assignment, target figure, and date by which the ask should be made.

2. **Tier Two** comprises those individuals and organizations who need more cultivation than those in Tier One. Usually these are prospects who need more connection to the organization. These are often potential funders whose concern for and capacity to support the programs and services of the organization are known because of the other funding they do in the community. They already may be donors of smaller gifts to the organization. Most often the weak aspect of their potential as a donor-investor is their connection; fortunately, cultivation can build this. The strategy for them will include initial or continuing cultivation to further explore the shared values, common interests, or connection with the organization or people in the organization.

3. **Tier Three** includes those about whom there is even less knowledge. These may be people whose names are revealed during electronic screening. Frequently these are people whose capacity is known because of their community position, income or investments, and gifts to other kinds of organizations in the community. They may be modest donors already. But little else may be known. They may require more research, and certainly will need cultivation. While there is a long-term priority for identifying values and building a relationship with those in Tier Three, principal energy is appropriately placed with Tiers One and Two.

The Key Prospect List is the strategic management tool for prospect development and solicitation and the basis for monitoring progress. In a well-managed prospect and donor development program, names in Tier Two will be moved into Tier One as those prospects are solicited. Tier Three prospects are moved into Tier Two for more focused cultivation if research reveals promising areas of potential. Otherwise, the names may be dropped from the Key Prospect List and other names moved on to the list.

Evaluate the key prospect list continually so that those in Tiers Two and Three, if they prove to have no potential as investors, can be moved off the lists to make room for those identified in subsequent (usually quarterly or semiyearly) silent prospecting sessions.

3. Cultivate

Planning moves into action with this step. Cultivation is more than random acts of kindness: It is a strategic, disciplined, time-sensitive, focused, and continual interaction with individuals (and institutions) with whom we believe we can establish a lasting donor-investor relationship.

Once again, the partnership is called on. Staff choreographs and participates in opportunities for board members and other volunteers to meet and talk with prospective donors. While these are primarily prospects in Tier One, initial strategy setting may also involve some prospects in Tier Two who are connected to prospects in Tier One and might be responsive to an event or opportunity to be with their friends. For cultivation to work well, volunteers should make themselves available for regularly planned events (concerts, receptions, lectures, etc.) to which prospective donors will be invited and also for special cultivation activities (tours, lunches with the executive director) planned with a particular prospect (or prospects) in mind. Volunteers also need to provide feedback to staff regarding meetings they have held independently with identified prospects.

Here are two good rules to keep cultivation moving smoothly:

1. *Communicate any volunteer interaction with potential funders from any tier in the Key Prospect List to staff.* To make this process easier, many organizations create and post to a volunteer-only Web site (or distribute for those who would rather fill out and fax) an "Action Update" form (see Exhibit 4.6). These forms are widely used in capital campaigns, but also in the process of cultivation for annual gifts. "E-reports" can be encouraged from volunteers who prefer to use e-mail. Whatever method, the point is the same: The information needs to get back to staff to integrate into the database and/or to take action.

2. *Coordinate any cultivation that takes place on behalf of an organization with the staff.* The reasons for this are several:

   - Staff may have information that is critical to any conversation with the prospect (e.g., previous gifts, previous outreach).

   - The prospect may be "on hold" for another opportunity or time for a reason not known to the volunteer.

   - The prospect may have already been assigned to another volunteer and the duplicate effort would send a confusing signal to the prospect.

   - The volunteer may benefit from special information that staff can make available from what is already known about that individual's connection or concerns.

We tend to think of cultivation as parties and events during which we introduce potential donor-investors to the people and mission of our organization. Although this is true, it is not the whole picture. Parties and events, without systematic follow-up based on a cogent cultivation plan, are ineffective. Follow-*through* is required. There is an important distinction between follow-*up*, which implies a renewed effort, and follow-*through*, which implies sustained effort. There is never any relaxing of effort in the fundraising sector (news that comes as no surprise to anyone reading this book).

After any kind of event or activity, a follow-through plan ensures a stronger connection with those who attended. Good follow-through techniques include immediate addition of names to the mailing list and thank-you letters that convey the success of the event or program to those who attended. Personal phone calls from board members or event committee members to patrons of the event also make a huge impact. If some of

EXHIBIT 4.6   ACTION UPDATE FORM

ACTION UPDATE

Today's Date: _____

Volunteer's Name: _____

Prospect's Name: _____

Date of Action: _____

What Happened: _____

_____

_____

_____

_____

_____

_____

Next Action Planned: _____

_____

_____

By When: _____

Comments: _____

_____

_____

_____

_____

Please fax to (number), e-mail, or mail to the Development Office.

those on the guest list are Tier One prospects, be sure a board member is assigned to look after those individuals at the event. Afterward, have the board member file an Action Update form, send an e-mail, or meet with a staff member to plan the next steps. At cultivation or recognition lunches or dinners, assign a board member to each table (unless the table has been bought by someone for a group and is completely filled). Where tables are hosted, a member of the board or dinner committee can circulate graciously at appropriate intervals among the seated guests.

The quality of the cultivation and the follow-through provided has a major effect on the ease and success of the eventual solicitation. Those responsible for monitoring the cultivation of key prospects need to recognize signs that a prospect is getting close to the point where he or she can be asked for the gift. Cultivation, because it is pleasant and painless, can easily become a consuming activity. Continuing cultivation staves off the inevitable: asking for the gift. Learn to pick (and savor) ripe fruit *before* it drops to the ground.

Role of Information in the Cultivation Process

Not all cultivation involves the kind of personal interaction just described. Providing information is another way to cultivate prospects. An electronic or mailed newsletter is a form of cultivation, and can be used very effectively for this purpose. Evaluate the newsletter and be sure it is conveying the message that the organization most wants readers to receive. Does it convey the *impact and results* of programs, or does it focus on the organization's needs? Does it portray—in words and images—the kinds of people the organization is serving and its programs? Does it balance volunteer information, donor recognition, and program impact? Apply the same questions to the Web site, and be sure the Web site is kept current. Far too many Web sites list events that happened months before. This sends a poor signal to constituents.

The organization's newsletter and Web site are two forms of nonpersonal cultivation, but there are others as well. If a special program is of known interest to the prospect, have the program director prepare a "white paper" relating the program to an article in a magazine or newspaper that focuses on a local, national, or international need that the organization is addressing through this program. A family service organization focused on its child abuse prevention program with a group of donors. An excellent article on the importance of child abuse prevention education was pulled from a major newspaper with national circulation and prestige. The position paper prepared by the staff person focused entirely on what this family service organization was doing to address this national issue locally. The clipping, with the article, was mailed to prospective funders as well as current investors. The mailing to prospects included a note drawing their attention to the local agency's efforts to address an issue about which they knew the individual or institution was concerned. It was a strong cultivation tool. For current donor-investors, the articles were mailed with a note that thanked them for helping to make such programs possible. Both notes had a high impact on the funders and prospects to which they were sent.

"E-updates" are similar to white papers in intent, but vastly more simple to create and send out. These brief notes convey a program-related success to donors, and include appreciation for their continued support of the work of the organization. An organization that works with homeless and runaway youth let its donors (some of whom had given $100 or less but were known to have higher potential) know of the success it had attained in reuniting a runaway girl with her parents. The organization thanked the donors for helping make this possible. The story told was detailed and touching: The impact was profound. When considering this approach, be sure to use an e-mail program that individualizes each recipient's email address—the organization can be working from a 2,500-name list-serve, but be sure only one address appears on the e-mail. Consult a provider of software or service for more information on how to make this kind of "e-mail blast" work.

Cultivation also occurs unexpectedly. Favorable press coverage of an event or a program will heighten potential funder awareness of an organization and its mission. Enthused board members and other volunteers become informal advocates, often unwittingly arousing great interest among those with whom they interact socially and professionally. The largest gift from an individual (nearly $500,000) to a campaign for a social service agency in California was made anonymously by a person who became interested in the organization because of the enthusiasm and advocacy of one of its staff members. The donor had no prior connection to the organization but, over time, respected the commitment of the staff member.

In yet another instance, a bequest in excess of $1 million was received by a children's services agency from a woman who had no direct experience with the organization. During the woman's years of illness, her neighbor, a volunteer for the organization, would bring her lunch from the agency's volunteer-run restaurant, which benefited the organization. The woman asked the volunteer regularly about the organization, about the children served, and about her involvement. When notification came about the provision in the will, everyone—including the volunteer—was taken by surprise. There had been no previous indication.

No deliberate cultivation took place in either of these instances. Both gifts were the spontaneous result of a relationship with an individual who was committed to an organization. These stories underscore the importance of staff and volunteers being informed and enthusiastic about the organizations they represent. We never know when someone's commitment—that sustained passion that people recognize and respect—will be a catalyst in converting casual interest into a gift with impact.

Most cultivation is more formal. Organizations, as part of their overall development plan, should have a component that describes cultivation strategies. The plan should include a set of calendared activities (e.g., tours on the first and third Tuesdays, lunch with the CEO or program staff on the first Wednesday) to which board and nonboard volunteers can bring prospects. It should also include a commitment to be responsive to those individuals or institutions for whom calendared activities may not be appropriate. They require individualized cultivation experiences. The cultivation plan should also include a timeline and an estimate, based on the Key Prospect List, of the number of people needed for each activity or step. Critical to successful cultivation is sufficient budget to support these activities. If organizations are to go beyond fundraising, they must be willing to invest in cultivation that will result in meaningful investment and be the beginning of lasting relationships.

4. Involve

This is a powerful concept and a powerful process. To truly involve someone means to engage them in the work and the results of the organization in such a way that they begin to feel that they are participants. Involvement encourages a deeper exploration of the values of the potential funder and the way in which the values of the organization can bring that individual or organization satisfaction as an investor. Although involvement sometimes begins with the donor–investor making an initial gift, most involvement of major donors develops out of the cultivation process.

Involvement differs from cultivation in the nature of the relationship. Cultivation can be a somewhat one-sided process, with the organization providing information and participation opportunities and both the organization and the potential funder observing and listening/learning. Involvement is a more dynamic stage of the relationship. The potential funder may become personally involved with a project or may be enlisted to serve on a committee or task force.

A regional repertory theater created a unique way of involving its potential funders for a proposed capital campaign. They were invited to become part of a "Play Support Group" that formed at the beginning of preparation for each of the company's eight season productions. The Play Support Group, which included prospective funders as well as board members who had been assigned to cultivate and solicit these prospects, was present at the first reading of the play and attended subsequent readings and rehearsals. The director shared his or her interpretation of the playwright's script with the group and invited conversation around its themes and nuances. Costume and set designers showed the group their preliminary sketches as well as their evolving creations. Play Support Group members were organized to take out-of-town cast and production staff members to dinner and to look after their needs, if convenient. On opening night, the Play Support Group was given special seating and recognition. As a result of their involvement, new potential funders became enthused about the theater company. Not incidentally, board members who participated in the Play Support Group had a renewed and deeper commitment to the organization. Their capital campaign, conducted several years later, benefited from a strong base of informed and passionate supporters.

Although a performing arts organization has more obvious opportunities for such involvement, other kinds of organizations can fashion creative ways to involve potential funders—and their possible solicitors—in programs that will bring them closer to the organization. In 2004, NET (Nebraska Educational Telecommunications) produced a moving and significant program on the Nebraska Canteen that served soldiers who were traveling by train across country for deployment overseas during World War II. They invited World War II veterans to come see the making of the production and were honored and gratified that word of mouth increased the number of "Canteen veterans" who came to be interviewed and see the making of this historic and touching documentary. Some organizations have issues of client confidentiality that preclude such direct involvement. However, involvement with program staff in presentations and discussions can be quite engaging. And, using another approach, an environmental organization in the San Francisco Bay Area takes potential funders and board members out on their patrol boat for excursions during which they watch for signs of oil spills or other hazards to the fragile balance of the bay. Museums often find that involvement in docent or other classes has a high impact on a person's eventual commitment as a donor, and schools and colleges can find an abundance of ways to get potential funders involved.

Recognize involvement as a critical step, and set up systems to ensure it is a regular part of the development process. And remember that it is another opportunity for the board/staff partnership to work together effectively.

The involvement phase should reveal much about the strength of the common values and interests that the potential donor shares with the organization. Involvement is a time for testing ideas with the prospect and for handling initial questions or objections the prospective funder may raise. Encourage questions, answer objections candidly, and provide information requested by the potential funder openly and honestly. Transparency, accountability, and disclosure of information are critical factors in building an investor relationship.

5. Evaluate and Determine Final Strategy

At this point in the process, the relationship that is growing between the organization and the potential donor must be evaluated. These are some of the questions to ask:

- Are the right board members (or other volunteers) cultivating this prospect?
- What are this person's principal interests, concerns, motivations?
- Have we provided the necessary and right information for this prospect?
- Has he or she met with those individuals with whom there will be the greatest shared values?
- Are there other connections we need to build?
- Have we done adequate cultivation?
- Have we assessed capacity correctly?
- What amount do we feel would be the appropriate ask? And for what project or program?
- What is the best timing for the ask? Has that changed since our original strategy?
- Who should be included in the solicitation meeting?

Evaluation and determination of final strategy requires focus on the results of the first four steps in order to plan the solicitation. Draft a written prospect evaluation, based on the above questions, and keep it on file so that a confidential copy can be provided to those who will be assigned as solicitors in the next step.

6. Assign

There is an old saying in fundraising: A successful solicitation occurs when the right person asks the right prospect for the right amount for the right purpose at the right time. Wishful thinking? Not necessarily. Such inspired assignments are possible if we are attentive to the steps that lead up to them. The development partnership is critical in the assignment phase. Staff and volunteers work together on this step to ensure the highest possible success by making the best possible solicitation assignment. During cultivation, certain relationships probably formed between the prospect and individuals involved with the organization. Assignment is based on these relationships. Current donors, active board members or former board members with continuing involvement in the organization, or members of the community for whom the prospect has respect and with whom the organization has a strong relationship are all potential candidates for the assignment.

More than one solicitor may be assigned to a prospect. Team solicitations are best. Two or three individuals who represent board and staff may call on one or more individuals who have been appropriately cultivated and are ready to be asked. Board members provide vital community linkage; staff members offer expertise and familiarity with program and administrative issues. A board member needs to be on every solicitation team, paired with program, administrative, or development staff or with another volunteer whose linkage to the prospect or commitment to the cause would be persuasive to the prospect.

Regardless of whether two or three solicitors are assigned, it is still very important for one person to have the primary responsibility for coordinating the solicitation, making the appointment, and bringing the prospect to the point where the solicitation can be made. Information about the assignment should be entered into the database. Preparation for the solicitation should be made with the entire solicitation team, but may be preceded by a strategy meeting with the lead solicitor and the development director. In this meeting, a solicitation plan leading to the next step should be developed.

7. Solicit

If the previous six steps have been well planned and implemented, this step will follow naturally. As relationships develop, the thought of asking for the gift becomes less troublesome. At this point in the process, the prospect should be ready and, in fact, will begin to wonder why he or she has not been asked. The details of the solicitation process are covered in Chapter 5. However, some essential points regarding all solicitations are listed here because they relate to the entire donor development process.

Gauge Your Timing Carefully
A solicitation that comes so late in the process that the prospective donor has lost interest or patience with the organization is as doomed as a solicitation that is made prematurely.

As the donor development process moves forward, be confident about merging or skipping steps that may not seem necessary for a particular donor or about extending certain steps for others who do not seem as ready. The "new" philanthropists who emerged in the late 1990s and early twenty-first century in America are impatient with lengthy processes. Often they have researched an organization extensively before getting involved. They approach nonprofit giving as social investment, and apply the same due diligence as they do to their other kinds of investments. When they are ready to invest, they do not want to be delayed by the organization's idea of what it wants them to know or learn.

The development process should be fluid and flexible. It is intended as a description, not a prescription. If prospects start asking how they can help the organization, be prepared to move into the solicitation by offering some gift options. If, in conversations, prospects share information that would indicate their interest in making a gift at that time, act on it. One of the things we have learned about the development process is that it requires intense listening skills, a great deal of intuition, and the courage to move ahead somewhat rapidly when prospects indicate that their connection and concerns have been brought to the point of action.

Be Specific about What Is Wanted

Always ask the donor for a specific amount of money, and describe the results that gift will have. We talk to donors about *major gifts,* which is an internal definition attached to a development goal or benchmark. It is more appropriate to talk with potential donor-investors about a *gift that will have an impact.* The size of an impact gift varies, as does the size of a major gift. However, the word "impact" reminds us to focus on results—and conveys the idea that this gift will have an impact on the organization and its programs. Be clear with the donor regarding the purpose of the gift. If the donor wishes to restrict it to a particular program or building objective, state how the donor's wishes will be ensured. Likewise, if the keenest priority in an organization is for unrestricted annual or endowment money, make the case to the donor for an unrestricted gift. Be sure that those who make unrestricted gifts are recognized as appropriately as those whose gifts are restricted to a particular building or program.

Have a Menu of Recognition Opportunities Ready for Discussion, But Be Alert to How the Donor Wants the Gift Recognized

When asking for an impact gift, communicate the ways the donor can be recognized. However, exercise caution in describing these opportunities. Some individuals prefer no recognition at all and would rather not give than be recognized inappropriately. Test the water. Find out if and how the person would like to be recognized if the gift is made, and build a response around those desires. The reluctance of some funders—both individual and institutional—to be recognized publicly (or even privately) should always be respected.

Approach the Solicitation from the Shared Values Basis of Philanthropy and Development

Even at this final "fundraising" stage, remember to make the ask in the context of the larger philosophical and strategic functions of philanthropy and fundraising. This keeps the ask values-driven and mission connected and helps solicitors keep the tin cup firmly out of the process (see Chapters 1 and 2).

Relax and Enjoy the Moment

As developed in Chapter 5, the ask should be a moment of *release,* not *pressure.* All the donor's desires and the organization's opportunities should come together at this moment. The solicitation team is the catalyst for giving donors opportunities to act on their values, bringing to fruition their connection, concern, and capacity in an investment that will have an impact in the community and help ensure the advancement of the organization.

8. Follow-through and Acknowledge

Whatever the result of the solicitation, there is an opportunity to further the relationship by follow-through and acknowledgment. Even if the final answer is no (tips for converting nos or for accepting them as merely temporary setbacks are provided in Chapter 5), handwritten personal notes thanking prospects for their time are a gracious gesture. There have been countless instances where a no, acknowledged kindly by the solicitor or the organization, has turned into a yes (and an immediate gift).

The board/volunteer/staff partnership is particularly critical here. Organizations should provide staff support to volunteers in assembling information needed for follow-through, or provide stationery and postage for the notes that are written. Follow-through is required if the answer is still pending following the solicitation: If the prospect needs more time or information, both must be provided with a clear indication of the next steps that will be implemented. The follow-through schedule for each pending solicitation should be suggested and carried out by staff working with the volunteer leadership. If financial or program information has been requested, it needs to be supplied as quickly as possible. If the prospect has indicated an interest in meeting with other funders, certain program staff, or would like to tour the facility, the request should be arranged as part of this step in the process.

There is great urgency in this step. Failure to follow through appropriately can negate the entire effort that has gone into the process to this point.

9. Steward

Stewardship of the *gift* is a venerable concept in good nonprofit management. Stewardship of the giver, fully explored in Chapter 8, is a newer concept and one of equal importance. In some denominations in Christian churches, "stewardship" is the name given to the annual campaign for congregate pledges. Originally, to be a "steward" was to be a "keeper of the hall" (old English). In the context of the development process, stewardship is the organization's privileged responsibility to be watchful "keepers" of those who, through their gifts, are "keeping" the organization healthy.

Most organizations recognize the importance of accountability in the use of donated funds. But in many organizations there is an alarming laxness in stewardship of the donor that results in difficulty and resistance during the gift renewal process. Low annual giving renewal rates may be a symptom of poor stewardship. The results of poor stewardship often are revealed most sharply during a campaign feasibility study or, sadly, after a campaign has begun. Neglected investors are not apt to reinvest. Saying thank you is not enough. We must convey the continuing value and impact of the investment in order to solidify relationships.

Stewardship can be viewed as "cultivation after the fact." It affords donors the same attention and thoughtfulness as prospects. Stewardship stops the too-common practice of stuffing donors into the donor file as soon as the gift is made and closing the drawer until it is time to ask for money again.. As soon as a prospective donor–investor makes a gift, he or she begins a new relationship with the organization. We must not look on that same moment as the end of a somewhat long, exhausting, and tedious transaction. We must view it as the beginning of a transformational relationship that will be grown through stewardship.[1]

Stewardship should be based on the donor's, not the organization's, desires. While certain stewardship practices (prompt thank-you letters, accurate data entry that prevents duplicate or incorrect records, courteous and timely notification of upcoming events or activities of interest to the donor) are standard, we must be willing to tailor our other stewardship practices to fit the needs of the donor. For example, at one museum, a donor who had made a gift of significant impact was offered membership in the highest recognition level. He refused that recognition, saying he was already involved in too many recognition groups. Rather than immediately offering another alternative or accepting the idea that he did not want to be further involved, the board chair asked him what *he* would like to experience in recognition of his very generous gift. The donor knew what he wanted: "consulting" time with the curator of the museum's collection in which he had the keenest interest and was himself a modest collector. It was arranged, and the donor's connection with the museum increased along with his knowledge. Today, more than a decade later, the relationship between the individual and the curator thrives, and the museum's building program and collections have benefited tremendously from his increasing level of investment.

Astonishingly, sometimes the best stewardship is no contact at all—*as long as that is what the donor wants!* One of the principal funders for a midwestern university capital campaign, when questioned in a postcampaign survey designed to assess funder satisfaction with the development practices of the university, was asked how he would describe the stewardship the university had provided. "Excellent," he said. "The best of any organization we fund." Pressed to describe what the university had done to warrant this praise, he said, "Nothing. They leave us alone." Questioned further, he revealed that his foundation wants neither recognition or follow-up after the formal thank you. This information is conveyed to those they fund, and nearly all choose to ignore the foundation's request. The university, by honoring the request and "leaving them alone," was, in fact, providing the best stewardship of all: the kind the donor wanted.

The importance of strong stewardship—consistent and based on the donor's needs and preferences—cannot be overstated. It is one of the most critical factors in strong organizations. It is covered more extensively in Chapter 8.

10. Renew

Donors like renewing their investment if they feel the gift has made an impact. Feedback that focuses on results, and proper stewardship of the gift and the giver will ensure the organization's right to renew the gift. Those who fear going back to the same donors in the following year miss the point. An organization does not seek funds because it *has* needs, but because it *meets* needs. The needs that are met seldom diminish; in today's social and cultural environment they only increase. If an organization is doing a good job and can point to results, and if the growing need in the community for the organization's programs and services can be substantiated, then it should be able to turn with pride of achievement to investors and invite them to increase their investment so the organization can have even greater impact.

Renewal of donors who have made impact gifts starts the cycle over again, with all its partnership implications. Requalify donors based on their recent gifts and then proceed (albeit more quickly) through the other steps leading up to the solicitation. Donors, if treated like partners with the fundraiser and the organization in meeting community needs, will want to reinvest.

Remember, too, that "renewal" is not just renewal of the gift: It is renewal of the relationship. It is an annual or less frequent opportunity to bring someone ever closer into the mission, vision and values of an organization and offer them opportunities to renew their values-based investment and their relationship with an effective community organization.

SUMMARY

The nonprofit sector depends on multiple partnerships within their organizations and in the community to deliver on their mission. Of all of these partnerships, the development partnership is the most powerful and inclusive. It involves staff and volunteers and engages funders too. It is the pivotal partnership for all nonprofits, and ensures the success of donor and fund development that is based on the mission and values of the organization.

The development partnership is grown and nurtured around a 10-step donor development process, each step of which is a partnership between staff and board and only two of which require asking for funds directly. Forging strong partnerships for the development process is an important activity for all nonprofits, one with great immediate and long-term rewards for the organization and its staff, those it involves on its board and in other volunteer capacities, and its funders.

NOTE

1. Kay Sprinkel Grace and Alan L. Wendroff, *High Impact Philanthropy: How Donors, Boards, and Nonprofit Organizations Can Transform Communities* (John Wiley & Sons, 2000).

CHAPTER 5

Inviting Investment

Solicitation is the opportunity to invite investment. As the culmination of the first six steps of the development process, solicitation is the action that enables those who have been cultivated to act on the values they share with our organizations. Although *solicitation* may feel like a one-sided equation, with the labor and the benefit focused on the not-for-profit organization, positioning the process as *investment* balances the organization and the potential donor-investor as equal players in the transaction.

The organization has, by this point, discovered the concerns, connection, and capacity of the prospect (see Chapter 4). The potential donor-investor knows the organization and is familiar with not only its programs but with their results. The invitation to invest is a logical and fulfilling conclusion to this process for both the organization and the prospect.

Just as "development" is not a euphemism for fundraising, "investment" is not a euphemism for donation. Development and investment are different, stronger concepts, and they bring different, more powerful results. All investors in not-for-profit organizations are donors, but not all donors are investors. The investor relationship is not measured by the size of the gift, but by the *intensity of the connection* the donor and the organization feel with each other. Although we may easily identify donors of impact gifts as "investors," we need to make sure that we consider all donors as investors. The investor relationship is dynamic; the donor relationship may be passive.

The investor relationship is not measured by the size of the gift, but by the *connection* the donor feels with the organization. The purpose of the 10-step development process, presented in Chapter 4, is to develop and strengthen that connection with as many investors as possible. As organizations move potential and current donors through the 10 steps in the development process, they are building investor relationships, not just a donor base. These relationships require more effort on the part of board and staff to nurture and maintain, but the long-term benefit is substantial. The existence of these investor relationships enables organizations to go beyond fundraising.

Some major or impact gifts are given by people who do not yet have an investor relationship with the organization—their gift is a signal of alignment they feel with programs, impact, and/or values. Many smaller gifts are impulsive, and may also lack the true "investor" motivation—but in both cases, a relationship can be cultivated by the organization. The investor relationship is dynamic (see Chapter 2); the donor relationship may be passive. Organizations that follow the 10 steps in the development process build more than a donor base: They build a base of investors with potential for sustained involvement. Investors require more time and energy from board and staff to identify, nurture, and sustain, but the long-term benefit is substantial.

Defining Donor-Investor

An investor, or a donor-investor, is an individual or organization whose financial commitment to a nonprofit is guided by a belief in their shared values and in the ability of the investor and the organization to mutually benefit each other and the community.

Investment should be approached as if it will be long term and renewable. Quick-fix fundraising does not stimulate investment. Investors in nonprofits look for two bottom lines (financial and values) but one principal return: the knowledge that their investment will have the intended results and make an impact on the organization and the community. Investors are more willing to renew gifts given to meet the *community's* need for a particular program or service than gifts made because of the *organization's* need for money. The wise investor knows that the community's need for these programs or services is always apt to be there and will be proud to renew when the impact of a first gift is communicated.

Building a Base of Donor-Investors

It takes new strategies to bring potential long-term investors into an organization. Engaging donor-investors takes hard work by board and staff, and requires a deep institutional commitment to create and sustain an environment in which investments will flourish. The effort required to involve potential donor-investors with organizations demands follow-through that many organizations may feel they cannot provide. Driven by an urgent need for funds and by lack of understanding about the development process, organizations end up asking for money without benefit of proper strategic relationship building. Once the gift has been made, they let their donors lie fallow, reactivating the contact only when another gift is needed or given. The result is a disjointed, exhausting, and frustrating cycle of hand-to-mouth fundraising.

The investment concept is based on an understanding of the difference between development and fundraising. Development is a sustained and systematic multistep process; fundraising is a focused and immediate transaction. A successful development process facilitates effective fundraising. Successful solicitation of new or renewed gifts requires organizations to cultivate their prospects and be stewards to their donors. It does not just happen. Many campaigns get off to very slow starts because there is so much "remedial stewardship" required. Time has to be spent building connections with current and past donors that have either been severed through neglect or never established. Too many organizations have assembled the bicycle while riding it.

CHALLENGES TO IMPLEMENTING AN INVESTMENT ATTITUDE

Internalizing a commitment in all organizations to the value of development as an investment process could revolutionize fundraising and cause both communities and organizations to look on the activities of our sector more favorably. Doing this implies a massive program of educating communities and donors not only in America but also western Europe and other parts of the world where the development process is even less understood. In eastern Europe, where existing systems of government support were completely stripped from the infrastructure, there has been a remarkable acceptance of American development practices. In other parts of Europe and throughout the world, there is still a tremendous need to undo old beliefs. Governments, which were often the sole supporters of charitable organizations, have reduced their support and will continue to shrink as sources of both steady funding and influence. But the specter and hope of renewed government support does not fade in countries around the globe, and there is a lingering dream that it will be restored. This is highly unlikely, given the current global economy and a growing belief that private funding must match or augment public funding around the world. This is a time to heed the advice given by Bob Waterman, in his book *The Renewal Factor,* and "surrender the memories." Until there is acceptance that things will not return to what they were, the impediments to change will persist.

To a smaller extent, the same is true in the United States. The increased fiscal conservatism by the government will not change substantially regardless of the politics of the party in power. The resources are just not there, even if the will or passion is. Some cities and states in the United States are nearly bankrupt. Nonprofits have to increase the services they provide. To do so, we must change the way we do business. We must establish ourselves as excellent investment opportunities for strengthening our communities at local, regional, and national levels.

If our sector is to survive and serve society, we will have to continue educating our communities about the importance of their ongoing investment in nonprofit organizations.

ASKING FOR INVESTMENT

How we ask for the gift is one of the most critical aspects of inviting investment. Tin cups, as discussed in Chapter 2, are out of fashion. We must turn the needs-benefit equation around and move the giving process to one in which we promote and respect the *mutual* benefits that accrue to the donor, the organization, and the community in a true investment partnership. Asking requires volunteer and staff participation and diligent coaching and training. Effective solicitors are those people whom we are confident can bring donor-investors into our organizations.

Here are some observations about masterful solicitors.

- They are always well prepared, but never seem rehearsed.

- Excellent listeners, they remember they have two ears and one mouth and they use them in that ratio, particularly in the step where they are engaging the prospect.

- Because they are well prepared, they anticipate and are able to respond to unexpected objections.

- They are willing to admit they do not have an answer and are willing to get the answer from the right person.

- Firm in their own belief and support for the organization they represent, they have made their own gift before asking anyone else to invest.

- Their commitment and enthusiasm characterize the interaction and positively influence those with whom they meet.

- Focused on the purpose of their meeting, they get right to the point after a minimum of small talk.

- They become so familiar with the steps in the solicitation that the process appears seamless.

INVITING INVESTMENT: THE SOLICITATION STEPS

The solicitation steps in Exhibit 5.1 are a sequential subset of Step 7, Solicit, in the development process (see Chapter 4). They become seamless when they are practiced, used, and internalized.

1. Make the Appointment

This is often the hardest part of the solicitation. Getting the courage to pick up the telephone and call someone to make the appointment to ask for a gift—even someone you have been cultivating and with whom you have developed a good relationship—may be very difficult. The appointment can be made by the lead volunteer assigned to the prospect or by a staff person. In some cases, it may be made by a friend or business associate of the prospect who calls on behalf of the organization or the lead volunteer.

There are ways to make setting the appointment easier. If the appointment can be set while *with* the person at a meeting or event, it seems more natural and logical. "Ed, we'd like to get together with you for a half-hour sometime next week and tell you a little more about what you've just seen and talk about some of the ideas we have about the support you (and/or your company/foundation) might give to this project. Do you have your calendar with you, or may I call you tomorrow and find out what days next week are good for you?"

EXHIBIT 5.1   THE SOLICITATION STEPS

Step 7—Development Process

1. Make the appointment.

2. Plan the solicitation carefully.

3. Coach.

4. Gather and go, meet and greet.

5. Engage the prospect.

6. Say what you came to say: State the case.

7. Invite the investment.

8. Keep the silence.

9. Work with the prospect's answer and close.

10. Follow-through.

If it is not possible to make the appointment while you are with the potential donor-investor, you will have to call. When you call, keep your tone natural and consistent with the rapport you have developed with the person so far. If you are working with a secretary or associate of the prospect, gain his or her confidence by being very clear about what you want. Often a secretary or associate, when treated as a key player in making this important transaction happen, will make a great effort to help you get the appointment. If you treat people as if they would not understand or find interesting what you have to say, often they will see to it that the appointment does not happen or is difficult to get.

Although a volunteer-initiated meeting may be easier to arrange, the staff person can call and say, "This is Zed Matthews from the Florentine Agency. I'm calling on behalf of Donna Jones, a board member of our organization who has met several times with Mr. Smith over the past several months and would now like to set up an appointment to discuss a campaign gift with him. Can you help me arrange a half-hour appointment with her and our executive director, or should I speak directly to him?"

Settings for the Ask

Although common practice is to "do lunch" with someone, the solicitation meeting is really too confidential for a public setting and the general distractions (food, other people, noise) detract from the focus this meeting must have. People are more comfortable on their own turf. Suggest that you will come to the prospect's office at a convenient time.

If an individual is being solicited for a personal gift, it is very important to include the spouse or partner if decisions are made jointly (and, increasingly, most are). In that case, you will want to suggest coming to the home either during the day on a weekend or in the evening, so you can meet with both individuals. When the appointment has been set, follow up with a confirming note or letter. Be very clear about purpose, time, location, and who will be present. Reconfirm the meeting by telephone the day before.

2. Plan the Solicitation Carefully

The solicitation meeting with the prospect is the culmination of the entire development process to this point. It must be planned carefully. The development director, executive director, or designated board person (development committee chair, campaign (annual or capital) chair) should coordinate the planning meeting. The meeting should involve all those who will participate in the solicitation meeting. Have these materials ready for review: confidential prospect profile, the organization's case statement and other pertinent materials, and a written proposal if required or requested. At the planning meeting, decide what roles each person will play in the solicitation. Designate one person, preferably a board member, as the designated asker. Otherwise the meeting can drift. Another member of the solicitation team should provide program, administrative, development, or financial expertise. There may also be a representative from a program or capital needs area in which the prospect is interested in investing.

Lay out the structure of the meeting based on the time you will have with the prospect. Allow time for:

1. Small talk (but not much)
2. Open-ended questions that will encourage the prospect to speak at some length about his or her connection to the organization and concerns for the community need the organization is meeting
3. Presentation of the campaign objective or annual gift opportunity you want the prospect to consider
4. Request for a specific gift for a designated or unrestricted purpose
5. Subsequent discussion that will certainly follow the ask

In a half-hour meeting, you need to keep the conversation moving to cover all this ground. If you can present the campaign objective or annual gift opportunity at a separate earlier individual or group meeting, you have more time at this meeting to discuss the terms of the ask. Also, arranging a longer meeting, if possible, could be worthwhile, particularly if there are two or three solicitors meeting with the prospect.

3. Coach

No matter how experienced a person may be in asking for money, a little coaching before a meeting can help raise confidence and comfort levels. The staff or board person in charge of organizing the solicitation teams for the annual or capital campaign should develop a brief outline of the solicitation process and review it with the solicitors. She should brief the team on the prospect's profile including giving history and other relevant confidential facts. She should also provide the team with an easy-to-read fact sheet on the organization's case for support: budget, mission, size of campaign, current campaign status, people served, brief history, and so on. In the actual solicitation meeting, the team may also give this to the prospect as a snapshot of the longer case statement. The fact sheet is an important resource for dealing with objections. The more facts and information with which solicitors are armed, the more adept they will be at turning objections into positive learning experiences for the prospect.

In the coaching session, encourage solicitors to role-play. Most adults dislike the thought of role-playing. However, experience verifies that those who have role-played a solicitation with each other are much more confident during the actual solicitation. Call the role-play a "practice" session, and be sure each solicitor has an opportunity to learn and try appropriate words and phrases, implement strategies for keeping the meeting focused, deal with objections a prospect may raise, and make a practice ask or close.

An alternative form of role play is called the "freeze frame." In this exercise, three people from the board and staff who are comfortable with the solicitation process are asked to demonstrate an ask (playing the roles of two solicitors and a prospect). Give them time to plan their solicitation strategy, providing information about the three roles if that is helpful, and then ask them to model the ask in front of the group. However, they understand that they will be interrupted by the facilitator at intervals. During these "freeze frames," the group of volunteers being trained are asked to comment on the progress of the solicitation, offer ideas for shifting focus or presentation, and say whether they think it is moving smoothly. The people on the demonstration team must be highly confident, but, when this procedure works well, it is very effective in engaging the observers in the solicitation process.

Whatever process you use, when coaching the solicitation team impress on them the importance of listening to the prospect and to each other. The solicitation meeting will stay balanced and focused if team members listen and support each other, picking up on an interest or concern of the prospect that may be strategic in the presentation of the ask.

4. Gather and Go, Meet and Greet

If you have an appointment for 2 P.M., you should all arrive at once. Either you can all come together, or you can agree to meet outside the person's home or office at 1:50 P.M. If some team members are chronically late, be sure they are brought by someone who is always early or on time. A ragged beginning to a meeting throws off timing and momentum. People drifting in have to be brought up to speed, and the carefully assigned roles each person has been asked to play are disrupted when one person does not get there at the beginning.

Even after you have made sure the prospect knows how many of you are coming, who each person is, and why they are there, you should still introduce everyone and explain their role in the organization and why they are there. "Ed, I think you remember Alice Magpie, who serves on the board with me. Alice is the chair of the Program Committee this year, and it is in large part due to her efforts that we have been able to leverage the grant from the city [if you have already submitted a proposal to him or told him what you want] that we would like you to consider helping us match." Such an introductory statement removes much of the guesswork from a meeting like this. Your time is too short for people to sit there, wondering who is there and why.

At the beginning of the meeting, there are two critical things you should do. First, restate your understanding of the time frame: "We have planned a 30-minute meeting. Is that still good for you?" If the prospect's schedule has changed, and you have more or less time for the meeting, you want to know at the outset and not 15 minutes into the solicitation when suddenly Ed announces he has to leave. Second, restate the purpose of your visit. "Ed, as you know, we're here to talk with you today about an investment—a gift, if you will—that we would like you to consider making toward the renovation of our job training facility for women transitioning out of our alcoholic treatment center."

5. Engage the Prospect

The most common mistake in solicitations is jumping right from the opening "stage setting" into the presentation of the funding opportunity. Unless you have met just recently with the individual and have already begun your discussions, it is better to engage the prospect in some conversation using open-ended questions before getting into the presentation. There are exceptions to this, of course. The most important exception is prompted by the prospects themselves. If they are impatient and just want to get to the point, then do not press forward with more open-ended questions. Get to the purpose immediately. Be gracious but brief. If, however, you get signals that they are enjoying the conversation, continue.

Remember to use active listening skills. Listen to what the person is saying and not saying. One of the major reasons for having two or three solicitors present at a solicitation meeting is the assistance in listening. If you are alone, it is hard to notice both the dynamics of the meeting and listen to the words. During their downtime in the meeting, solicitors should listen and watch so their reentry into the conversation is more valuable.

Open the conversation with the prospect by referring to a common experience you have had that relates to the organization. Here is some dialogue that might happen when a solicitation team calls on a prospect for a gift to the local community orchestra: "We were just delighted you could be at the concert last week. I appreciated your making a special effort to find me afterward to thank us for the tickets. It was great to hear how much you enjoyed the performance. Didn't you mention that this was the first time you have heard the orchestra in a few years?" (Listen for an answer, then continue.) "We know you're very busy, and we appreciate not only your attendance at the concert but your willingness to have lunch with our music director a few weeks ago. We also enjoyed having you at our education program at Martin Luther King School last month." You can then easily segue into appropriate questions that will lead to the ask.

If, instead, you start with very personal small talk—"Say, Andrea, I saw you out on the golf course last Saturday with Donna Ranchert. I haven't seen her in years. What's she up to now?"—you not only exclude the others in your group, but you also send the conversation in a direction whose course will be hard to correct. Keeping the focus on the organization, even in the small talk, creates a more seamless solicitation.

From the conversation about the orchestra, you can begin engaging Andrea more directly by asking her open-ended questions like the following. If, after the first one, she seems to want to get to the point of the meeting, do not continue with these questions. Examples of open-ended questions are:

- "I seem to remember you played the flute for a few years. How did you get started with music?"
- "Having not heard the orchestra in a few years, what were the changes that you noticed?"
- "What types of orchestral music do you enjoy most?"
- "With the decline in cultural resources in our city, what role do you feel the orchestra should play in the ongoing debate of giving the public what it should have or giving it want it wants?"

Open-ended questions are powerful. They can stimulate answers that reveal a great deal about the person's interests and values.

Even at the beginning of the meeting, watch for body language and other nonverbal indicators of how the meeting is going. Crossed arms and legs are often a negative sign, as is lack of eye contact. If a person is distracted—going through papers, taking phone calls, getting up and walking around—you may want to ask if this is still a good time for the meeting. Two responses are possible: The prospect will realize she needs to focus on her visitors and will eliminate or ignore distractions, *or* the prospect will admit that this is a bad time, and she is diverted over a business problem. In the latter case, you can make a positive impression by suggesting that you return at another time. (Be sure to make the appointment before leaving.) The prospect will be very grateful. Sometimes people stick with appointments that have been difficult to arrange because they do not want to disappoint anyone. Being intuitive to their distraction ultimately enhances the invitation to invest.

6. Say What You Came to Say: State the Case

Once small talk and engagement are behind you, say what you came to say. Adjust the length and detail of your presentation according to how much you have already presented to the prospect about the project, program, or campaign in prior meetings. In your discussion, be clear, succinct, and on point about the project or your organization. Refer back to the shared values you have uncovered during the development process: "Ed, I recall when we first visited the job training site. You mentioned that you wished more recovering alcoholics could have an opportunity like that. You felt that it would prevent them from sliding into alcoholism again. We believe that the renovation of this job training site—which will enable us to increase our trainees by 60 each year—is one of the most directly beneficial things we can do as an organization to try to reduce the long-term effects of alcoholism in our community. I remember those statistics you gave us about days lost on the job in your factory because of drinking—incredible! And I think you know that, in our other counseling program, we also work with families to help them be more active partners in the long-term rehabilitation process. We'd like to think that we can make a difference—and, with your help, I believe we can. The grant from city redevelopment funds covers phase one of the renovation and we'd like you to consider helping us match their gift so we can do phase two and get this facility running at full capacity." Constructing a statement like that allows you to reinforce the prospect's beliefs and values, lets the prospect know you valued their advice or opinion, and seamlessly introduces the invitation to invest.

If you are going to provide a written proposal, do not refer to it during the meeting. Give the prospect the written proposal at the close of the meeting, or send it later if it needs to be revised due to information or interaction that arises during the meeting. You will lose vital energy and eye contact—to say nothing of the participation of the team you have brought in for a lively conversation—if the prospect starts reading a proposal in the middle of the meeting. If you have already sent the proposal, as follow-up to a previous meeting, be sure that all the members of the solicitation team and the prospect have read and are familiar with it. Otherwise, refer only briefly to the proposal, stay focused on the conversation, and delay discussion for a later phone call or meeting.

7. Invite the Investment

Once you get this far, you are almost there. You have introduced the idea of investment, and you must keep moving into the close. Take a breath and plunge forward. "As you know from the materials we went over at the site visit, Ed, the city's gift to us was $100,000. We've raised $25,000 from the board, one-third of whom, as you may know, are former clients of the program. That was a very heartening result for us. We'd like you to consider a gift of $25,000, and it is our plan—already well under way—to solicit the remaining $50,000 in midrange and smaller gifts from the community, plus a few corporate gifts, which we hope you might be able to help us identify. I have the plans for that fundraising program with me, and I can leave them with you. I'm confident that, with your gift, we will have the $100,000 for phase two by the end of the year. That means the construction can be completed by April, and we'll be able to let those on our waiting list know that job training is just around the corner. Would you be willing to consider a $25,000 gift?"

8. Keep the Silence

After extending the invitation to invest, *keep silent*. There is a saying in sales training: The person who talks first loses. In these delicate negotiations in which our community and organizational stability is often at stake, we need to keep silent while the prospect considers the request we have made. As a society, we do not seem to seek or welcome silence; we move from car radio to home stereo to mobile phone to personal stereos with earphones. Yet at this moment in the long process of bringing the prospect to the decision point, we must respect silence.

Honor the prospect by allowing him time to think about this major request you have just made. People who have accrued the capital to be prospects for impact gifts have done so by carefully marshaling their resources and investing wisely. They are seldom impulsive about financial decisions. But be forewarned: Time is never more relative than when we are waiting for the answer to an important question. Fifteen seconds seems like minutes; two minutes seem like an hour. In our haste to bring what is perhaps still an uncomfortable process to a swift end, we mistakenly rush to break the silence by saying something that will not only end the negotiation for that meeting but send a confusing signal to the prospective donor-investor. We say things like:

- "If you need more time to think about this, I can call later this week."
- "If that amount is too much, let us know what you would consider."
- "If this doesn't sound like something you want to do, we'll understand."
- "Maybe our timing is off—perhaps you would like to wait until the community campaign is completed?"

Unfortunately, these comments are not merely a harvest from a rich imagination; they are drawn from real-life confessions.

We need to maintain faith while waiting and not second-guess our prospects. We should not play bad tapes in our heads, ones that say the prospect is not really interested and we have made a fool of ourselves. That is nonsense. The prospect would not have spent time with you if he were not interested. He is just trying to formulate a response. Be patient.

9. Work with the Prospect's Answer and Close

You will hear one of three basic answers: yes, maybe, or no.

If the answer is yes, be enthusiastic but businesslike. This is not a time to be overly cool; it is all right to show your pleasure. Your solicitation team and the donor should be feeling a level of joy over your mutual decision to solve a community problem or provide a community enhancement. Determine how the gift is going to be made and over what time period, discuss the kind of recognition that is available and what the donor desires, ask what kind of follow-through is needed from the organization (letters, reminders, etc.), and have the donor-investor sign the pledge form if the gift will be made over time. *Never* leave the pledge form behind when the transaction has not been closed; you give up your reason for returning and give control of the transaction to the prospect.

Avoid the impulse to "sell after the close." Also borrowed from sales training, this behavior is inspired by relief over getting the gift. Suddenly the tension is gone; you remember all the things you wanted to say. You remember reading somewhere once that you should relax and enjoy the moment. Instead of directing this newfound excitement and energy into making a gracious and timely exit, you start restating your case as part of your thank-you: "Thank you so much! Your gift means we'll be able to provide job training to 60 more people each year. Do you know what that means? Blah, blah, blah." The donor-investor who has made the commitment does not need to hear all of this again. In all likelihood, your 30 minutes is more than up, and everyone should get back to work. Exit smiling, and be happy for the gift.

If the answer is maybe, hide your disappointment. This is an easier response to deal with than you may think. The conversation is far from over, and the answer could be yes within a few minutes or days. The prospect (Ed) says, "Well, that's an intriguing proposition. You're right, I'm very interested in the project. But I think I need to be more informed about your overall financial picture, not just this campaign, before I'm ready to make a gift of this size." If you have come prepared with backup material, including budgets and financial statements, you can review them. You can also offer to arrange a meeting for him with your chief financial officer (unless you thought to bring your CFO along too). Whatever the strategy required, keep it on track and set a timeframe to retain the momentum. Don't say, "Sure. I'll drop that information by for you tomorrow. When you have had a chance to read it, give us a call. Then we'll set something up." That is too vague. Instead, say you'll come by and go over it with him. Set a time right then. Keep the process moving. Most maybe answers convert to yes before long.

If the prospect says no, be gracious. This can happen, even with a well-cultivated potential investor. However, by the time someone agrees to see you and has entered into a relationship with you, chances are strong that a gift of some size eventually will be made. The operative words here are "of some size" and "eventually." With people who have been treated like potential investors during their interactions with the organization, the no that you hear will probably be a qualified no. Sometimes you have to ask what no means. "Naturally, we are disappointed. Would you mind saying what led you to this decision?" Avoid the direct question *"Why?"* when someone says no: it puts people on the defensive.

Most often, the prospect will qualify the no for you without your asking, especially if you maintain a short period of silence after hearing the answer. The prospect may then say, "I just couldn't do that large a gift this year." Your response should be "What amount would you consider giving this year?" Or "If it were possible for you to make the gift over two years, could you consider our request favorably? We could continue construction with a bridge loan if you would be willing to make the gift over that period of time." Note no "counteroffer" (lower amount) was suggested. In philanthropy, it is not in good taste or judgment to enter into a series of offers and counteroffers. This is not a real estate transaction or other commercial negotiation. In nonprofit organizations, we diminish the donor-investor attitude when we put people on the defensive by asking for repeated levels of gifts that they are unable or unwilling to make. We also don't ask "How much could/can you give?" because the prospect may be very capable of making the gift we have asked for or even a larger one. Capacity to give is not the issue. We want to know what they would consider giving to this project.

Another qualification for a no response is timing. "I'd love to help, but you've come at the wrong time. Between now and the end of the year I'm just overwhelmed with financial responsibilities with the business and personally, what with two kids in college." The response is obvious: "What would be a better time for you? I am sure we could work out a schedule for financing the construction that would enable you to give your gift next year instead." When no is really just a postponement, be sure to follow through in an agreed-on time period. Gifts are sometimes lost to organizations because of failure to follow through. Set up a manual or computer-based tickler file to ensure closure on all pending solicitations.

One way to phrase the follow-up question to a no answer based on timing or amount is an "if/then" response. "If you could make this gift over a period of two years, then would you consider our request?" Often this alternative lets the prospect see a way to make a larger gift.

Sometimes no really means no. "You folks know how much I like your organization, but, quite frankly, I just can't get excited about this project. I am concerned that we are running head on into what the youth symphony is doing with their outreach program, and I don't think there is a big need for this additional program. I think there are enough resources already to meet this need." There are several options that help keep the door open.

- Continue talking with the prospect about ways in which the youth symphony program and yours are different.

- Do additional research and cultivation to find out if this is really the objection or whether it is deeper (the arts in general, redundancy in community programs of any kind, etc.).

- Find another program that will capture her interest and present it to her—underwriting a concert, funding the first flute chair for a year, and so on.

When you hear the absolute unequivocal no, you cannot help but feel disappointed, perhaps puzzled, and certainly chagrined. "I hate to turn you folks down, but as I have listened to you and gone over your materials I have to say that this is just not our priority. We feel that programs like this are good for the community, but I don't think this is where we want to put our charitable dollars this year. It has been a tough decision, and we are sorry." You have invested a great deal of time in this potential donor-investor. You need to find out if there was anything about the cultivation or solicitation that you could have done better. You will want to keep the relationship alive. You may say, "Naturally, we are very disappointed, but we appreciate your interest in what we are doing and hope that you will want to stay informed and, to the extent possible, involved. May we call on you next year and tell you how the project is progressing?" The person who has turned you down is feeling uncomfortable at this point and will welcome this gracious exit line. Keep the prospect informed during the year, and remember to make an appointment as promised.

10. Follow-through

Do whatever needs to be done following the meeting. Each response (yes, maybe, no) has its own set of follow-through requirements. Be sure you follow through quickly, professionally, and warmly, no matter what the response has been.

- If the answer was yes, remember that this individual or institutional donor-investor has just entered into a new or renewed relationship with you. Investors expect stewardship that includes information, attention, and involvement.

- If the answer was maybe, follow through with required information or meetings with others until you have closed.

- If the answer was no, keep the door open if at all possible and try to find an opportunity or time that will be right for the gift.

This 10-step sequence is straightforward and relatively easy to implement once an organization understands the entire development process. Its success increases with experience.

Shedding Old Attitudes

The success of the 10-step process increases as fear of rejection subsides and solicitation teams put away their tin cups. Confidence is also a fundamental success factor. Turn negative phrases, which recur in our minds as we prepare for a solicitation and cause us to be tentative and ineffective, into positive statements:

- "I'm sure they won't want to give."
  "I think this is an opportunity they will really like."

- "They just made a gift—we can't ask them again so soon."
  "This giving opportunity is very exciting. While they may feel it is too soon after their last gift, let's ask anyway. It's their decision."

- "I don't think they are ready to be asked yet."
  "We've been tracking this cultivation very well, and I think they are ready to talk seriously about a commitment. Let's arrange a meeting and see how they respond to some initial ideas."

- "I'm sure they wouldn't want to come . . . they are so busy."
  "Their good friends, the Ryans, are coming to the event. Let's call and extend a personal invitation, and see if they and the Ryans would join us for cocktails before the larger reception. They could meet the conductor and some of the musicians."

- "He wouldn't have time for an appointment: I'll just write a letter."
  "Seeing him face-to-face would be a major advantage to us. I'll call him so he'll know how important this effort is to me. After all, we have been friends a long time."

- "I know I'll say the wrong thing."
  "Getting into these conversations is always hard for me. I do better when someone else is with me. Could you join me on this call?"

- "I can't possibly ask for that much."
  "I want to make sure that is the right amount. Have we done adequate research and cultivation to know we're on target? If so, I'm glad to ask. My gift was smaller, but it was a stretch for me and I can ask her to stretch also."
- "I am probably the wrong person to be asking for the gift."
  "I just want to make sure I am the right person to ask for the gift. This is a very important solicitation. If you feel I am, then I'll do it."

Undoubtedly, you have heard others say these negative things or said or thought them yourself. This focus on ourselves, and the tendency to second-guess the prospect, is a major deterrent to successful implementation of the solicitation process. Positive phrases, whether said or thought, build confidence in you and others.

We must not approach those who have the capacity to benefit our organizations with an attitude that we want something they do not want to give. Instead, we must approach them with an attitude that we have something they want—an opportunity to invest in an organization that is strengthening their community, solving problems of concern to them, and providing programs or services in which they believe.

The Donor's Perspective

We need to look at fundraising—the process of inviting investment—from the potential donor-investor's standpoint. Put yourself in the potential donor-investor's shoes. You have been cultivated over a period of months (or perhaps years) by an organization whose values and purposes are consistent with yours. You have concern, capacity, and connection with and for the mission and, increasingly, the organization. A relationship has been built through the effective application of all or most of the steps in the development process. There is synergy and involvement between you and the organization. You have attended events, been taken to lunch, met the executive director, and been asked for your opinion on matters within your expertise. At this point, if you are an individual investor prospect—or an individual representing an organization over whose resources you have some influence—you will *want* to do something for this organization.

Testing the Waters

In one major campaign, the president of an educational organization met during the campaign planning phase with a longtime friend of the organization who was a previous large investor. The purpose of the meeting was only to *test* the concept of a particular capital campaign objective. The objective was a favorite of the president's, and his passion and enthusiasm were apparent. By the end of the meeting, both individuals were on the edge of their chairs with excitement about the potential for this particular project. The potential funder immediately said, "I want to make this happen. How much do you need?" Those last four words, along with "How can I help?" are the words you want to hear after you have made a presentation to a potential donor-investor. They signify a true investment attitude.

In this instance, however, there was a problem. The project was so embryonic that there was no cost estimate yet. The president could not ask for an early gift. So he did the wisest thing possible; he asked this individual to join the project planning task force. As the planning progressed and the project was defined, the organization asked for and received a substantial lead gift from him. This was a true investor partnership; the external funder teamed with the internal organization to create a project that would enhance the organization and its constituents.

Unasked Prospects

Some potential donor-investors self-identify and make a gift on their own initiative, but most wait to be asked. Fairly experienced donors, when finally asked by an organization for a gift, have often expressed their relief: "I thought you'd never ask." Timing greatly influences successful asks. Too early or too late, and the results may be doomed or diminished. Untold gifts are "left on the table" because we let our fears, anxieties, or disorganized follow-through get in the way of the relationship between the potential or renewed donor-investor and the organization.

In a major campaign for a cultural organization, an individual who was being cultivated for the lead gift had no real relationship with the organization. The pursuit of the gift was based on the prospect's known desire to attain community recognition through a significant naming opportunity. After months of discussions with the individual and her family, the negotiation broke down and the potential donor withdrew. The organization's board of directors, which had been meeting more often than usual and was very involved in some exciting facilities and program planning, had been kept regularly informed of the progress of the solicitation (although the name of the prospect was appropriately kept confidential) and were promptly informed when the solicitation discussions ended. A few hours after this grim news was announced, the chair of the board received a call from one of the board members, an individual who had made a substantial gift to the organization the previous year. Although this individual was on the key prospect list, the board development committee volunteers felt that his recent gift was so large that they should not go back to him right away (a conclusion with which staff and consultant did not entirely agree). In his phone call to the board chair, the board member asked why he had not been asked to make the leadership gift, and then proceeded to offer an eight-figure investment.

Although the size of this gift may be far beyond most organizations' ambitions or needs, the story has some fundamental points that apply to organizations of all sizes and to all investor gifts.

- The individual was *already invested* because of his involvement with the organization and his previous gifts. As a member of the board, he was very aware of the organization's impact in the community and very involved with the substantial and carefully crafted future plans.

- He had solid relationships with board and staff.

- Happy with the results of his previous investments, he was delighted to make another investment to ensure the success of the campaign and the future of the organization.

- Through this gift, he was ensuring the maximum possible benefit to the organization from his *previous* impact gift as well. With the new facility, the program he supported would have more space and prestige. The naming opportunity was very appealing to him for deeper reasons than recognition in the community. He already felt pride from the impact of his previous gifts on the institution.

- The organization had decided *not* to ask him for the leadership gift and chose instead someone with whom there was no relationship and for whom this was more a business transaction. They had second-guessed the objections of the person who did make the gift, instead of thinking of the leadership gift as an opportunity for him to act further on his values and deepen his investment.

How Investment Leverages Investment

Another story is pertinent. The success story of the campaign for the San Francisco Museum of Modern Art, completed in 1994, was widely reported at the time. The museum's highly committed board members and friends, determined that San Francisco should have a world-class museum for modern art, were willing to make huge commitments themselves in order to leverage gifts from others. They wanted to inspire the people of San Francisco that this was an important civic venture whose success depended not only on leadership gifts but on a broad base of community supporters. So effective was the campaign in involving the community that the number of patron ($1,000) and smaller-gift donors exceeded all expectations—most of them coming from a direct mail piece to members that was positioned in terms of this being an investment in the cultural future of the city. The letter was a superlative example of an investor appeal (see Exhibit 5.2), framed as an opportunity to be part of something very special. Although the $70 million given by the board of directors attracted widespread publicity and admiration, it is equally important that museum membership swelled threefold during the campaign (even though the museum was not open) and that 10 years later the new museum has maintained its high level of membership and is extremely well attended by residents and visitors. The base of midlevel donors also increased impressively.

Inspiring Investment at All Levels

The investment attitude should frame all development and fundraising activities. Although this chapter has focused on the face-to-face invitation to invest, other kinds of fundraising materials and programs require similar attention.

Be sure direct (mass appeal) and select (personally addressed) mailings reflect the investment opportunity a gift to your organization offers. Coach phone volunteers not to use phrases like "We're desperate. If we don't get the matching funds for this grant, we will lose it." Inspire, do not discourage, potential donor-investors.

EXHIBIT 5.2   A DIRECT MAIL LETTER THAT INVITES INVESTMENT

December 15, 1995

_____
_____

San Francisco, CA 94123

Dear Ms. _____,

Let me introduce you to San Francisco's newest landmark—the new SFMOMA.

It's an imaginative design of galleries, learning areas and performance spaces, integrating collections, exhibitions and educational resources with greater accessibility for everyone.

Quite frankly, when I agreed to chair the final phase of the New Museum Campaign—soliciting the Bay Area community and SFMOMA members—I was flattered to have the privilege to invite members to help complete this project.

If anybody's been waiting for this museum, it's you.

In fact, I believe your question is not whether you will help support the new museum, but how much to give.

All in the community will be given a chance to participate in the museum's completion and we're confident the response will be strong. But the reality is we must ask, and rely on, museum members like yourself for the bolder commitments.

In a few days you will receive a call from an SFMOMA representative who will be speaking with you about your participation in the New Museum Campaign.

Right now, before the call, I'm asking you to consider a pledge of $83 per quarter over three years for a total gift of $1,000, placing your name in the New Museum Grand Opening Commemorative Book.

And because this may be asking you to consider a larger gift than you may have given to SFMOMA before, I want to make some points with you, in advance of the call, about the new museum.

In addition to the distinctive Mario Botta design, planning for the new museum has involved consultation with an array of professionals with expertise ranging from museum curatorship and education, to installation and lighting design,

The impact of the new museum will be immediate and enduring:

- Improving educational resources for all sectors of the community, opening its doors to children, adults, students, and teachers;
- Attracting exciting exhibitions from the U.S. and abroad;
- Increasing donations of art to a facility capable of showing and interpreting those collections and gifts;
- Creating a cultural landmark of regional pride for Bay Area residents and tourists alike.

EXHIBIT 5.2   A DIRECT MAIL LETTER THAT INVITES INVESTMENT
(Continued)

The new SFMOMA provides a rare event: a new modern art museum in America's most deserving city. There are few philanthropic activities that offer such far-reaching impact and continuing influence. It's an occasion for you to share ownership of an exhilarating new concept with a different world view than other museums, just as San Francisco is so different than other major cities.

The museum representative who calls will speak with you about the schedule of choices available for your pledge. Again, I encourage you to consider the New Museum Grand Opening Commemorative Book naming opportunity.

I'll add my appreciation for your faithful support and my hope that we'll add your name to the new SFMOMA.

With sincere thanks,

Steven H. Oliver

Steven H. Oliver
Chairman
New Museum Campaign Council

The whole development process is really an investment process. People who have been properly "developed" *want* to invest. The chronic fundraising problems of many organizations can be attributed to their unwillingness to invest in the process of investment. They do not put the time or resources required into the steps described in Chapter 4. These organizations find themselves exhausted year after year, trying frantically to fund raise from a donor base on which they have records (maybe) but with whom they have no relationship.

Board members in these organizations usually confine their "development" activities to signing the year-end appeal, selling a few tickets for a raffle or event, and/or providing board approval for foundation and corporate grant proposals developed by staff. Most often they are relieved that this is the extent of the demands on them. They are shy and uncomfortable about talking with people personally about giving. They routinely refuse to participate in phone appeals, using the excuse that they themselves hate to be disturbed at dinner. A cartoon shows a person answering the phone, with a spouse or friend still at the dinner table. The cartoon caption reads, "And to think, if I hadn't been home having dinner tonight I might have missed this wonderful investment opportunity." Although these exact words may never be heard during a phone appeal, volunteers should not underestimate the interest and willingness of people in their communities to support their organizations.

Fear of Rejection and the Face-to-Face Ask

Even in organizations where "PS-athons" (signing letters at a group meeting) and phona-thons are regular board activities, actually asking someone face-to-face for a gift fills board members with paralyzing fear. Because they view the transaction from their own personal involvement in it, rather than from the perspective of mutual benefits, they submit to the most commonly expressed fear, rejection.

No one wants to be told no. Remember that the fear of rejection comes from the belief that the most common response to a request for funds will be negative. Believers in the development or investment process know that those who will turn us down have self-selected out of the process, for the most part, before the ask is made. Those with whom we seek that precious investor relationship become increasingly involved with the organization through the development process (see Chapter 4). If they were not interested, they would not keep responding to requests or invitations.

We should not fault or criticize boards and staff that are fearful and reluctant about fundraising, and in a state of urgency regarding the need for their campaign to be a success. Instead, we should fault the legacy of misunderstanding about the importance of the development process, about the concept of investment, and, most of all, about the powerful role board members play in building a better community. When these things are understood and believed, solicitors can approach the previously daunting task of asking for money with much more confidence and comfort. The tin cup is retired.

People involved in development know they are not asking for money because their *organization* has needs, but because the *community* has needs that their organization has or will meet.

Pressure and Release

Positioned in this way, the solicitation steps guide a transaction in which investment in a vital community resource is requested from an individual or organization whose values, interests, capacity, concerns, and connection have been reinforced by the cultivation process. Operating in the context of the three-part model of philanthropy, development, and fundraising (see Chapter 1), fundraising is the activity that gives donors an opportunity to act on the things they value. It is the invitation to invest. As such, the solicitation should never be a time of *pressure* for the prospect. Instead, it should be a time of *release*.

The person being asked should know the sense of fulfillment that comes from being able to make a difference—large or small—in the lives, futures, or well-being of people in the communities served by the institutions they support. The asker should also find satisfaction in knowing that an opportunity has been for offered the donor-investor to become further involved. If the prospect declines the opportunity, the asker should not take this as rejection. Instead, he should view the transaction from the prospect's perspective. This may be the wrong time, the wrong project, the wrong amount. But keep the door open. This person is interested and, when the conditions for investment are right, may invest.

OVERCOMING OBJECTIONS

Objections are really masked values. If potential donor-investors express concern about how money is managed in your organization, you can infer that they place value on sound money management. Other investors will focus on different areas: program, planning, board involvement. Listen carefully to those objections, and respond to them with these guideposts in mind.

- Never *beat* an objection. Meet it instead. "I can understand why that would be upsetting to you." "You certainly have a right to be concerned about how your investment would be handled."

- For strong objections, use the "feel, have felt, felt" sequence: "I know exactly how you must feel. I have felt that way myself (only if you honestly have), and others have said they felt that way too." This assures the objector that these feelings are not only accepted, but understood.

- Know the four levels of objections, each of which requires a slightly different response:

  - *Misunderstanding.* This is the simplest. You can respond with facts. "That is an excellent question. While it was true that 70 percent of our board used to be parents of current or former students, we now have a board which is half parents and half representatives from the community. The self-interest concern you have expressed was the reason for altering that balance nearly a decade ago."

  - *Skepticism.* This requires an outside opinion or objective evidence to dispel. "I can understand why your previous experience with scholarship funding at your university was unpleasant. Let me arrange for you to meet with one of our community college scholarship donors. She can answer your questions about the way we interact with our students and donors—and how we encourage them to get to know each other. I think you'd enjoy meeting Naomi Windust, and I'd be pleased to set that up so the two of you can meet by yourselves."

  - *Disinterest.* Often this is *seeming* disinterest. Probing reveals that there is a strong and sometimes emotional basis for apparent disinterest. An example would be donors who have stopped giving to their local symphony. A volunteer telephones and gets a somewhat cool response, accompanied by the comment "I really just don't care about the orchestra anymore." The caller can say, "I'm sorry to hear that. We're really excited about the things that are happening now. Have you been to the concerts recently? Are you getting our publications?" This may trigger a revealing response: "Yes, I'm getting the publications. I can't believe they fired the conductor! He was the best musical director I ever heard. I just cannot imagine what they were thinking." Having uncovered the real objection, you can determine what kind it is. It may be very serious (the conductor was fired), or it may be a misunderstanding (he resigned).

  - *Real drawback.* This is usually a game breaker. Most often these come up early in the development-investment process or on a phone solicitation. Seldom do people with this kind of feeling about an organization allow themselves to be drawn deeply into the investment process. With such objections, seek balance. Help them see that, although the organization has failed or offended them in some way, there are some worthy aspects of the outcome or the organization. Parents whose children are qualified for admission but not accepted to the parents' alma mater(s) are primary examples. They are angry and disappointed. The first phone call or letter they receive after the rejection triggers a whole array of feelings and the volunteer solicitor is the recipient. First, listen. Then restate what you just heard. "If I understand you, your son, who had a 4.0, was student-body president, editor of the yearbook, and ran cross-country at the national level, was not admitted to the university." Then add: "I don't blame you for being disappointed. Was your son counting on going to the university, or did he have other alternatives?" Sometimes this shift away from the injured parent to the student (who is probably by that time enjoying another university) changes the focus of the parent's feelings.

- Coach all volunteers on the objections they may confront, and provide materials that will help them respond. Several organizations have developed objection-response lists that pinpoint specific objections and provide precise responses. The danger is that the volunteer, on hearing an objection, will say, "Oh, that's number seven on my list. Let me look up the answer." Volunteers must internalize and master these responses. For training purposes, such lists are vital.

- Know **CLASP** techniques. This acronym summarizes critical listening skills that are helpful in handling objections and in keeping the entire solicitation negotiation on track.

  ○ Clarify if you don't understand what the person has said. If you feel you would like to have them repeat it, say so. Otherwise, you may end up building an entire case around erroneous information.

  ○ Link by listening for interests and concerns expressed by the potential donor-investor. Link them back into a program or opportunity in which you want them to invest. "A few minutes ago you mentioned your concern about the loss of music in our schools. I'd like to tell you about one of our programs. . . ." Such statements please the prospect because they indicate you are listening. They also connect what you are about to say to something he or she already feels is important.

  ○ Acknowledge the feelings evidenced when expressing objections or the interests and ideas during other parts of the meeting. "I know just how you feel." "That's a great idea. Let me tell you something we're doing that relates very well to that." Convince the prospect that you are genuinely interested.

  ○ Summarize at intervals which will keep the meeting moving forward and within the time frame and to signal a shift in the conversation. "This opportunity to review how our community must address the needs of the homeless, and to hear your ideas about our programs, has been very enjoyable for us. Our time is passing quickly, and we'd like now to make our proposal to you regarding the financial commitment we hope you will be willing to make."

- o **P**ace involves the speed and nature of the communication. If you speak at a rate that is too fast or too slow for the person with whom you are trying to communicate, the exchange will be less effective. This point is good to remember when working with older people, visually or hearing impaired people, or people whose native language and yours are not the same. The signals will be obvious to you. If you speak too quickly or too slowly, you will lose their attention, and MEGO (Mine Eyes Glazeth Over) will set in. As you get to know your prospects, gauge their pace and make any necessary adjustments to yours.

INCREASING ORGANIZATIONAL INVOLVEMENT IN THE INVITATION TO INVEST

Board members, other volunteers, donors, and program staff need to feel that they can be helpful in many stages of the development process and that asking for money directly is not the only way to bring investors into organizations.

Because the development partnership is complex and inclusive, it provides opportunities for people to become involved in numerous ways. Here are two examples.

The Reluctant Board Member

In one organization there was a longtime board member who told each new board chair that she would "do anything but fundraise." Remaining on the periphery of development, she was always a willing hand when it came to stuffing envelopes or sorting lists or being a superb hostess for visitors. And her contribution to the success of a small campaign was impressive. When only 6 of the 25 board members provided lists of potential prospects for the campaign, her list was among the first to be received and was the longest and most detailed. When asked to review the list with the campaign committee, she spent a great deal of time providing some rich insight to her already complete written comments. As the campaign committee met with the people on her list, their praise for her as the person who had connected them to the organization and kept them in touch over the years was glowing and consistent. And she was diligent about reporting to staff any conversation she had with people on her list regarding the campaign. As the campaign evolved, several of the people she recommended were in the top tier of prospects. She was responsible for connecting this organization with many people whose continuing investments will have long-term impact on its development and successful fundraising. But, by her own admission, she preferred not to fundraise.

The Satisfied Donor-Investor

In another campaign, an individual in the community with tremendous capacity and concern for the mission of the organization was brought in initially through a personal relationship with the campaign consultant. He developed an immense admiration and respect for this organization as he came to know the staff and board who were involved with the campaign. On several occasions, he made it a point to say how impressed he was with the way in which the organization was managed; low profile and high productivity. It was his kind of organization. His expertise relative to the project was carefully sought by campaign leadership. His limited time was used wisely. He was kept well informed as several potential sites for the new building were evaluated. His own gift was definitely an impact gift. In spite of his other major commitments in the community, he "stretched" for this organization, which had come relatively late into his giving interests. But what he did after making his own gift was very significant. He leveraged a gift from a local foundation on whose board he sits that was larger than the one requested by the organization in its proposal.

Satisfied investors not only commit their own resources. They are also willing to become advocates for the organization. It is not unlike someone who has made a fantastic investment on Wall Street and wants to tell everyone what a good deal it is and encourage them also to invest.

Inviting investment extends beyond the actual ask. The entire 10-step development process is a process of *investing*: time, research, and resources by the organization and its board and staff; time, interest, and concern by the prospect.

WE HAVE LEARNED TO LOVE THE NEW APPROACH

When the phrase "investor" or "investment" first surfaced in not-for-profit circles more than a decade ago, there were voices of resistance. Now that seems hard to believe. The context of giving has shifted to social investment, social entrepreneurship, donor investment, and return on investment. And huge changes are still happening as philanthropy grows as a thriving part of our economy and reveals itself as our greatest vehicle for building and strengthening our communities. The root of the early objections is important to review.

For some, it seems to put nonprofits on the same funding footing with businesses, thereby denying their unique position in the community. This may actually be a good comparison to make. We still have a great distance to go in "capitalizing" our sector; we need more than ever to provide the solid foundation of endowment or rotating operating reserve funds that will ensure an organization's ability to consistently meet the needs of the community even if its annual funding or earned income sources temporarily run "dry." If people with capacity and concern would view a substantial investment in endowment or operating reserve as a way to not only strengthen the organization, but also to ensure the continuation of the program or service in the community, it would make a vast difference in our ability to consistently meet human needs. It would stabilize our communities.

For still others, it implied that donor-investors would want more say in the management and image development of the organization, and the thought made some nonprofit managers uncomfortable. This happened particularly during the most active part of the venture philanthropy movement in the late 1990s and early twenty-first century. But what is wrong with that? Managers of nonprofits should welcome community input and set standards for involvement that clearly distinguish between governance (board) and management (staff). Hostile or friendly take-overs of nonprofits by donor-investors are rare (!), occurring only when board or staff management is not doing its job or stonewalls volunteers and funders so strongly that they become alarmed. Organizations should actively seek wise investors who want to give their time, opinions, and ideas as well as their money. Those are all true gifts.

For still others, it conveyed the notion that there would be some kind of monetary return or payback on the investment. This was a misunderstanding, although at least one organization reportedly tried to launch a "loan program" disguised as an investment opportunity. This thinly veiled emergency funding effort invited "investors" to make "gifts" now, which would be returned in their entirety five years later. The "gifts" were really no-interest loans. Although its failure to generate funds was blamed on the lack of tax benefit for the donor, another major reason was the absence of philanthropic values and principles. This was a purely financial transaction that benefited the organization alone. The only payback in the kind of investment discussed in this chapter is the satisfaction and values reinforcement derived from seeing the results of the investment. Today, increasing numbers of new and veteran philanthropists are reaping huge returns for their social investments: stronger communities, healthier children, more independent seniors, a cleaner environment, and other attributes of our society that have been made possible by their philanthropy.

Summary

The investment attitude has the potential to shatter the myths that keep our sector in a supplicant posture, myths that still exist in communities across America and around the world.

Inviting investment is the high point of the development cycle, the culmination of the six preceding steps in the development process. It requires board and staff members to act within their development partnership to ensure the most meticulous planning and implementation of the ask itself. Fundraising is a contact sport. We cannot invite investment from a distance.

The framework and the process for inviting investment are critical strategies and skills for volunteers and staff. True investment comes only when the potential donor-investor has been engaged in a relationship with the organization that stimulates a desire to invest.

CHAPTER 6

Capitalizing on the Community's Investment

Part One: Annual Campaigns

Individual and institutional funders become involved donor-investors when they are offered regular opportunities to renew or increase their support for community organizations whose work they value. The techniques most commonly used for building a base of donor-investors are annual and capital campaigns. Viable community-based organizations maintain a cycle of annual fundraising programs and occasionally find themselves seeking capital funding for buildings and/or endowment.

This chapter examines annual campaigns as they relate to the overall organizational purpose of building a base of donor-investors who will be partners with the organization in ensuring the continued delivery of programs and services. Chapter 7 presents capital campaigns in the same framework.

A view of annual and capital campaigns as they relate to overall capitalization of organizations provides a valuable comparison.

ANNUAL AND CAPITAL CAMPAIGNS

The specific objectives and structure for each type of campaign differ, but the general purpose for both is the same: to increase capitalization of an organization. In the non-profit sector, capitalization is defined as the production and retention of sufficient financial resources by an organization to ensure its ability to withstand changes in the flow of earned or contributed revenues and keep programs and services healthy. Increased capitalization is achieved through annual campaigns that ensure an adequate cash flow to support current programs without incurring debt. Capital campaigns increase endowment and/or raise overall capacity to deliver programs through the acquisition, remodeling, or building of a new facility or the purchase of needed equipment.

Annual Campaigns

Annual campaigns involve both major and general donors in yearly opportunities to provide current program support. These funds are spent in the year they are received, and at the end of the fiscal year, any surplus is assigned to an operating reserve fund. Annual does not mean "once a year"; it means all year round. Fundraising activities include mail, phone, Web-based giving, e-mail appeals, and special events. Annual campaigns keep the mission and impact visible in the community.

Capital Campaigns

Capital campaigns for buildings, equipment, or endowment are conducted very occasionally by most organizations. Some universities are now into a regular once-a-decade cycle of capital campaigns. In the United Kingdom and western Europe, capital campaigns are now being conducted with success by educational and arts organizations, using proven but culturally adapted American development practices. Organizations in Australia and New Zealand and in some Asian countries have also become skilled capital campaigners. Capital campaigns, wherever they occur, usually require increased staff, outside consultation, and an infusion of new or renewed leadership. They are short term, very intensive, and provide an excellent opportunity to increase organizational capacity overall.

Annual and capital campaigns differ in several ways, as illustrated in Exhibit 6.1.

Capital and Annual Campaign Similarities

Both capital and annual campaigns raise vital funds and are a key way to sustain donor relationships and a sense of investment. Annual fundraising involves the donor-investor as a participant in keeping the mission evident in the community. Capital fundraising provides a rare or occasional opportunity for a donor-investor to play a major or supporting

EXHIBIT 6.1	DIFFERENCE BETWEEN ANNUAL AND CAPITAL CAMPAIGNS	
	Annual	**Capital**
Duration	Ongoing, all year round	Limited time period (1–5) years
Source of gifts	Discretionary income or from assets (stock)	Assets or estate for some; income for others
Range of gifts	Small to major	Emphasis on large
Focus	Current program support	Building, equipment, and/or endowment
Purpose	Donor acquisition, renewal, upgrade; infuse cash flow	Major capitalization of buildings, endowment, equipment; involvement of major individual and institutional funders

role in helping an organization build its long-term capacity, capability, and resources. By maintaining strong program support (annual campaigns) and building a solid foundation of endowment and facilities capacity (capital campaigns), an organization can position itself as an attractive philanthropic investment. The two kinds of campaigns complement each other and are catalysts for maintaining donor-investor relationships.

ANNUAL CAMPAIGNS

A successful annual giving program will involve many activities.

- *Direct (impersonal) mail or Web-based giving opportunities* to acquire new donors
- *Select (personalized) mail and e-mail* to renew or upgrade donors
- *Personal (handwritten or specially tailored on the word processor) mail* to make a very personal ask for a larger annual gift or set an appointment for a face-to-face call
- *Personal phone calls* to follow up on personal letters or to solicit a gift directly (the personal call to ask for a gift should be followed up by a personal letter)
- *Face-to-face meetings* for the solicitation of larger gifts or gifts of any size from board members and other special friends of the organization
- *Phone-a-thons* in which groups of volunteers participate in an evening of calling previous or prospective donors for their gifts
- *Special events* that are both *friend*-raisers (cultivation and stewardship of prospects and donors) and fundraisers
- *Foundation and corporation* annual funding

ANNUAL CAMPAIGNS: DEVELOPMENT AS WELL AS FUNDRAISING

Direct Mail

Direct mail, whether e-mail or "snail" mail, is, in the purest sense, an impersonal approach using a form letter. It is appropriately reserved for those prospective donors with whom the organization has little or no existing relationship. Although these mass mailings can be personalized with inside addresses and salutations even to those we do not know, people are not fooled. It is still direct mail that fills mailboxes and annoys many recipients. Direct mail has a low response rate because most is never opened.

The purpose of direct mail is the *acquisition* of a new donor who is then brought into a relationship with the organization. Yield from direct mail is typically small: 1.5 percent to 2 percent is an excellent response; 0.8 percent is common. Such letters are mailed to "cold" or "warm" lists. These lists, which may come from the organization's own database of referred names or from an exchange with another similar organization, or be rented from a mailing service, provide names of those whose philanthropic interests or demographic profile make them likely investors in the organization. Organizations are cautioned not to buy lists, because the percentage of those who will give from a direct mail solicitation is increasingly smaller. It is not good practice to burden an organization's database with a list that may be 99 percent deadwood. When a list is rented from a mailing or direct marketing service, only those who give become part of the organization's database. If a list has been exchanged with another organization or purchased, it is retained as a prospect list; those who give are moved to the donor list. Periodically, evaluate these prospect lists and remove those names that have not responded for a several-year period.

The letter itself is important. Direct marketing ideas have changed, and what seems to be most effective are letters that use short sentences, a great deal of open space, crisp words that catch attention, and have a compelling ask. A simple formula for constructing a letter is: (1) touch my heart; (2) tell me what the problem is; (3) tell me what you are doing about it; and (4) tell me how I can help. An easy-to-use reply card and envelope should be included, along with a brochure or other information if appropriate and cost-effective.

E-mail and Web-based Solicitations

We have experienced an accelerated acceptance of e-mail and the web in philanthropy. The outpouring of gifts after the terrorist attacks in September 2001 and following the Indian Ocean Tsunami in December 2004 were breakthroughs in people's awareness that Web-based giving is increasing significantly. Web sites almost universally include a way for people to give, and e-mail appeals—particularly for renewal of gifts from certain donors whose preference is to give via the web—are increasing, as well. Because these are "messages in a hurry" that cannot be folded, reread easily, or put into the bills-to-be-paid file for later action, crafting a message for the Web or an e-mail appeal requires greater simplicity and directness. People who visit your Web site are predisposed to be interested in the organization—you do not have to do as much selling as you do with a direct mail piece. And if you have already had contact with the person you are e-mailing, the same rule may apply. In both cases, be absolutely clear about how the gift can be made and the kind of acknowledgment donors can expect. Make sure it is easy to give. Many Web sites are very frustrating to use, and result in people giving up before they complete the transaction. Organizations that cannot support their own on-line giving are contracting with companies that provide this service. Check out the clarity and ease of the process before signing up. Once a person has given, be sure to move them into a more personal program as soon as you can. Include them in your thankathons (see below) and use brief questionnaires on your Web site to learn more about them. Web-based tools for more effective management of the stewardship process by organizations are being developed. They are geared to the nonprofit sector and will help revolutionize personalized interaction with donors in the decades ahead (see Chapter 8).

Personalization of Mailings

One way to enhance the results of a direct mailing is to really personalize it (with notes and real signatures, not just with a computer-generated inside salutation). A newly formed hospital foundation in a small semi-rural but rapidly growing area of California broke all records for an acquisition mailing (22 percent response) and received initial gifts of nearly $38,000 by using a simple technique known as a "PS-athon." During the course of an afternoon, more than 20 volunteers wrote personal notes on nearly 3,000 pieces of mail. The printed letter, well constructed with a compelling message, had been signed by four prominent citizens who were already involved with the foundation. Labels had been generated using numerous lists, and each participant in the PS-athon selected labels from the lists, put them on envelopes, and then added a personally signed PS that urged the recipient to join this wonderful new organization that would support the hospital under construction. The response was gratifying and gave the foundation a solid base on which to build. A range of donor levels was included in the mailing, and gifts spanned those options ($25 to $500). Although the personalization of large mailings requires using first class rather than bulk postage, the results usually justify the cost.

Following Through on Donor Acquisition

The follow-up to an initial mailing is critical. An acknowledgment letter sent 24 to 72 hours after receipt of the gift is an excellent policy to adopt. In the United States, the IRS-appropriate wording must be contained in that letter or receipt. But the acknowledgment process should be more strategic. For too long, organizations have used an internal gift threshold ($100, $500, $1,000) as a way to determine whether a donor is brought into a more personal relationship. At these levels, donors are offered opportunities to come to special events or receptions, or they receive a personal call or letter from a board or staff member thanking them for their gift. These internal thresholds do not build relationships, they discourage them. Donors can be in a database for years and never receive the kind of personal outreach that could convert them into donor-investors. Many potentially large donor-investors may be hidden in the database for want of some kind of outreach that will reveal their values and their connection to the organization. An initial personal contact, after the first gift, can serve both the organization and the donor.

The Thankathon

"Thankathons"—begun two decades ago on college campuses—should by now be a mainstay in the donor development techniques of all organizations. They provide the first step in stewardship of all donors. The thankathon serves a purpose besides thanking donors: It also provides volunteers with opportunities to interact with donors in a conversation that is not driven by asking for money. This increases both the willingness and the comfort level of the volunteers. Shortly after a wave of gifts have come in from the Web site, e-mail, or direct mailing or after a special event, organize a thankathon. Put the chair or a member of the development committee in charge of organizing other volunteers to participate.

A thankathon uses some of the same structure as a phonathon, which many organizations use for raising money directly or for following up on mail or e-mail appeals. The key ingredients of a successful thankathon are the same: willing volunteers, a location where there are adequate phones, accurate lists with phone numbers, and relevant non-confidential information including previous gifts and any volunteer involvement, and supervision by a volunteer or staff leader.

A central location for the thankathon works best: the organization's office (if there are enough telephone lines) or a real estate or stock brokerage firm office of a board member or other volunteer. Sometimes active donor-investors are generous with their offices, as well. Volunteers, with or without staff participation, are provided with lists of those who have made a recent gift. According to the policies of the organization, the volunteer may or may not know the size of the gift. Volunteers then call donors, using "talking tips" that have been prepared by staff or other volunteers, and thank them for their gifts. Messages can be left on answering machines. When contact is made, the response is warm. Donors are surprised and gratified, and many will ask if this is a call for more money. The answer, of course, is no. This is a call to thank them for their most recent gift. If donors are willing to chat, provide the callers with a few questions (what the donor knows about the organization, what inspired them to give, etc.) so the body of information about the donor can begin to build. More than one thankathon has been followed by an additional unsolicited gift from donors who were touched by the outreach they received. And more than one potentially large donor or estate donor has been initially identified through a thankathon.

Select Mail

Select mail is used for renewing or upgrading gifts from existing donors. In donor development, the renewal and upgrade are critical steps in building long-term relationships. Because computer technology with mail merge allows all mail to be personalized easily, "select" mail must accurately and honestly reflect your relationship with that donor. At a minimum, the letter should indicate the amount of the previous year's gift as a basis for requesting a renewal or upgrade. The letter must also be accurate with all program statistics and donor information, and have a focus on results. Donors want to know what impact their previous gift(s) made in the community through the work of the organization: how many people were fed, how many children were served, how the reviewers welcomed the concerts, and so on. Donors also want to know the status of the need the organization is meeting: how many more seniors still need meals at home, how many more families need child care assistance, how many more schools need the performing or visual arts program. Profile a recipient or participant in the program by way of illustrating, through one example, the impact the donor's investment made on others, as well. Keep the message positive, even if the problem you are solving together remains difficult. People want to invest in progress, success, and results. Whiny or depressing letters may garner some sympathy gifts, but true investments are made in those organizations that position themselves as problem-solvers and show their results. The response to letters positioned in this way is strong: Donor-investors feel as if they are partners in pursuing the mission and opportunities with the organization. They feel as if their investments are working.

At this level, renewal and upgrade of the gift begin to form the basis for an organization to move beyond fundraising and into true donor development and relationship building.

For both direct and select mail, organizations may use telephone or e-mail follow-up after the letters have been sent. When a gift comes in, the follow-up to select mail is the same as for direct mail: letter with appropriate receipt and a thank-you call either through a thankathon or, in some cases, personally from a board member or staff person.

Personal Mail

Personalized letters generated on the word processor or written by hand from one individual to another are highly effective in solicitations. These letters may be sent to existing donors as a next-level solicitation technique or may be used as the first outreach to a special prospect from someone who knows that prospect well. The power of the handwritten message cannot be underestimated: a full letter, a note on a word-processed letter, or a thank-you note all spiral in their effectiveness when handwritten. A lost art, especially in this age of technology, the handwritten letter is read and valued far more than word-processed letters. In the donor-investor development cycle, there is a noble place for the handwritten letter or note.

Even those who claim their handwriting excludes them from such an exercise can be persuaded that just a few sentences added on to a word-processed letter can make all the difference. In one organization, the CEO writes handwritten notes at every opportunity. These notes are often saved by their recipients and clipped inside the front of the board or committee member's binder. Volunteer and staff leaders should add this idea to their array of techniques for building donor relationships. In a major university campaign, the chair of one program was a talented amateur photographer who made photo note cards for her personal use. The university regularly supplied her with lists of volunteers and donors who deserved or needed special recognition or attention. She would write a handwritten note on one of her photo note cards. During the course of the campaign, more than 200 of these photo notecards were sent to volunteers and donors. The response was very positive, and several volunteers and donors reported they had framed the photos from the cards. At the end of the campaign, the program chairperson wrote the final thank-you note on cards created with photographs of the university. The relationship-building impact of receiving these special handwritten notes was measurable in volunteer retention and donor feedback. Drawing on the leader's talents, the recipients received unique acknowledgment.

Presolicitation Letters

Letters that state a solicitation is impending, but do not ask directly for the gift, are called "presolicitation" letters. No amount is suggested in this kind of letter. Instead, the letter requests that the individual read brief materials that are enclosed and expect a telephone call from the letter writer within a prescribed period of time. It is essential to make the follow-up phone call within the stated time period. Many prospective and previous donors have been puzzled by failure of the writer to follow through with the stated intent to call and ask for a gift or discuss a campaign. These letters should be very personalized, and may be signed by the person who is going to call. Or the writer may say that another volunteer will be calling.

Acknowledge a gift that comes as a result of a personal letter with an appropriate letter and receipt, plus a very personal phone call. This is a potentially transforming step in the relationship-building process and has to be carried out with professionalism and heart, and within the right time frame.

Face-to-Face Solicitation of Gifts

Face-to-face solicitation of gifts is, of course, the most successful and proven way to engage or reaffirm the investor relationship, reinforce previous giving, share enthusiasm and results, and convey the sense of partnership between the organization and the donor in accomplishing the mission of the organization. There is no substitute for this type of solicitation. Every organization should strive annually to increase the number of prospective and previous donors who are solicited in this manner. Doing this requires increasing the number of trained volunteers who are willing to and capable of participating in this kind of solicitation.

The obvious prospects and donors for face-to-face solicitation are those from whom the anticipated gift is the greatest, which includes not only individual donor-investors, but those individuals who represent corporations and foundations. The techniques for making the ask are covered in Chapter 5. The focus in this chapter is the importance of those asks in the annual funding cycle and in relationship building. The face-to-face ask, in an organization that is dedicated to developing its donor base into a solid constituency of donor-investors, will be extended beyond major donors, corporations, and foundations to include these individuals, whether their gifts qualify as "major" in the organization's giving level listing or not:

- All board and key nonboard committee members
- Those whose gifts represent a major commitment and investment to the organization relative to their capacity to give
- Those who have committed a planned (estate) gift to the organization

Each of these individuals is a major stakeholder in the organization, and each should be given the courtesy of a face-to-face solicitation.

Board Member Solicitations

Too many organizations solicit their board members by letter, phone call, or "group ask" at a board meeting. These same board members are then expected to go out and solicit gifts face-to-face from others, when they have not been asked themselves in the way they are expected to ask. It is small wonder that board members are hesitant about making a personal solicitation: They have not had a model to follow based on their own ask. In organizations that understand that going beyond fundraising begins with the board, the annual solicitation of board members is the benchmark for all other major solicitations. The executive director and the board chair have a personal meeting with each board member, individually, on an annual basis. Details of this meeting are discussed in Chapter 9.

Solicitation of Nonmajor "Major" Donors

In every organization, there are certain donor-investors whose gifts, relative to their capacity to give, are significant. These are the individuals, often living on a fixed income, who send in $25 a month, or $5 a week, or make an annual gift that represents nearly all of their discretionary income. Often these are individuals who are elderly, who may have a sense of involvement with the organization based on some previous service or volunteer experience. An annual visit with them, just to thank them and tell them how much their gift means to the organization, can do a great deal to build the kind of relationship that dignifies our sector. Sometimes the relationship will demand other extraordinary actions. In one unit of the American Cancer Society, the staff was asked by one of their longtime donors, who was widowed, had no family, and lived alone on a farm outside of town, to call him every morning just to make sure he was alive. They did. They also made frequent visits to him when they were in the area. One morning, about two years into their outreach to him, he did not answer the phone. The staff called the local fire department, which went to the farm. They found that he had died sometime during the night. Had these staff people not carried out their promise to him, it could have been considerable time before he was found. His estate, while modest by some standards, was left entirely to the ACS local unit and had a significant impact on programming for many years to come.

Personal Solicitation of Those Who Have Made Planned Gifts

Personal solicitation will strengthen the relationship with those who have made this long-term commitment to your organization. These people are the futurists of the organization. They have made an investment in programs and people they will never see. A planned gift is an act of faith. It is an expression of the donor's belief that the organization in which he or she is investing is sound, stable, and important. It is also an affirmation of the donor's belief in the importance of the need that is being met and that the need will not go away. Donors who have made it known that their estate plans include your organization should be treated like major donors even if their annual support falls below the level the organization has targeted for special attention.

Encouragement to give annually, no matter the size of the gift, keeps the planned gift donor involved in the organization. It encourages and strengthens the relationship, and may lead to an increase in the estate gift or a more vigorous participation in annual giving programs. All planned donors should be asked for an annual gift, unless specific instructions prohibit such solicitations. A personal call on these individuals, at least yearly, is critical. Even if an annual gift is not made, the stewardship aspect of such visits is powerful.

The Board's Role in Face-to-Face Solicitations

Board members need to be very active organizers of and the primary participants in face-to-face solicitations. In the United States, where there is a higher comfort level in speaking with people directly about a contribution that reflects knowledge of the potential donor's financial capacity, face-to-face solicitations are increasingly common and more comfortable. Elsewhere, particularly in western Europe, where there is still much privacy associated with financial capacity and philanthropy, such solicitations are still rare. There reliance on personal letters is strong. As the need that western European organizations have for private funds increases with continuing government pull-backs, solicitation patterns will have to shift. Education about philanthropy and its accomplishments will have to be coupled with an easing of taboos on discussing financial capacity so that appropriate personal solicitations can occur. Australia and New Zealand have a somewhat more open attitude about the implied understanding of an individual's wealth and capacity, but hesitations still remain about the face-to-face solicitation in which those issues could be probed. In the process of evolving donors into donor-investors, these obstacles to personal solicitation can be reduced if the organization approaches the solicitation from the sensitivities of the donor rather than from the desires of the organization.

Phone-a-Thons

Raising money by telephone has declined in recent years as web-based fund raising has increased. This news delights many would-be donors who consistently complained about the calls that invariably came during dinner. However, in certain parts of the United States it is still a common practice, and among certain organizations in all parts of the United States and in some other countries, phone appeals are used for special appeals or for "cleaning up" annual or capital campaigns. Historically conducted by volunteers, phone-a-thons have become largely the responsibility of paid callers. Even on most university campuses, the student callers are paid. In the spirit of transparency and to comply with a growing number of laws that allow people to take their names off direct marketing (including nonprofit) call lists, when initiating a solicitation by telephone, callers need to identify themselves as paid or volunteer callers. It is now more common to have volunteers conduct the thank-a-thons and leave the phone appeals to paid callers. However they are conducted, these calls should be done with consideration for the donor, the culture and tradition of the community and the integrity of the mission. If hiring paid callers, be sure to understand clearly what they will keep as their fee. Scandalous revelations of paid calling organizations that have kept up to 97 percent of the money they raised have plagued the sector and given philanthropy a setback in community perception.. Whether paid or volunteer, callers need to be trained or coached in the mission of the organization, basic facts about its financial and program impact, what the money will be used for, what the cost of fund raising is for the organization and other pertinent information that those called may request. This coaching can occur on the same evening as the calling, thereby minimizing the time required of the callers. Following a phone-a-thon, be sure to do whatever is required to ensure that the loop is closed: thank you note, thank-a-thon, additional information or personal letter or visit.

Special Events

Special events are both *friend-raisers* and *fundraisers.* Organizations that depend on an exhausting cycle of special events to raise their annual current program support funds will never go beyond fundraising. Special events are one form of donor acquisition (along with direct mail), and they are useful as stewardship strategies. Even when an event makes a considerable amount of money, two factors must be considered carefully:

1. The *real* cost of the event, including staff time and other indirect expenses
2. Follow-up to the event

If community members only interact with an organization at their annual spectacular Haunted House Ball and receive no other outreach or information during the year, then the relationship-building opportunity is lost or diminished. Only when the event is positioned in the annual cycle of development activities and when careful follow-up is done, can the value of events be increased. A few planning and follow-up procedures will heighten the long-term value of a special event to an organization:

- In planning the event, use a checklist or questionnaire that assesses the true costs in time and money, the consistency of the event with the mission of the organization, the resources available (volunteers, staff, and money) to allocate to this event, its position relative to the calendar of other community events, and so on (see Exhibit 6.2).

- Draw up a realistic budget and stick to it. Costs of events have a way of mushrooming unless the budget is carefully controlled.

- Have program/organization description brochures at the event along with a photo display or other means (DVD, video) for presenting the purpose and activities of the organization.

- Have an action plan in which all tasks and assignments are carefully defined and on which there has been agreement by all those who will work on the event.

- After the event, review the list of attendees and devise follow-up for each. At a minimum, conduct a thankathon in which each participant is thanked and informed about the net amount raised (if solid) and the impact it will make on the organization and the community.

- Send copies of your organization's newsletter, with an accompanying note, to all attendees. Keep them informed throughout the year about the organization's other activities.

- Add these names to your prospective donor lists for the next acquisition mailing.

- Do a special "volunteer opportunities" insert or separate mailing the first time you mail to these individuals. Include a nonfundraising program description brochure about the organization.

EXHIBIT 6.2   EVENT PLANNING FORM

This form is to help volunteers in planning events for [the organization]. If you have an idea for a special event, please fill in this form as completely as possible, then bring it in to the office. Thanks!

  I. Description of the Event:

 II. Purpose(s) of the Event, in measurable terms:
     II.a. Audience(s):

III. Planned date(s) of the Event:
     _____ I (we) have checked this date with the following calendars:

IV. Chair for the event:

 V. Committees:

	Number of Volunteers/Hours Needed	Number of Staff Hours Needed

Planning/Oversight
Chair:

Underwriting/Sponsorships
Chair:

Advertising: selling ads in the
printed program
Chair:

Printing/Mailing
Chair:

Publicity/Media
Chair:

Ticket Sales
Chair:

Program/Entertainment
Chair:

Finance/Budget/Records
Chair:

Food/Wine
Chair:

Logistics: Setup, Decorations, Cleanup
Chair:

EXHIBIT 6.2   **EVENT PLANNING FORM** *(Continued)*

VI.   Planning Timeline — Day and date of event: _____

Three months in advance: _____
    To do: (activity deadline date)

Two months in advance: _____
    To do:

Six weeks in advance: _____
    To do:

One month in advance: _____
    To do:

Three weeks in advance: _____
    To do:

Two weeks in advance: _____
    To do:

One week in advance: _____
    To do:

Day Before Event: _____
    To do:

DATE OF EVENT: _____
    To do:

Follow-up Activities: _____

_____

_____

_____

_____

Please mark at least two interim "bailout" dates for this event. "Bailout" dates are deadlines by which certain tasks *MUST* be accomplished in order for the event to proceed as planned. Consider changing, postponing, or canceling the event to cut losses if these deadlines are not met.

(continues)

EXHIBIT 6.2   EVENT PLANNING FORM *(Continued)*

VII.   Planning Budget

Item	Projected/Estimated (Expense estimates based (on firm bids)	Actual
Expenses:		
Facility Cost	$ _____	$ _____
Facility Prep	_____	_____
Equipment Rental	_____	_____
Stationery/Invitations	_____	_____
Printing	_____	_____
Postage	_____	_____
Photography	_____	_____
Supplies	_____	_____
Meal Cost	_____	_____
Complimentary Meals	_____	_____
Wine	_____	_____
Decorations	_____	_____
Centerpieces/Flowers	_____	_____
Door Prizes/Awards	_____	_____
Recognition Materials/Gifts	_____	_____
Security	_____	_____
Transportation	_____	_____
Insurance	_____	_____
Other	_____	_____
Contingency _____%	_____	_____
Expense Total	$ _____	$ _____

EXHIBIT 6.2   EVENT PLANNING FORM *(Continued)*

Income:	Projected/Estimated	Actual
Attendance/Ticket Sales	_____ × $_____ = $_____	# _____
		$ _____
Cash/Sponsorships/Contributions		
1.	$ _____	$ _____
2.	_____	_____
3.	_____	_____
4.	_____	_____
5.	_____	_____
Gross Income	$ _____	$ _____
Gross Expenses	$ _____	$ _____
NET INCOME	$ _____	$ _____

In-Kind Contributions

1.	6.
2.	7.
3.	8.
4.	9.
5.	10.

Don't forget:

☐ Liquor License   ☐ Parking   ☐ Handicapped Accessibility

☐ Insurance   ☐ Child Care   ☐ Emergency Planning

Source: Form developed by Lisa C. Bennett.

Corporations and Foundations

Corporate and foundation fundraising fits into the annual cycle to the extent that these gifts are solicited annually and represent a form of modest but regular support. Large corporate and foundation gifts for campaign or other special purposes—like those for very large gift individual donors—do not fall into this cycle, but the relationships built during the annual outreach are those on which the success of the larger asks will be based. Often employee fund gifts are given annually, even if corporate gifts are not. Corporations that match gifts also deserve recognition and a sustained relationship. With the mergers and economic hammering many corporations took in the late twentieth century and are still taking in the early twenty-first century, nonprofit organizations have had to develop patience with the recovery of this source of income. Increasingly, we look to the marketing budget in companies for event support and underwriting. One trend, cited by the *Washington Post* in July 2003 and later reinforced by the *Chronicle of Philanthropy,* is a back-to-the-1980s practice by corporations of giving more in-kind gifts (equipment and services) than cash. This type of gift reflects management's concern for the corporation's bottom line and their obligation to their own shareholders.

The harsh damage to many foundation investment portfolios in the late twentieth and early twenty-first centuries also affected nonprofit fundraising even after economic recovery began. During the crumbling of the stock market, many foundations maintained their commitments to nonprofits by drawing off more interest from their investments than anticipated. When those obligations were completed, they had to make an adjustment in payouts to ensure future capacity. Many operate on a three year averaging basis and used the end of their cycle to recalibrate. This resulted in some severe reductions in foundation giving that are only now beginning to be restored.

Sustaining an annual relationship with corporate and foundation representatives is an essential part of donor development. Even in years when your organization is not funded, extend outreach and stewardship to those institutional investors who have played a significant role in capitalizing the organization in the past. These relationships become the basis for planning and implementing larger funding drives, or when assembling community advisory boards for general or capital campaign purposes. Funders, whether institutional or individual, must never gain the impression that their only value to you is the money they give. They must believe that their opinions and feedback are important as well. And they must know the impact of their gifts.

Regular communication to donors from the organizations they are funding should convey results: number of people fed in a hunger program, how the dropout rate among high-risk students is declining, what treatment breakthroughs have been attained with a new piece of medical equipment. If donors are satisfied with the impact their gifts are making and the way in which their gift is being managed, they will continue to support the organization. A common myth among organizations that focus on needs, rather than results, is that it is not a good idea to go back to donors who have recently given substantially to the organization. A *needs* focus leads to apology for coming back to the donor for more money; a *results* focus invites the donor to reinvest in a program that is making a major difference in the community. It is the latter approach that gives energy and spirit to fundraising.

Cycling Annual Fund Activities

Annual fundraising should be energizing to an organization. A carefully crafted cycle should reflect an evaluation of resources, needs and potential market and be timed to provide a regular influx of cash to meet current program support requirements (see Chapter 11). The development staff should set an annual fund goal that is a carefully derived figure within the larger budget. For arts organizations dependent on season or individual ticket income, or organizations that rely on regularly calendared grants from government sources, there are usually periods of diminished cash availability. One important role the annual fund plays is to ensure that periods of scarcity in earned or grant income are countered by annual fund programs that will raise the needed funds.

Develop an annual fund cycle in which the appropriate annual fundraising activities are planned in such a way that the cash flow from earned and contributed revenue stays balanced. Program, administrative, and development staff should all be guided by this annual calendar. Exhibit 6.3 shows a sample performing arts organization's cycle. It is a tool for managing fundraising, involving volunteers, and anticipating and responding to cash flow management needs.

EXHIBIT 6.3   SAMPLE ANNUAL GIVING CYCLE: PERFORMING ARTS ORGANIZATION

Month	Annual Giving	Earned Income
January	Follow-up phoning to year-end appeal	Recital (January 11)
February	No new funding activity Thankathon for year-end gifts Foundation grants	Single-ticket sales
March	Spring mailing out 3/26	Subscription renewals begin
April	Spring mailing returns Corporate funding drive	Subscription renewals
May	Spring phone cleanup by volunteers Corporate cleanup by development committee Thankathon for spring gifts	Renewal cleanup by telemarketing firm
June	Annual major donor campaign; board solicitations	None
July	Thankathon; no new revenue-generating activity	7/4 Concert in park Single-ticket sales
August	Foundation proposals researched and scheduled for fiscal year	Subscriber phone drive
September	Autumn mailing	Single-ticket sales
October	Harvest Ball event	Single-ticket sales
November	Phone cleanup to autumn mailing; second round of major asks Harvest Ball Thankathon	Single-ticket sales

December	Clean up all pending solicitations;
	   conduct holiday thankathon with
	   volunteer young musicians calling
		Holiday concert
		Single-ticket sales

Using the Annual Fund Cycle to Capitalize Community Investment

Although we think of capitalization as periodic infusion of major dollars into an organization through endowment or building campaigns, the annual fund also functions as an important element in long-term capitalization. An organization whose annual fundraising is weak, even if the endowment is strong, will erode its capital holdings through annual or accumulated deficits. Several of America's symphony orchestras failed because annual and earned income was insufficient to sustain rising costs. Endowments were invaded, and the orchestras eventually closed their doors. Although at least two (Oakland, California, and Denver, Colorado) have been reorganized (Oakland Symphony as the East Bay Symphony and Denver Symphony as the Colorado Symphony), even the temporary demise of these important cultural resources was damaging to their communities. Moreover, the donor-investors who had sustained these orchestras through their regular annual and occasional capital funding programs were reluctant to provide further capitalization to the new organizations. When they did, they placed certain restrictions regarding budget, endowment, and general management.

Annual fundraising should be guided by the understanding that key donor-investors want to protect their investments. Major individual donors to capital or endowment needs should be included in the annual fund unless they have specifically stated they wish to participate only in endowment or capital funding. Certain institutional funders, including corporations and some foundations, may also participate in annual as well as capital fund drives. As they become increasingly committed donor-investors, they will respond to requests for a variety of investment opportunities within the organization.

The regional research facility of a national computer company had established a donor relationship with a local children's agency. Its annual gifts were consistent but modest, and the nonprofit agency practiced good stewardship. The agency had an opportunity to purchase an important set of reading books for its therapeutic day school; however, all the funds for books and supplies had been spent for the year. The development director called the computer research facility and talked with her contact there. He put her in touch with the employees' organization, which became interested in the project. From funds collected from employees for community and social activities, the company made a grant that enabled the agency to purchase the books. The following year, frustrated by not having the database on a computer, the development director talked with the head of the employees' organization again, but this time about the possibility of the employees donating time to computerize the database. They were delighted to do this, and contributed more than 500 hours to the project. At the end of that year, the agency honored these employees with a special reception, at which time they also met the teachers and saw some of the students who had benefited from their earlier gift.

PRESENTING MULTIPLE GIFT OPPORTUNITIES TO DONORS

When seeking multiple gifts, the approach has to be right. Donor-investors will be open to requests for multiple kinds of funding if they are always provided information about results achieved and continuing needs that must be met. Solicitations should reflect program priorities and results, not funding goals alone. Annual fund solicitation letters that begin "This year our annual fund goal is $75,000. It is important for us to meet this goal, and your gift will help us make it! Please give generously to our annual fund with a gift of $100" miss the point. People do not invest in annual funds, they invest in organizations. The annual fund is a vehicle for investing in an organization, just as the organization is a vehicle for investing in the community.

"Annual fund" is really an internal accounting and function title for the means by which nonprofits raise current program support. It implies that fundraising is driven by the organization's fiscal year, rather than by the external needs the organization is meeting. Stanford University, following its successful Centennial Campaign in the 1980s, dropped the word "Annual" and now involves donors in The Stanford Fund. This name change, while seemingly subtle, is powerful. Removal of the word "annual" gives the fund a sense of permanence and places it appropriately in its role as an element in the overall capitalization and stability of the university. Dropping the word "annual" creates a greater opportunity to focus on multiple opportunities to contribute on an ongoing basis.

Potential and current funders who have been brought into a relationship with an organization look at an organization in a somewhat holistic way. The annual fund, a capital campaign, and/or endowment fund are ways for them to support an organization in which they believe. They see an orchestra that presents quality programming and solid educational outreach into the schools; a hospital whose emergency and care facilities are of unique service to the community; a feeding program for the elderly that gives meals and companionship; or a child care program that enables young parents to work or attend school without worry. Those who share the values that underlie these programs invest in the *organization* providing the program. The annual fund, a capital campaign, and endowment funds are merely ways they can give to the programs in which they believe. We can confuse donors by thrusting at them the internal labeling we give to the various pockets in which we place our contributed revenue or the way we categorize our donors. Although we track donor-investors internally according to size and frequency of gifts, it is important for us to reserve these labels for internal use only. Consider this example of a failed donor relations outreach: A donor of $200, uncertain if his gift had been received, telephoned the nonprofit to talk with a development staff person. After several minutes on hold, he was connected with an individual who identified herself as the person in charge of "intermediate donors." For this donor, $200 was a major stretch. The donor was insulted and never contributed to that organization again.

ELEMENTS OF A SUCCESSFUL ANNUAL CAMPAIGN

Board Leadership

Although it is assumed that all successful capital campaigns will have board and community leadership, annual campaigns too often are staff-driven and staff-led. All fundraising should be a partnership between board and staff, but the visible leadership in the community should be that of the board. The building of the kind of long-term relationships that enable organizations to go beyond fundraising begins with board leadership of the annual fund. An annual fund committee of board and other community members has to work with staff to design and implement the process for the campaign, including review of prospect lists, affirmation of the goal, recruitment of solicitation teams, strategy development for prospects, follow through on assignments, and successful wrap-up of the campaign.

Participation of Volunteer Teams

These teams include not only board members, but those from the community who have a values and financial investment in the organization (former board members, committed donors). Prospect assignments to solicitors should be done with the team's participation. Motivate teams with a three-part goal:

1. 100 percent contact with all prospects assigned
2. 100 percent calls completed within the established time frame for a particular funding drive
3. A minimum dollar amount raised by each team

For example, if the autumn annual appeal drive has a goal of $100,000, and there are five teams, each team has a *minimum* goal of raising $20,000. Because the contact and completion goals are also in place, the organization is assured that everyone on the assigned lists will be contacted. Goals that focus only on a dollar goal may lead teams or individuals to decide not to call on remaining prospects once they achieve their minimum. It is important to have all three goals. Friendly competition among teams and recognition for goal achievement spur teams on to complete all their contacts.

A Plan

Construct a plan for each year's annual fundraising as part of the overall development plan. Base it on an analysis of the previous year's process and results, establish a goal that is realistic yet a stretch, provide a gift range chart based on the goal and the known prospects for the campaign, offer strategies for acquiring prospective donors and for renewing and upgrading previous donors, set firm timelines for the various components of the annual campaign that are keyed to the earned or granted income cycle of the organization, and provide objectives that will engage and guide the volunteer and staff leaders toward a successful completion in that time frame.

A Financial Goal that Is Realistic but a "Stretch"

Viewing the annual campaign as a means for increasing the capitalization of the organization means setting annual goals that are realistic but that are "stretch" for the organization's donors and volunteers. Most organizations need more donors and larger gifts each year. In the budgeting process, the annual fund goal is often set without adequate consultation with development staff. It is viewed as a "plug" figure: Whatever projected expenses cannot be met through earned income, endowment income, or a capital fund drive that may be planned or under way are "plugged" into the annual giving goal. If this figure is too ambitious, the organization is doomed to a year of cutting expenses or readjusting the contributed income line. Just as detrimental as overstating the amount that must be generated through annual contributions is an overly cautious approach that provides no challenging increment from year to year. Avoid these problems by including the development director in the budgeting process and by encouraging volunteer leadership to provide the incentive, inspiration, and contacts needed to meet a more ambitious goal.

Carefully Constructed List of Prospects

Attempting an annual campaign with a prospect and donor list that has not been refined, evaluated, screened (by staff and board or electronically), expanded, or cleaned up from year to year creates both internal and external problems for the organization. The campaign becomes difficult to implement because the lists and assignments are flawed. Previous and prospective donors (who may receive more than one appeal, a letter addressed to a deceased spouse, or not be acknowledged for their previous giving) gain the impression that the organization's systems are in disarray. This reflects poorly on the organization as a whole. An otherwise well-respected social service organization saw its major gift campaign nearly derailed when the accuracy, quality, and relevance of its lists fell dramatically short. List management is a year-round task, the value of which is most apparent when implementing the annual fundraising programs. Keeping the donor-investor base accurate is essential for a successful campaign. A good database management software program is no longer a luxury. Far too many organizations work with systems that do not serve them well. There are few more important investments than in the technology that supports donor relations. For very underfunded organizations, capacity building grants for equipment and software may be available through community or other foundations. If your organization is struggling with an outdated system, and if you simply have no budget for this kind of investment, seek grant funding. Otherwise, you will not be able to serve the donors you have or attract new—and increasingly demanding— donor-investors.

Strategies that Include All Donors in a Continuum of Investment Opportunities

Very often, organizations separate "annual" and "major" campaigns, rather than viewing them as a seamless continuum that can be integrated in a very powerful way. This integration builds solid relationships and enables donors to feel invested in the *organization* rather than in a particular funding effort.

In planning for the annual contributions to an organization, analyze data on *all* potential new or renewed donor-investors. You may want to take different approaches for the same donor from year to year, based on the previous year's gift, the donor's concerns, other investments that may have been made in the organization by the donor (e.g., a planned gift or a special gift), or the individual's particular circumstances. In one year, the donor may be asked for a gift of $5,000 to lead the annual giving program. The following year, the same donor may be asked to increase his or her gift overall, assigning a portion of it to the unrestricted fund for current program support and another portion to a particular capital need. In yet another year, that same donor may be asked to make a leadership gift to an endowment or capital campaign and only a modest gift to the fund for current program support.

When organizations get tangled up in their own internal funding compartments, they often miss great opportunities to engage donors creatively in funding opportunities that reveal the range and impact of the organization and spark new enthusiasm in donors.

Energize Volunteers with Training and "Product News"

Many board members are reluctant to participate in fundraising because they feel uncomfortable with the asking process (see Chapter 2). To cure this reluctance, provide training that will raise the comfort level of all board members who will make phone or face-to-face asks and acquaint them with the remarkable investment opportunities you offer. In the training, cover the philosophy, strategy, and techniques of development and fundraising and provide practice in the ask itself (see Chapter 5). The training can be done by a qualified board member, a development staff person, or an outside consultant. To be most effective, the training should occur as close as possible to the actual time the volunteers will be using their new skills. Otherwise, the information retention is poor.

In addition to the basic skill orientation in the ask, all training sessions should include product news. For at least 15 minutes, but preferably a half-hour, have one or more individuals who benefit from the organization's programs and services speak to the board and other volunteers about the impact the organization has had on their lives and in the community. This is not a report from a staff person *about* a program. For social, medical, human services, religious, educational, and similar organizations, it is a presentation by an individual (or the individual's family, employer, coworker) that comes from the heart and is compelling in its impact on the board members who must go out and ask for funds. For arts and cultural organizations, it may be from a schoolteacher whose classes have benefited from the in-school programs or docent-led tours, or it could be from a performing or visual artist who speaks with passion about what it means to be a part of the nonprofit. One orchestra had two musicians come in and explain and play their rather unusual Baroque instruments and share their gratitude for having such a superb group to perform with.

Also include important informational reports about the organization's accomplishments, finances, and vision. Provide fact sheets for volunteers that summarize these reports. Finally, be sure that you motivate your volunteers. See Chapter 2 for full details on training sessions for volunteers.

Be Sure Staff and Materials Are Ready to Support the Volunteers

Staff members—as part of the staff-board partnership—are responsible for preparing professional materials and providing support. Staff, working with volunteer committee members, should create volunteer packets containing all pertinent information required by the volunteer for completing his or her assignments. These materials should include, but not be limited to:

- A fact sheet about the organization and/or the campaign
- Campaign or organizational case statement
- Program and budget information
- Timeline for the annual campaign
- Tips for making successful solicitations
- Principal objections the volunteer may encounter, and the appropriate responses
- Lists of key individuals involved with the board and/or the campaign and of current donors (without amounts and only with their permission)
- List of fellow volunteers, with phone numbers
- A staff list (some staff members even offer their home phones for those weekend questions)
- Pledge and/or remit cards
- Stationery and envelopes for thank-you letters

Professional and support staff, or the volunteer leadership team if there is no professional development staff, are there to assist board and other volunteers in every facet of their solicitations. They can help:

- Review assignments to ensure the greatest degree of knowledge regarding the prospect's capacity, concerns, and connection with the organization
- Coach in solicitation techniques
- Set appointments if necessary
- Accompany board members on calls
- Help with follow-up, including timely thank-you letters and receipts
- Develop appropriate stewardship strategies for each prospect

The partnership between board and staff is recognized by donors, and helps solidify the investor relationship. Having a sense of shared initiative and responsibility in the solicitation process strengthens the feeling of investment and ownership on the part of board and staff.

Summary

Annual campaigns provide the income stream that is the lifeblood of the organization. These consumable funds are also a form of capitalization, as they prevent an operating deficit that can erode institutional image and stability. A strong annual giving cycle invites donor-investors to participate in numerous opportunities for funding and keeps the mission visible in the community. Annual giving is periodically complemented by the more common form of capitalization, the capital campaign. Chapter 7 explores capital funds drives.

Capitalizing on the Community's Investment

Part Two: Capital Campaigns

Capital campaigns allow organizations to further capitalize the annual investments of donors and keep their base of financial support strong. Coupled with successful annual fundraising, these two kinds of campaigns help ensure the safety of community programs provided by nonprofit organizations. The similarities and differences between these two kinds of campaigns are summarized in Chapter 6. The focus in this chapter is on capital campaigns as they relate to the long-term capitalization of an organization.

A capital campaign, designed to raise money for a specific purpose within a particular time frame, is an exhausting, draining, exhilarating, and tightly focused effort that challenges the stamina and human resources of even the most stable organizations. When well conceived and executed, a capital campaign has four major results:

1. The targeted financial goal for the campaign is met or exceeded.

2. The organization's visibility is increased in the community and among its constituencies.

3. The overall base of donors is increased.

4. The organization achieves the next level of performance and results.

Decades ago, only the most established educational, cultural, and healthcare organizations—universities, independent schools, hospitals, museums, symphony orchestras—dared undertake such an ambitious effort. Now the pendulum has swung (some would say too far), and organizations large and small with a wide range of missions and readiness are launching community-wide campaigns for construction or equipment, programs, and/or endowment.

RATIONALE FOR CAPITAL CAMPAIGNS

There are numerous factors to consider when deciding whether to undertake a campaign. These factors are often examined in a feasibility study, which tests both the internal readiness (case, fundraising expertise, staff and board commitment, etc.) and the external support (potential funders and leaders, community perception of the organization, other conflicting campaigns, etc.). Before discussing how to test for a capital campaign, this section looks closely at the rationale for a campaign within the context of building donor-investor relationships that enable an organization to go beyond fundraising.

Capital campaigns are conducted to provide buildings or equipment that cannot be funded out of earned income, annual fundraising, endowment income, or capital reserves. They are also undertaken to launch or increase an endowment fund. Well-reasoned campaigns grow out of careful analysis of existing resources (facilities, staffing, annual and endowment income) relative to predicted community needs. These needs are identified through market and program studies that are conducted regularly in conjunction with institutional long-range planning. Anticipation of significant growth in the demand for services, without concurrent potential for significantly increasing fees or annual fundraising revenues, requires prudent organizations to consider alternatives. The same is true when confronting the need to move from a leased or inadequate building. Alternatives exist in both instances. These options will vary depending on the organization and the circumstances, but a capital campaign is almost always among the choices.

Because they see a capital campaign as a solution to their problems, organizations are surprised to discover how complex and difficult they are to plan, organize, and implement. This is particularly true when organizations have failed to develop investor relationships with their donors. Because a capital campaign gift is so obviously an investment, it is given in the belief that the organization is a vital community resource whose future will be strengthened by a new building or an increased endowment fund.

Some very complex organizations, particularly major universities, conduct comprehensive capital campaigns in a nearly predictable cycle every 10 to 15 years. Because of their complexity, these organizations have a broad enough menu of purposes (buildings, scholarships, professorships) to justify these cyclical efforts. For other kinds of nonprofit agencies or institutions, whose mission and programs are more single focused, a capital campaign is rare or very occasional. Smaller organizations often find it hard to develop the rationale, or the energy, for once-a-decade major fundraising efforts.

Ironically, seed funding for an organization—the initial capitalization—is seldom (if ever) raised through a capital campaign. Seed funding is most often obtained from a few institutional or individual donor/investors who are involved in the founding of the organization. Capital campaigns require the backing of an organization as well as a vision. A recent and notable exception was Sage Hill School, the first independent nondenominational high school in Orange County, California which opened in 2000. There, the founders successfully conducted an initial $36 million capital campaign for the building and for scholarship endowment before the school opened. Their success was a tribute to the vision and values of the founders, who had spent many years sharing their dream with those who would, when the time came, fund it. Now they are successfully conducting annual campaigns for program support from parents and the community, have met a foundation challenge for additional scholarship endowment, and are in the next phase of their building campaign. This story constitutes the exception rather than the rule.

NEED TO CAPITALIZE NONPROFITS

The concern about "capitalizing" the nonprofit sector is authentic. Trends in funding suggest that organizations need to build endowment, raise operating reserve funds, and, increasingly, own their own buildings if they are to remain vital service providers to their communities. By capitalizing organizations—providing the base of endowed and annual funds that permit adequate programming without deficit financing—investors can prevent the year-to-year funding crises of many organizations. These crises are often well publicized and pose a threat to the community's perception of the stability of the organization and of the programs offered. Capitalization increases donor confidence and invites greater investment.

If the organization serves a valid role in the community, and if its annual fundraising efforts—combined with revenue from services, interest on endowment, or other earned sources—do not generate funds sufficient to support current programming and create/increase an endowment, renovate, or build a facility, and establish an operating reserve, then there is no alternative other than the capital campaign or a reduction in services.

ATTRACTING DONORS TO CAPITAL CAMPAIGNS

Capital campaigns provide a major opportunity for funders to assess their philanthropic priorities. Competing campaigns for the arts, culture, education, health, or social services are presented to those who are capable of making impact gifts. Experienced donors put their options in priority order, considering several factors:

- Benefit to the community
- Benefit to the organization
- Benefit or recognition for themselves
- The other funders involved

The order of these considerations may vary according to the motivation of the particular donor, but donors consider these four principal issues when making capital campaign gifts.

Benefit to the Community

Community benefit is the bottom line for many people. In a campaign for a local food bank, leadership gifts were secured from several foundations, corporations, and individuals who had no previous record of giving to the agency. The food bank had made a compelling case, citing the more than 300 feeding programs dependent on its resources, describing the way in which enhanced facilities and equipment would increase the amount of food it could process and distribute each year, equating the increased capacity with the importance of preventing food waste in the community, and assuring potential donors that the warehouse design was functional as well as attractive to the neighborhood. The message was very clear: An improved food bank was part of an improved community. Feeding programs made possible by the organization touched all ages, races, neighborhoods, and conditions: children, seniors, people with AIDS, religious and secular groups, African Americans, Hispanics, women, and families. With dedicated leadership and a few inspired donors who were willing to ask others to be investors with them, the campaign exceeded its financial goal of $5 million, increasing its community visibility among corporations and individuals and multiplying its donor base twofold.

Hunger is an obviously compelling issue in any community. Many arts and culture organizations hear too often that the arts are not as urgent or important. The array of social and human problems may be so overwhelming that funding for an orchestra, ballet, museum, or opera seems somehow frivolous. There are proven strategies for engaging community support for arts and culture and for positioning the need for the arts in society as a compelling case. Years ago, a highly regarded dance company wished to produce a new, full-length *Cinderella*. The price tag was high: nearly $1 million. Unsure about community response to this ambitious undertaking, the ballet's CEO arranged a facilitated focus group with volunteers and potential funders. Structured questions led them into a lively discussion of the balance of arts and social services in their community. So strong was the feeling about the need to resolve chronic problems with the homeless and other civic concerns that one participant suggested that *Cinderella* could be promoted as a ballet about child abuse! This approach was discouraged, but the message was clear: Somehow, the arts had to be relevant in order to capture funding. The CEO listened thoughtfully to the entire discussion about community priorities and then offered this idea: If, in the course of solving all the human and social problems in our communities, we neglected and lost the arts, our society would be a sadly diminished one. His message was clear and convincing. The focus group realized that investing in this ballet production was a way of investing in a balanced future for the community by ensuring its arts programs. Group members also gained a greater appreciation for the urgency of funding the arts in a society easily overwhelmed by the compelling social and human needs it faces every day.

Benefit to the Organization

Keeping focused on this potential motivation for donor investment—the benefit to the organization—may present problems from time to time in the campaign. At the outset of the internal planning for a capital campaign, the focus of the board and staff planners is almost entirely on the potential benefit to the organization of undertaking such a monumental funding effort. Those closest to the organization see its needs: more space, endowment, or equipment. They want the campaign to alleviate these needs. Volunteer and professional campaign planners speak passionately about the impact of the campaign on the organization. Volunteer workers are enlisted with the campaign goals clearly stated. Case materials are drawn with these benefits featured. Donors are persuaded by volunteers and staff that the campaign will produce strong and lasting benefits.

Unfortunately, sometime after the campaign is under way, doubts among staff and volunteers begin to emerge, and even the most dedicated leaders find themselves asking if the venture is worth the effort and time. It is sometimes difficult to sustain the passion when things go slowly or badly in a campaign. Internal resources are stretched. The cost of increased staff, although needed, may erode the net financial gain from the campaign. Program staff, asked to accompany board members and administrative staff members on calls and to welcome potential donors to observe programs or tour facilities, may grow impatient with the process and the time drain. The heavy front-end investment required for a campaign (feasibility study, staffing, materials) seems to bear no dividend after the initial gifts. The surge of leadership gift funding, seductive in its seeming ease and size, fades. The campaign "troughs," and volunteer and staff leaders begin to question whether there is any benefit to the organization. Concerns arise as to whether the campaign goals can be met or whether those initial gifts will have to be returned. All of these thoughts contribute to what can be the darkest moment of the campaign, and a dangerous threat to the success of potential donor involvement. It is imperative that these concerns not be conveyed to donors nor be allowed to sap the enthusiasm of those who must do the cultivating and asking.

Antidotes for Discouraged Campaigners

Patience is required at this point, as well as some reflection on other campaigns and their course. All campaigns hit a low point after the first rush to get started. Because the initial gifts are usually from those closest to the organization, they are relatively effortless to solicit. Often a campaign will not be given the green light to move ahead until one or more of those gifts have been secured, not just promised. The euphoria that prevails at the beginning of a campaign—when the feasibility study indicates adequate support, a few key gifts have been identified or committed, leadership is excited and ready to go, and the quiet phase can hardly be kept quiet—may fade. If you expect this to happen, you will not be thrown into turmoil when it does.

Neither will you despair, in the plateau period of your campaign, that there is no obvious benefit to the organization and find yourself unable to convey your initial fervor to your prospective donors. There is plenty of benefit to the organization. Reflect on the community need that brought you to the point of undertaking the campaign; consider the long-term impact of the investment in additional staff, publications, volunteer training, and cultivation of donors; and be confident that the outcome of a well-managed and successful campaign includes an enhanced organization as well as a delighted group of donor-investors. Stay optimistic, because this plateau will pass once enough qualified prospects have been cultivated, enough potential prospects are in the pipeline, and enough donors are solicited who will be willing to engage others.

Keep the features and benefits of the campaign and the organization fresh and removed from the doubts that may be felt. Maintaining optimism will attract the new donor-investors who will pull you securely off the plateau and on to the next pinnacle of achievement. Some specific techniques for alleviating midcampaign depression are:

- Secure a challenge gift from an individual, foundation, or corporate donor. This will give people incentive to give within a particular time frame.

- Increase the number and variety of cultivation events.

- Enlist new volunteers who represent new constituencies for the campaign.

- Conduct another prospecting session, with new lists and some new people involved in the review process.

- Hold a board or campaign steering committee retreat. Focus on the "SOS"—Share Our Success—aspects of the campaign.

- Offer a refresher training course in the solicitation process, using one or more successful solicitations and a few unsuccessful ones, to guide the learning process.

Benefit or Recognition for Themselves

Benefit or recognition for themselves is a common motivation for donors who contribute major or stretch gifts to a capital campaign. It guides the preparation and publicity of naming opportunities for buildings or endowments. An appreciation of this motivation is critical in working with prospects and donors, and this motivation or need should never be ridiculed or denigrated by staff or volunteer leadership of the campaign. There has been considerable exploration of donor motivation in recent years, including writers who have examined, in particular, individuals who give generously to the arts. The apparent need of these donors for recognition and social position as a result of their giving has been identified and, in some cases, criticized, as if it were a lesser motivation than that of someone who might give less, but be perceived as more altruistic.

The motivation of individuals and institutions who seek recognition and/or benefit to themselves from making a major or stretch gift should be examined against the standards and values of the organization. If there is no harm to or demand on the organization, and if the gift results in the bettering of the organization and an overall benefit to the community, then it does not make sense to deride the motivation or the gift, even privately. Throughout the world, philanthropy has given individuals and organizations recognition and a sense of immortality through the naming of institutions, buildings, and endowments. For the peers, families, and friends of these donors, such gestures provide pride and inspiration and may ignite a similar desire to give that will also benefit the community. Museums in France, universities in the United Kingdom, hospitals in Israel, schools in China, and concert halls in the United States bear the names of or are supported by endowments from people and institutions whose vision and capacity combined to help strengthen the future and services of these organizations. Capital campaigns provide vehicles whereby donor-investors can benefit an organization and a community and be recognized appropriately for it.

Remember that a gift *to* your organization is really a gift *through* your organization into the community. Hospitals and universities are generously funded by individuals and foundations that want to ensure certain long-term benefits to the community—and educational and health programs that will benefit themselves and their families directly. Medical programs are frequently funded by those who have a family history or experience with a particular disease. Community hospitals are able to attract donors by letting them know the benefits of having a trauma center or heart surgery center in the community: When the time comes for them to use the service, it will be there. More immediately, some private secondary schools find that current parents are highly motivated to give to campaigns that will provide facilities and programs that will directly benefit their children. One such individual, with another like-minded parent, raised nearly $800,000 in six weeks to finish the construction of a vital building on the campus of his children's school. He was impatient with the school's process for getting a campaign in place, and wanted to see the facility built while his children were still enrolled. When asked what had inspired him to do this, he remarked that it was less philanthropic than it was a strong desire for his children to have the best preparation possible for college. Without the facilities and programs that this building would create, he felt their education in a particular subject area would not be competitive with students in other schools. This individual, a very philanthropic and generous member of his community, who supports health, human services, and the arts, was in this instance very open about his motivation.

Ours is a donor-centered universe, and those organizations that understand that aspect of the development process are much better at building donor-investor relationships that will take them beyond fundraising. Individual as well as foundation and corporate prospects will seek to make community investments for which there is a "return" on their investment: satisfaction, benefit, recognition, involvement.

Involvement of Other Funders

Funders like to know who else is giving. This reality of capital campaigns is becoming more widespread. Perhaps because of the proliferation of capital campaigns, including a disturbing number that are unsuccessful in their dollar goals or time frame, funders are reluctant to be the first to step forward with a gift. They do not wish to make an initial investment that will not be supported by others. This is particularly true of some foundations, which wait to see what other foundations will fund the program or project. It is also true for individuals, many of whom want to know who else is involved before they will make a gift. It is rather like the dilemma of getting your first job: You need experience, but you cannot get experience until you get a job, and you cannot get a job unless you have experience. At some point, someone—the employer for the job, the funder for the campaign—has to take a risk. Capital campaigns are the same. Organizations need champions in the community who can convince funders to be the first.

One of the many benefits of building strong long-term donor-investor relationships with funders is their willingness to take the risk of being one of the initial investors in a capital campaign. They are also willing to go out and talk with other donors and leaders in the community. These are the individuals and institutions to which an organization should take the embryonic dream for the new building, equipment, or endowment. Share with them the excitement of the planning and the development of the case for support. Their role and importance to the success of the campaign cannot be overstated.

In one campaign for a religious organization, two longtime trustees and supporters of the organization held on to an architectural and programmatic vision for the institution for decades. In the interim, a brief, largely unsuccessful campaign for endowment intervened. But they held on to their dream until it was embraced by new religious and lay leadership. Finally, in the waning years of their lives, as the organization's trustees created a vision and plans for the completion of the facility, they each offered a very large gift to get the campaign started. Their initial gifts inspired volunteer and institutional leadership to initiate a successful capital campaign, and were responsible for leveraging the gifts of hundreds of others. The results of this campaign, in which the vision they and others had held for so long was finally fulfilled, will stand over time as a tribute to them and will be used and respected as a vital community resource.

Although confidentiality, cultural mores, and other constraints may prevent an organization from revealing the exact amounts that donors have given to a campaign, most donors understand that their gifts provide leverage for raising others. When leadership gifts are secured in a campaign, discuss with the donor the way in which information about that gift can be used to inspire others. In the initial or quiet phase of a campaign, the list of donors can then be conveyed to other potential donors in one-on-one meetings. When a campaign is announced to the public, the list of donors and the size of their gifts —plus the total raised to date—is often provided. Clearance with donors is obviously essential. However, early contributors to a campaign want others to join them and are most often very willing to not only have their gift made known, but may participate in future solicitations themselves.

WHAT TO CONSIDER BEFORE UNDERTAKING A CAPITAL CAMPAIGN

Most organizations conduct a feasibility study before embarking on a capital campaign. Productive feasibility studies have these qualities:

- They are conducted by an outside objective consultant, thereby ensuring the candor and confidentiality of the feedback from the community.

- They test both the internal readiness (systems, staffing, enthusiasm, board involvement) and the external feasibility (potential funders and leaders, perception of the organization, impact of programming).

- Organizations trust the results and are guided by them.

- Consultant(s) employed are one(s) in which the organization has confidence regarding skills in marketing the project, interviewing community members, analyzing the data, and preparing a cogent and useful report.
- The organization works cooperatively with the consultant(s) in list preparation, interview scheduling, setting of meetings, and other mutually determined aspects of the study is understood at the outset.
- A written contract is developed and agreed to, including a clause permitting either the organization or the consultant to terminate the agreement if necessary.

Determining Whether to Go Ahead with a Campaign

The feasibility study will test an organization's:

- Visibility
- Potential for support based on a gift range chart that is reviewed with all those interviewed and from which they are asked to select their approximate potential gift
- Projected goal
- Potential for enlisting campaign leadership
- Image in the community
- Perceived capacity to fund raise
- Mission importance among other community priorities
- Credibility
- Rank among the potential donor's other charitable priorities
- Potential for identifying additional likely prospects

Conducting the Study

A feasibility study should be conducted by consultants in whom the organization has confidence to be the front-line marketing advance team. These individuals will make the first impression on your potential leaders and funders. They must be fully and honestly informed about the case for support and coached about the sensitivities or importance of any of those interviewed for the study. Consultants should also be willing to show you a report format and an executive summary (with confidential information obscured) of a previous study. References are essential. Check them out.

A study will take at least two to three months, and sometimes as long as four to five months if there are many interviews or scheduling difficulties. Most studies are based on approximately 40 to 50 interviews, with some larger campaigns and institutions requiring as many as 100. The cost of the study varies from place to place in the United States and abroad: consulting costs tend to differ dramatically, depending on geography, type of organization, and the qualifications or reputation of the consultant. The cost will increase with the time required: More interviews will mean a higher fee. Those selected for interviews should represent the constituencies that are important to the community and the campaign, including civic, social, financial, corporate, foundation, and opinion leaders as well as board members, current and previous donors, and former board members. Organizations need to identify 20 to 30 percent more names than they intend to interview, as some will be unable or unwilling to participate.

The feasibility study builds potential donor relations. Organizations need to participate in the preparation, review, and approval of the letter and questionnaire that are used by the consultants. Be sure, as well, that all materials look professional. Again, this may be the first contact an important potential donor has with your organization.

Getting People to Participate in the Study

Send out a preliminary case for support, no longer than two pages, with the letter of invitation to those you want to interview. This "prospectus" is a combined fact sheet and marketing statement. It has to have a bit of a "marketing spin" to be compelling, and it may be the first information some people receive about the organization. The prospectus should be prepared by staff and consultants working together. You hope that those who read it and are interviewed will become donor-investors in your organization through the proposed campaign. Send the letter out over the signature of someone highly respected in the community. Ask a volunteer leader or high visibility administrative leader of the organization to sign the letters.

In a study for an endowment campaign for a city-sponsored cultural center, a letter from the mayor inviting people to participate resulted in nearly 97 percent of those invited wanting to participate. At the opposite end of the success scale, the executive director of a social service organization, impatient to get the letters out, signed the letter himself. The consultants had a very difficult time getting appointments, and only 40 percent of respondents participated. Those who knew the executive director viewed him as controversial; the majority receiving the invitation had never heard of him or the organization.

If you engage a consulting firm with several partners or consultants, be sure you know who will conduct the interviews in your feasibility study. Sometimes the consultant you interview and select is not the person who does the actual interviewing for the study. In the context of building donor relations, the person doing the interview is critical.

Working with the Results of the Feasibility Study

After the consultant has assessed the internal readiness of the organization to undertake a capital campaign and the external community interest for funding and leading the campaign, he or she will prepare a comprehensive report. Do not be satisfied with reports that say "A majority of those interviewed felt the campaign would be successful." You should:

- Know the percentage of those who felt it would be successful
- Be able to read comments (never attributed, as that would breach confidence) that give insights as to why or why not

- Be provided with the number of responses to each question so you know what percentage of the sample was involved in the conclusion (on scaled and weighted questions, it is very important to know what percentage of interviewees answered as that can skew the results)

The table of gifts needed for the campaign, developed prior to the study and reviewed as part of testing the overall goal, will show how many potential gifts have been identified at each level. This information answers the most fundamental questions: Is the lead gift there? Are there enough gifts to go ahead? For most campaigns, if the sample is valid, an indication of one-third to one-half of the needed gifts is sufficient to go ahead. Any less, and the results are doubtful. Consider these study examples:

- With a $20 million endowment campaign, gifts of $8.7 million were identified in the study. It proceeded and is on course.
- With an $11 million proposed campaign, gifts of $4 million were identified in the study, and there were already two significant lead gifts in place. The campaign raised over $13 million.
- In a $3.7 million campaign that raised $4.2 million, an amount slightly more than $1 million was identified. Obviously, the campaign succeeded in spite of not reaching the one-third mark.
- In a $500,000 campaign, nearly $300,000 was identified. The campaign went over its goal.
- In a proposed $2 million campaign, only $300,000 was identified. The campaign did not go forward.

Pegging the campaign goal against early indications identified in the study is the standard practice. Some campaigns have also lowered their goal as a result of their study, and they have succeeded in raising the revised amount. The gifts identified in the feasibility study are not binding in any way, and interviewees are assured of that. It is good to test the likelihood of that gift by asking another question during the study: "Among your current philanthropic priorities, where would you place this campaign?" Offer respondents a choice of high, medium, low; or give them a numerical scale. This can be another way of interpreting the eventual likelihood of the gift and, therefore, of the reliability of the identified funds.

The results of the feasibility study should be accompanied by comprehensive findings and recommendations. The findings will probably be tied to the questions on the questionnaire, providing an easy reference for those who must use the study to implement the campaign. The recommendations should provide detail and direction for getting ready for the campaign. This is not a campaign plan, but it is the preliminary set of guidelines the organization will have to follow. A feasibility study will have one of three basic outcomes:

1. *Do it.* The money and leadership are there.
2. *Delay it.* Do not go ahead unless and until certain actions are taken (this may include steps toward internal readiness, board preparedness, etc., or external factors, such as

establishing and implementing a communication and public relations program to enhance organizational visibility in the community before the campaign gets under way).

3. *Forget it (at least for now.)* Do not go ahead in the foreseeable future. This negative outcome may be based on low public esteem for the organization, conflicting campaigns that are consuming the time and funds from the most likely prospects, no financial support indicated, deep concerns about management and/or current fundraising practices, and so on.

Organizations have gone ahead with campaigns in spite of the recommendation to implement certain measures or to not proceed at all. Some of these campaigns have succeeded, others have failed.

The Quiet Phase of a Campaign

Campaigns are "top down" (large gifts first, closing with the small) and "inside out" (start inside the "family" with the board and reach out, over the course of the campaign, to those who have less connection with the organization). The campaign constituency is often depicted as concentric circles, with the board in the middle. Board gifts come first, whether they are "major" in size or not. Once the board is 100 percent committed to the campaign, then other gifts can be solicited from previous or potential major donors who are strongly connected to the organization.

The quiet phase is gift, not time, determinate. In the quiet phase, an organization should raise 60 to 70 percent of the total campaign funds. Although organizations can plot a timeline and predict that the quiet phase will take a year, or 18 months in some very large campaigns, length is difficult to gauge. In one $5.5 million campaign, the "quiet phase" ($3.7 million) took two years, but the balance of the funds were raised within six months. At the end of the quiet phase, the campaign is announced to the public. Usually capital campaigns are not well-kept secrets among those closest to the organizations. There should be no media or community announcement until the leadership gifts have been raised and the goal has been validated or adjusted. When some organizations get into the quiet phase of the campaign, they determine that the goal was either too high or too low. This is one of the main purposes of the quiet phase: It is like a second feasibility study.

You can build strong donor relations during the quiet phase. The campaign's founding donors are a special group of people, and should be treated with the highest respect and stewardship. These early visionaries should be honored throughout the campaign and afterward. In one extraordinary campaign, in which a community performing arts center was completely funded ($70 million) by private nongovernmental sources (individuals, foundations, and corporations), the initial study for the campaign was funded by a group who were called the Founders. Their financial contributions were not as great as some that came later on, but they were the individuals who were willing to put up the seed money for the fundraising and architectural feasibility studies. As the campaign took off, and other much larger funders were involved in the actual building campaign, these individuals were forgotten. Today, their connection with the organization has been sev-ered, and many of them no longer support the center at all. Founding funders, whether they turn out to be the top funders for a campaign or not, should be accorded the stew-ardship they deserve for their pivotal role in making the project possible.

Going Public: Making the Announcement

When the benchmark 60 or 70 percent of the campaign funds has been reached, and the goal has been validated or adjusted, the campaign can go public. Dozens of books can provide detailed information about running a capital campaign once the public phase is announced, but a few ideas about making that announcement are worth repeating. They are offered in here in the context of helping organizations initiate good stewardship prac-tices and create true donor-investor relationships.

- Invite all early funders to the public announcement.
- Include annual donors and members, even if not yet solicited for the campaign, to the kickoff and announcement. Get them excited.
- Plan an event that is appropriate for the scale and purpose of the campaign and the organization so that donors do not feel their contribution is being used unwisely.
- Create a media "hook" to ensure good coverage of the kickoff linked to the impor-tance of the need this campaign will be meeting and arrange interviews with donors.
- Engage civic dignitaries if possible and introduce them to key donors.
- Whether it is a ribbon-cutting, groundbreaking, sky-breaking (as one building proj-ect had), quiet announcement of an endowment at the organization's headquarters, or any other kind of symbolic event, be sure the *beneficiaries* of the building or pro-gram are present (clients, performers, teachers, etc.)—not just funders and digni-taries—and that the beneficiaries and the donors and dignitaries are honored.
- Keep speeches and ceremony to the minimum, but be sure to include a funder who can speak from his or her heart about why a large gift was given.
- Be sure all board members are asked to be there and are identified as board members.
- If the building is in a neighborhood, invite the neighbors and introduce them to board members and donors.
- Work with a representative community of volunteers, including one or more donors, to plan and implement the event.
- Keep the cost down by getting goods and services donated if possible and let that be known to those who attend, including funders.

Maintaining Donor Relations during the Campaign

Stewardship is covered in Chapter 8, but it is critical to remember that once a donor makes a campaign gift to your organization, the relationship is just beginning. It is our tendency, once a gift we have worked on for a long period of time comes in, to put that person into the donor file, close the drawer, lock it up—and then open the prospect file to find another potential donor to solicit. Meanwhile, the new donor languishes in the file drawer, wondering what happened to all the attention that was given before the gift was made.

Donors are allies in a campaign. They have already invested, so they want others to invest. They are convinced, and they can convince others. They have given and want to be recognized, and we need to afford them the recognition and stewardship they want and deserve. Often a donor will make a repeat gift toward the end of the campaign. By placing them in situations where they are convincing others to give, they often convince themselves to give more.

Donor-investors provide the solid base on which the campaign will succeed and future campaigns will be possible. They have capitalized the organization in which they believe, and they have a sense of ownership. We must honor that ownership and find ways in which they can exercise their stakeholder role. We can ask them to:

- Assist with solicitations.
- Review prospect lists.
- Participate in cultivation and stewardship activities (lunches, dinners, etc.).
- Review existing materials for appropriate updating.
- If they have comfort and skills in public speaking, let them be formal advocates for the organization and the campaign at service clubs and churches or other forums.
- Serve on the campaign cabinet or steering committee.
- Serve on the board.
- Provide leadership for a segment of the campaign or the organization.
- Be a resource and reference in difficult donor negotiations in which there is skepticism or uncertainty regarding the satisfaction the pending donor will receive when the gift is made.

Summary

Capital campaigns are unique, occasional, exhausting, exciting, and productive; they focus organizations on a particular goal during a finite period of time and allow us to sharpen our sense of purpose and impact.

Both capital and annual fundraising provide donor-investors with opportunities to ensure the long-term capitalization of the organizations they value. Well-run campaigns of both kinds serve to elevate our organizations to new levels of community service and provide incredible opportunities to engage and involve people as long-term investors in our organizations.

CHAPTER 8

Stewardship: The Heart of the Development Process

No practice is more important in the development process than stewardship, the continued involvement, cultivation, and care of those who give. Stewardship has always been important, but never more so than now. As competition for philanthropic investment and donor expectations regarding their relationship with organizations have increased, so has the need for a commitment to stewardship.

Stewardship is more than a practice, it is an attitude. It is more than recognition, it is the offered opportunity to stay informed and become involved. It is an organization's philosophical commitment to the value and importance of donors as well as their gifts. It is a belief that each donor contributes more than money and that gifts are a symbol of the donor's belief in the values, purpose, and importance of the organization. Donors who feel they are valued only for their gifts, or who feel neglected after giving a gift, quickly sour on an organization or even on the nonprofit sector.

WHY PRACTICE STEWARDSHIP?

A strong stewardship program is the single greatest contributor to an organization's ability to go beyond fundraising. Donors who are drawn more deeply into a relationship with an organization through effective stewardship become its advocates and promoters. A credible theory exists that part of the donor's self comes with each gift. The philosophy of stewardship is based in large part on that theory. Organizations that dismiss the importance of stewardship endanger their potential for successful donor and fund development. Disgruntled and disappointed donors voice their complaints to others in the community, intensifying the damage and warning others not to get involved. Satisfied donors draw others in. They become an organization's champions. They are worth an investment in solid stewardship practices.

All stewardship and recognition practices must be backed by an honest commitment to the philosophy of stewardship. It is a philosophy based on respect that is as detectable in its absence as it is in its presence. Increasingly, donors are experienced at giving. As they act on their range of values, they provide philanthropic support for numerous organizations. They have opportunities to experience firsthand, and to compare, the various ways in which organizations interact with their donors. In confidential interviews for feasibility or development audit studies, donors will candidly disclose what they perceive to be the level of sincerity toward donors in an organization. If the stewardship program is focused only on very large donors, then those donors with potential who are not currently large donors will become discouraged at the lack of opportunities for their involvement. If the stewardship program does not begin early enough in the giving cycle (with the initial or renewed gift), then donors with potential for larger gifts or strategic volunteer roles may be lost. If the stewardship program is sporadic, changing with turnovers in staff or volunteer leadership, these experienced donors quickly notice the absence of a consistent philosophy about stewardship even if some recognition activities continue.

WHAT STEWARDSHIP MEANS

The concept of stewardship has expanded as organizations better understand the sequential and seamless nature of an effective development process. As the sector has evolved, the word "stewardship" has had various meanings and interpretations. Some of those survive and are used today.

Stewardship is used frequently to describe the annual congregation pledge drive in some Christian churches in the United States. This specific application of the word does not inform its general use in development and fundraising. Others use it to describe their overall management and use of donated funds. Still others, drawing on the early English definition of "steward" as "keeper of the hall," give a broader interpretation. They use it to describe the ethical management and care afforded to all resources of nonprofit institutions.

Increasingly, stewardship is understood as the critical function by which organizations develop lasting relationships with their donor-investors. This includes the ethical management and care of all human and financial resources. Stewardship promotes a donor-organization relationship based on mutual respect for both the source and impact of gifts. When well implemented, stewardship is the catalyst for building and renewing long-term relationships with donor-investors and for creating loyalty and a sense of participation that ensures the success of the development program.

In spite of its importance, this vital function is often neglected. In their urgent need to fundraise, and in their relief and joy in securing a gift, organizations forget that the real relationship begins once the gift is made. What feels to the organization like the end of a transaction (getting the gift) is in fact the beginning of a new or renewed relationship for the donor-investor. It is often observed that in times of tight budgeting, the funding for staff and activities with direct fundraising results is maintained (direct mail, special events, etc.), while far less measurable stewardship practices (newsletters, receptions) may be cut. One individual, in charge of development for a large organization, expressed his frustration over this issue in a letter to a fellow professional: "I *only wish* we had adequate resources to truly create opportunities to build lasting relationships that promote loyalty and generosity." This remark is a sad commentary on institutional funding priorities. When it comes to long-term return on investment, few efforts pay as many benefits as a well-designed and implemented stewardship program.

Giving and Stewardship

Stewardship is essential because of the nature of giving itself. When people give, they are acting on their values. A certain level of emotion or commitment is associated with the decision to give, even if the receiving organization is not aware of it when the gift is made. Gifts sent through the mail in response to letter appeals, or those that stem from a newspaper article or special event presentation, deserve more than just a thank-you letter. Organizations must get to know donors, and find out what their values are and why they were moved to make a gift.

Most organizations have had unhappy experiences with angry or disillusioned donors. The emotions connected with giving can turn from a positive sense of fulfillment and satisfaction to irritation, frustration, or disappointment. In campaign after campaign, previous donors who have been identified as top prospects reveal, when initial contact is made, that they are upset with the organization because they were not kept informed about the results of their previous gifts. No one has connected them with the scholarship recipients they have funded. They have never met any of the parents whose children benefit from the preschool program. They do not feel appreciated for what they have done and are therefore unwilling to do more. Alumni donors of universities or contributing constituencies of community-based organizations resent being contacted "only when the organization needs money." People do not get angry with an organization unless they care. It is up to the organizations in the nonprofit sector to minimize the potential for negative donor interaction. Stewardship is a fundamental function in keeping the relationship both positive and vigorous.

Stewardship and Belonging

The act of giving is a transforming act. It transforms potential donors, and current donors with greater potential, into stakeholders. Donors become donor-investors, keenly interested in how their gifts are used and what impact they will have on the organization and the community. They want a sense of ownership and connection. Well-managed stewardship practices provide opportunities for donors to deepen their interests and values.

Powerful evidence shows that one of the major motivations for giving is the need to belong. People want to belong to the success of an organization; they want to feel as if they participated in its growth. They want to share in the future of an organization in which they have invested; they want to feel as if they can inform that future with their opinions and ideas, as well as their gifts. Even those who do not pursue an active role with an organization derive satisfaction from belonging to the group of donor-investors who have helped it attain its mission and goals.

Years ago, a wealthy, powerful, and reclusive board chair for a major arts organization, always impatient with the process of meetings, distractedly observed a consultant-facilitated board discussion about why people give. Standing at the back of the room, visibly removed from the interaction around the table, he seemed barely to be paying attention although he was apparently listening. After hearing all the reasons for giving that the other board members offered, he asked to add one. To everyone's surprise, he said he believed people gave because they wanted to belong. This startling comment from a shy yet powerful donor of a million dollars a year to this organization caused an awkward and momentary silence in the discussion because of its self-revealing intensity. It provided key insights into the motivations of this particular philanthropist who, year after year, chose to remain in a leadership role as a donor and board chair.

GETTING DONORS AND PROSPECTS INTO THE KITCHEN

The Oregon Shakespeare Festival once summarized in a membership piece the importance of belonging. "The Spirit, the Art of Belonging" was a moving piece written by the late OSF artistic director, Jerry Turner. He concluded his description of the way people get involved in organizations by quoting Berthold Brecht. He said that Brecht once wrote that he chose one restaurant over another not because the first did not have a delectable menu, but because the second invited him into the kitchen. In the first, he said, he was a honored guest. In the second, he was a participant. He belonged.

Stewardship is the process we use to bring our donors into an ever-closer relationship with our organizations. It is how we get them "into the kitchen." Those donor-investors who are closest to the organization—board members and other volunteers—are particularly deserving of the very best stewardship practices. When afforded this respect and acknowledgment, they will *stay* in the kitchen.

Although the concept of the "kitchen" is figurative as applied to stewardship practices, some organizations have translated this concept into unique strategies for both cultivation and stewardship.

A state-funded university launched a campaign to build a new fine arts building. The dean's approach to fundraising and stewardship of donor-investors was innovative and attention-getting. Not only did he have a "sky-breaking" instead of a groundbreaking for the new building, he created a very unusual office space during the campaign. He had selected for his office an open area of a barnlike campus building that served as an overflow space for art, television production, and drama studios. The building was one of several sadly obsolete structures that housed the fine arts programs. The architectural plans called for the new building to unite all the fine arts programs now housed across the campus. At one end of the room, he put a restaurant-size espresso machine and a conversation area with a sofa and comfortable chairs. At the other end of the room, he left the painted backdrop of a kitchen and equipment used by a university morning television show. The result was dynamic. Faculty, friends of the university, funders, administrative staff, prospects, and other visitors were brought "into the kitchen," literally. The setting was complementary to the dean's high level of charm and persuasion. He was delighted to mull the future with his donor-investors in the "kitchen" of a building that would soon be replaced by a state-of-the-art facility. He was successful in gaining a new base of donor-investors who had never supported a state-funded university, in gaining unexpected and substantial support from the university administration for some state matching funds, and in drawing on the arts and entertainment community, which was delighted with his innovative approach.

At a resident artists' program, housed in a building converted from an old military barracks, each room was an artist's project. The kitchen was no exception. Although the work area appliances were utilitarian, designed for large-quantity cooking, the artists had created an eating area connected to the kitchen. Its remarkable attraction was the chairs around the eating tables. Each chair was different, a work by an artist. Those who worked in wood or other sturdy materials *built* their chairs; those with skills in other media *decorated* chairs they had acquired at antique or garage sales. No two chairs were the same: Each artist had left behind a signature piece. At lectures, meals, donor gatherings, development committee meetings, and other related functions, a unique sense of interaction with the artists prevailed. The message conveyed was immediate: This was a working center for artists whose expression and creativity was encouraged by community giving and volunteering.

Although both these examples are from organizations with artistic missions and available kitchens, other organizations can also bring their donors "into the kitchen" by connecting them closely with the people, ideas, materials, vision, and future planning for their organizations.

Putting Priority on Stewardship

Organizations that successfully implement donor-focused development programs assign budget and personnel to ensure that donors feel appreciated and informed. Because most organizations cannot assign a separate staff person to the stewardship function, it should be part of every staff person's job description and every board member's stated responsibilities.

If the resources are available, stewardship can be a separate staff position. Two major universities, on completion of capital campaigns for which they had added professional and support staff, appropriately trimmed the size of their development offices. They reduced staff across all programs, with one exception: Both universities added professional and support staff to direct stewardship programs. These institutions recognized that during the postcampaign period, they had to implement strong stewardship practices.

Principles for Creating a Stewardship Program

Effective stewardship begins with the organization's philosophical commitment to the importance of the interests and needs of donor-investors and results in long-term commitment to the organization by its donor-investors. Eleven basic principles guide the creation of a strong stewardship program.

1. Begin involving donors in the stewardship program with their first gift.

The thankathon, described in Chapter 6, establishes contact after the first gift and gives donors an opportunity to hear personally that the gift is appreciated and will be used wisely. This is a critical beginning to what can become a relationship of great value to both donor and organization. Involve major donors who are interested and knowledgeable in the review of critical donor and community materials. Invest in a DRAFT stamp ($3 to $5) and use it on proposed materials. Send drafts of proposed fundraising letters, program and development campaign brochures, or funding proposals to those connected to you, especially if they represent the communities to which the materials may be directed. Pride of staff authorship is not the issue here. Donor and volunteer ownership is. A few will respond with suggestions, not all of which will be appropriate or applicable. Respond to the suggestions with a phone call, explaining why you will or will not follow the recommendations. Whether their changes are included or not, they will still have a heightened sense of ownership of the organization's activities. The same strategy works for engaging people in focus or discussion groups around a proposed program or direction. Involve the key donor-investors with your board members. They will bring a refreshing perspective and may have or develop an interest in supporting the program.

2. Alternate messages to your donors.

A trusted rule says that for every one time you ask someone for money, you should contact them two other times without asking for money. It is a sound principle. Examples of nonfundraising contacts are the thankathon, an invitation to a lecture or presentation, a no-fee tea or reception to meet a visiting or resident professional, a "white paper" prepared by staff to describe an agency program that is meeting a particular community need and that is accompanied by a note thanking the donor for his or her support, or opportunities for tours or meetings that will bring donors closer to the organization's programs.

3. Allocate budget to stewardship activities.

Make stewardship activities—donor receptions, special mementos for large gift donors, dinner or refreshments for a thankathon—an integral part of the development program. The budget for specific *fundraising* activities is usually easier to justify than the budget for *development*. Fundraising results are usually immediate and measurable. Development results may not be evident for years. But development, and stewardship as a primary function, makes fundraising successful. Stewardship, although difficult to measure precisely in its financial return, affects the entire bottom line: An overall increase in giving, and a growth in donor retention, will follow. Support budget requests with any anecdotal evidence you may have from a donor about the impact of your stewardship program on their willingness to give.

4. Be sure the stewardship practice is appropriate to the amount of the gift and the budget and image of the organization.

Donors are uneasy when they believe that a memento or event is too expensive or inconsistent with their image of the organization (e.g., socially responsible, fiscally conservative, etc.). They wonder if their gift has been used up by the acknowledgment. In the

United States, the Internal Revenue Service has enforced stringent standards regarding the reduction of the deductibility of a gift based on the goods or services received by the donor. This ruling provides a wonderful opportunity to scale back the tangible benefits afforded to donors and focus on communicating the real benefits: the impact of the gift on the fulfillment of the mission in the community.

5. Determine what kind of involvement major and planned gift donors, some of whom may be very involved and busy with other organizations and their own professions, want.

They may not want to belong to a particular giving "club," preferring instead to enter into some other kind of interaction with the organization. Some larger donors wish to be left alone except when they initiate contact with the organization. People do not have to belong to a giving "club" to derive a sense of belonging. This sense of belonging should transcend membership at any level. Find out what the donor expects at the time the gift is made, and honor the donor's wishes throughout the relationship. Information regarding the way in which people want to be involved with an organization should be part of the database information about them. New volunteers or staff need that information in order to effectively continue the relationship.

6. Coordinate stewardship and cultivation outreach, so that current donors have an opportunity to convey their enthusiasm and commitment to prospective donors.

These "bookends" on a solicitation are very similar. Each is based on the same principles of involving the individual in a way that will uncover and reinforce values. A widely published cartoon shows a hostess walking around a beautifully set formal dining table, putting out the place cards on which are written: "Donor, Non-Donor, Donor, Non-Donor. . . ." The hostess is, of course, exactly right. Mix those who have given with those who are still thinking about it. The results will be beneficial to the individuals and to the organization.

7. Tie stewardship outreach to the organization's mission.

Just as effective board meetings should have a "mission moment" to continually tie board members into the mission, so should stewardship events and mementos. Although plaques and mugs and other articles serve their purpose, seek more meaningful ways to thank people when possible or appropriate. A drawing by a developmentally disabled child, framed and given to a donor, finds a place in a Wall Street office. A model of a set for a regional repertory theater production is prominently displayed in the lobby of the sponsoring corporation. A piece of sandstone, remnant of an extraordinary building preservation project at a university, sits on the desk of an American corporate executive in London. A photograph of dancers, captured performing a production she helped fund, is displayed in the living room of a Los Angeles philanthropist. The visionary leader of an endowment campaign for a western European art museum is honored with a national award by that country's minister of culture. Imagination can open new avenues for cost-saving ways to appropriately thank volunteers and donors in a way that reinforces the mission of the organization and the values of the donors.

8. Focus on intangible, rather than tangible, benefits.

This principle supports item 7 and also helps curb the dangerous downside of donor recognition: Donors will become complacent with current benefits and not increase their gifts. This is the downside of recognition levels. Donors value their gifts by what they get, not by the impact the gift may have. In a campaign a number of years ago, a foundation donor challenged a particular constituency to increase its annual giving by promising to match the increase. For donors of the largest annual gifts—who received many "benefits" for their contribution, including parking privileges, events tickets, a special dinner with the CEO—the challenge was no incentive at all. They were not immediately moved to raise their level of giving because the "floor" ($1,000+) had become a "ceiling" for them. Not until some spirited outreach was done by program staff did the leadership of that particular donor group understand that the true benefits which accrued from their gifts were not what they *received,* but what they *gave.* They understood that the impact of giving more was not another parking pass or dinner, but an organization even more effectively positioned to provide its educational programs to the community. This realization—a shift in thinking from donor to donor-investor —was a remarkable passage in the donor development history of that organization.

9. Maintain stewardship with longtime and generous donors, even when their giving falls off for a year or so.

Organizations, as a rule, base their stewardship strategies on internal measures of size or frequency of gift. In most cases, this is appropriate. But organizations should be mindful that circumstances may change temporarily. To abandon the relationship with a funder who may be going through a period with limited discretionary income because assets are tied up, or interest or earnings are down, or due to another major philanthropic commitment could be foolish. Often we are reluctant to engage the donor in a discussion when a gift does not materialize. If the funder, through stewardship, has become involved with the organization, the organization should honor the relationship that has been built and find out the circumstances that led to a reduced gift or no gift at all.

One donor, who had made increasingly higher gifts to the annual fund of a university, found himself at midlife starting a new business and putting several children through college. The volunteer assigned to this person, who had made regular contact over the years, let the university know that the man's circumstances had changed and that the previous level of giving could not be sustained. The volunteer asked the university staff person if she could continue the personal solicitation relationship in spite of the fact that the man's gift fell below the requisite level. The relationship was maintained for a period of six or seven years, and gradually the gifts began to increase. The donor's business was a huge success, and the children graduated from college. During a major fundraising campaign several years later, the donor who had received this continuing stewardship made a gift in excess of $1 million to the university.

Performing or producing arts organizations may find that corporate sponsors are not able to fund them every year. In the years when they are not underwriting, they should still be honored and included in receptions and at performances because of the role they have played in building the organization and contributing to the growth of arts in the community. Continued participation will influence future decisions regarding renewed sponsorships or contributions. To honor the idea of "investment" requires us to look at the continuing impact of a major or special gift, even if it is not renewed for a long period of time. By dropping donors from our stewardship, we signal to them that we do not value what their gift enabled us to do.

When planning those to include in a stewardship event, do not forget the donor whose "stretch" gift, while perhaps modest by some standards, represents a major investment that is driven by the heart and values of that donor. Such donors, too, should be honored. And include, too, those committed volunteers (docents, information desk staffers, pediatric ward volunteers) whose gifts of time should be honored and whose potential for making a planned gift may be great.

10. *Keep all previous large-gift donors informed and part of your database, even those who make what seems to be a one-time-only gift, unless and until you hear they no longer want to hear from you.*

Extraordinary gifts from individuals with no previous giving history are often honored extensively at the time the gift is made, after which time the donor is neglected. The problem is further exacerbated when the organization provides inadequate reporting to the donor (individual or family, foundation or corporation) about the impact of the philanthropy. At a U.S. preparatory school, a personal relationship was not sustained with a mother and her son after a scholarship was established with the proceeds of the grandfather's estate. When a subsequent major campaign was under way, these two donors were not contacted because the school surmised they did not have the continuing resources to be included in the large gift campaign. After the campaign was over, the mother let a leadership volunteer in the campaign know that they were angry that they had not been approached. Because of their existing investment in the school, they felt they should have been offered another opportunity to give.

11. *Establish relationships between donors and program staff whenever possible.*

People and institutions become investors in an organization because of a belief in or connection with the mission. Their need to belong stems not from their need to become involved with the administrative or development staff, but to become partners with those who actually provide the community service. Only then can they understand how their values are being acted on. If a funder is supportive of a learning disabilities program, make sure that he or she gets to know the director of that program. Provide opportunities for the funder to attend talks or participate in discussions about that particular program area, thereby heightening knowledge, interest, and the sense of investment. One donor-investor to a public library, who had established an endowed book fund with her family, was provided with an annual detailed report by title of how the earnings from the fund had been spent. Additionally, she was given opportunities to meet the director of that collection, to see some of the books with the family bookplate affixed, and to observe the way in which the books were being used. Personal holiday cards from the library director and letters about other collections and activities were also part of the stewardship outreach mix. The result was an increased sense of investment on the part of the donor. She and her family continue to contribute annually to the fund, often with memorial or "in honor" gifts for other family members.

IMPLEMENTING A STEWARDSHIP PROGRAM

With the preceding 11 principles as your guide, you can create and implement a stewardship program following 10 steps.

1. If the board has never adopted a policy regarding stewardship, start by creating and approving one.

The board should have a policy that puts the importance of donors and stewardship securely into the systems of the organization. This is not a detailed plan for stewardship; rather, it is a commitment to the philosophy and practice. By ensuring that a board policy is in place, stewardship is more apt to be a steady practice, rather than an occasional spurt of activity. Once you have done this—which may require some education about stewardship from a staff, board member, or outside facilitator—then you are ready to proceed. See Exhibit 8.1 for a sample policy.

2. Form a stewardship planning task force involving board members, other volunteers, a development or administrative staff member, and some donors.

Donors are particularly important to involve in a stewardship program planning process. They are an excellent resource for setting up a program to maintain donors because they have experience and perspective. Listen to them. Give them a leadership role, and let them be part of the team that presents the proposed stewardship program plan to the board. Once the task force has coalesced, work from the guidelines of the board policy to develop a plan based on the next steps.

3. Analyze the donor base according to the way in which gifts cluster, and establish four or five preliminary (test) giving recognition levels.

Although recognition is not the only aspect of stewardship, it is the most visible to the community and to prospective donors. If yours is a new community-based social services organization and your gifts range from (e.g.) $5 to $99; $100 to $249; $250 to $499; and a few at $500 or higher, then these levels will frame your initial donor recognition and stewardship programs. For established organizations just beginning to systematize their stewardship, the levels may be higher. Recognition levels may not start until $100 or $250 and may go up to $10,000 or $25,000. Recognition is given every year, for initial, repeated, and upgraded gifts. Establish different levels during a capital campaign that will apply to those gifts only. Some organizations also acknowledge a donor's cumulative gifts when they reach a certain level (e.g., $50,000, $100,000, $1 million). All recognition levels should be presented to the board or development committee for review before they are made final.

EXHIBIT 8.1   SAMPLE STEWARDSHIP POLICY

POLICY (Adopted by the Board of Trustees)

Donors to our organization should receive appropriate stewardship for their generosity. Commitment to stewardship should characterize all interaction with donors of any amount to our institution and not be reserved solely for those who are considered our major donors. As an organization, we understand that early engagement of donors leads to long-term commitment and giving.

Stewardship begins with faithfully following the intent of donors relative to the use of their gift (whether spent or invested) but also includes:

Timely and appropriate acknowledgement of gifts

- Recognition that is offered according to the donor's preferences and the impact of the gift
- Annual reports regarding overall management and use of funds
- Newsletters and other communications about program accomplishments
- Personal letters
- Telephone calls to let donors know the difference their gift is continuing to make (as well as to thank them for new and increased gifts)
- Receptions with individuals whose work or visibility is related to the mission of the organization
- Personal visits in the homes or offices of donors

Guiding this policy is a stewardship plan which is part of the overall development plan for our organization. Stewardship is more than gift acknowledgement and recognition: it is continuing communication with donors, not only because it is part of our policy and plan but because we regard donors as our organization's best friends.

We view stewardship of our donor-investors and their investments as another aspect of our management ethic. It is based on respect for the investments others have made in us and recognizes that managers and board members of our organization are holding this money in trust for the community and are using it wisely and ethically.

Excellent stewardship depends on staff and board involvement in outreach to our donors, and it is a policy of this organization that all staff and board are aware of this policy, and of the practices that support it, and of ways they can advance our organization through ongoing stewardship of our donors and friends.

For practices related to stewardship, including acknowledgements, recognition, gift processing, use of the donor data base, gift receipts and acknowledgement letters within the requirements of the laws governing nonprofits in our state and a list of benefits offered to our donor-investors, see the Development Plan.

4. Assign names to the giving levels that will be easy to remember and manage. Avoid being too clever or too complex. If possible, try to keep the names linked to the mission; otherwise use generic names (e.g., donor, patron, benefactor).

A dance company named its top giving level the Masterpiece Society because funds from those donors are assigned each year to the creation of a new work or the revitalization of an existing work. Within the Masterpiece Society, there are levels: Silver, Gold, and Platinum. Churches and cathedrals throughout the world have used Angels to denote their large donors and Archangels for their very large donors. The Los Angeles Opera has also used those words to designate its most generous donors. Preparatory schools and universities often name their giving levels after distinguishing landmarks: Quad, Inner Quad, Tower Society. Others will name them after leadership positions in the institution: Dean's Circle, President's Club, Director's Circle, Founder's Circle. Some choose to use the name of a specific individual (founder, benefactor, first president, a distinguished leader in the field) for one or more of their giving levels. This is particularly true for planned giving recognition societies: the name selected will often be the name of a founding visionary whose own estate gift was pivotal for the organization.

5. Determine the "benefits" for each level.

In the United States, as mentioned earlier, the enforcement of tax rules is stimulating organizations to establish and maintain an array of benefits that do not significantly erode the value of the donor's gift. Because receipts must now reflect the *deductible* portion of the gift (total gift less the value of goods and services received), be sure the deductible portion stays as high as possible. Organizations are increasingly offering donors the option of declining all but the basic benefits (e.g., newsletter, free admission tickets, etc.). Many donors are choosing that option.

The array of benefits usually increases with the size of the gift. In conveying these benefits, most organizations have a simple schedule that shows basic benefits and the increment to those basic benefits at each level. This can be done in narrative form or shown on a chart. Exhibit 8.2 shows corporate benefits for a major art museum.

Guided by principle 8 from the stewardship principles, above, try to avoid excessive tangible benefits and focus instead on benefits that will connect the donor more firmly to the mission of the organization. Public broadcasting in the United States has begun addressing its dependence on premiums for its pledge and membership programs—realizing that the cost of premium fulfillment erodes their net revenue and that the message conveyed to members by the "givebacks" was not consistent with the investor messages they now want to send. Benefits for corporations tend to be more tangible than those for individual donors. The giveback provides opportunities for corporations to approach giving from both a philanthropic and a marketing perspective. One positive aspect of an array of benefits like the one in Exhibit 8.2 is the opportunity for involvement of key executives and employees who may then become individual donors to the organization.

Opportunities to participate in programs and to get to know those responsible for program delivery are, in the long run, less costly and more memorable for donors. Organizations in all countries, whether there are deductibility advantages for giving or rules

EXHIBIT 8.2   EXAMPLE: CORPORATE ANNUAL FUND BENEFITS CHART

Corporate Annual Fund Charter Corporate Partner Levels and Benefits

An Art Museum

	Porcelain Partner	Jade Partner	Bronze Partner	Silver Partner	Gold Partner
	$2,500	$5,000	$10,000	$25,000	$50,000
For Your Company					
Ability to bring clients/customers for private tours			◆	◆	◆
Company recognition in the membership magazine		◆	◆	◆	◆
Charter Partner designation in corporate partner brochure	◆	◆	◆	◆	◆
On-site recognition of company on donor plaque		◆	◆	◆	◆
Recognition on exhibitions and programs				◆	◆
Private use of/for company events	◆	◆	20% discount	Rental fee waiver*	Rental fee waiver
Use of company materials				◆	◆
For Your Employees					
Free admission	50 passes	75 passes	100 passes	125 passes	150 passes
Invitation to reception for corporate members	◆	◆	◆	◆	◆
Discount on individual Museum membership	10%	10%	10%	20%	20%
Private gallery tours		◆	◆	◆	◆
Art talks in your office			◆	◆	◆
For Your Senior Executives					
Executive memberships	4	6	8	10	15
Reciprocal membership in 13 western museums	◆	◆	◆	◆	◆
Invitations to Exhibition Openings	◆	◆	◆	◆	◆
Invitations to Corporate Partner Luncheons		◆	◆	◆	◆
Behind-the-scenes tours			◆	◆	◆

*All event costs, including Museum security, are the responsibility of the corporate donor.

that govern what is deductible or not, should construct a benefit program that is based more on a return on values than on the giveback of merchandise or events. In regions of the United States, as well as in many parts of the world, tangible benefits may be culturally inappropriate to the donor's motivation and need for anonymity or a low profile. Intangible benefits—belonging, recognition, a sense of investment—cross cultures in their acceptance.

6. Present the levels and benefits to the development committee or board for approval.

Although the specifics of the recognition program are the most visible side of stewardship, and require approval, they should be presented in the context of the overall philosophy and strategy of the stewardship program. Recognition is not the same as stewardship, but it is a part of the stewardship process. Benefits are the tactical aspect of stewardship: The philosophy and the long-term strategy shape and guide the recognition program. It is not enough to recognize a donor: The offer for involvement has to be made, as well.

7. Create a stewardship plan that includes promotion of recognition levels in all donor outreach: mailings, Web site, telephone solicitations and thankathons, personal solicitations, and corporate or foundation proposals.

Emphasize that these are recognition levels, and are designed to provide a way in which donors can become involved, if they desire, in the organization. Some individuals prefer not to be listed in donor recognition materials, and others, while not objecting to having their names listed, honestly prefer not to get involved. True stewardship, including successful recognition, is based on the needs and desires of the donor, not those of the organization.

8. Monitor the program by tracking the relationship between stewardship and recognition practices and renewal/upgrade of gifts.

The giving behavior of those who are afforded appropriate recognition and stewardship should differ from the behavior of those who are not. Establish baseline data for new donors, and do long-term tracking of their giving. In many organizations, repeated or renewed gifts have risen significantly in the fund drive that follows a thankathon. One hospital tracked donor retention after starting its thankathons and reported a 40 percent increase in donor retention during a three-year period. At all gift levels, and wherever the donor is on the investment continuum, stewardship heightens the potential for retention. It has also been seen, in organizations that experience administrative scandal or financial difficulties, that those donors who have been involved and informed regarding the organization and its programmatic impact in the community are more apt to remain loyal.

9. Review the program, benefits, and impact annually, and make adjustments based on donor feedback, donor retention, and changes in the levels at which gifts cluster.

A recognition level and stewardship program that is initiated for donors of $500 or more may find that it needs to raise both the floor and the ceiling in order to provide recognition and incentive for increasingly generous donor-investors. If the message to donors has been the benefit *to the program* of their gifts (results), rather than the benefits afforded *to them* for their gifts, then a demonstration of the organization's capacity to meet greater needs with larger gifts will help raise giving levels. These levels will have to be appropriately recognized.

10. Determine your "threshold" giving level, and place special effort on those donors.

One key area for analysis is determining at what level of giving your donors end up breaking through into a much higher giving level. By studying this threshold point, organizations can assign volunteer and staff efforts to building stronger relationships with individuals when they reach that transitional level. Twenty-five years ago, the business school at a major university determined that level was $750: Once someone gave at that level, he or she seemed to move easily up to $1,000, and the gifts grew from that point forward. Two of America's leading public broadcasters have noted a pattern among their most generous annual donors: Once they reach $600, they very willingly move into the $1,000 recognition group if they are afforded special outreach and opportunities for involvement. One of the challenges we face is the tendency for donors to become "habitual" in their giving, people who give the same amount year after year after year. With good stewardship practices, and identification of those who are at or near your threshold, you should be able to move people out of habitual giving and into what is called "thoughtful" giving (i.e., a gift the donor thinks about).

Creating a Culture of Philanthropy through Stewardship

It is increasingly important to create a culture of philanthropy throughout our organizations. Stewardship is a critical practice in creating that culture. If the attitude toward donor-investors is embracing, and if your organization's desire to engage donor-investors so they feel as if they belong is honest, then those positive attitudes will begin to seep through to all parts of your organization. Take time at a staff meeting to invite a donor to talk for 10 minutes about why he or she is a generous investor in the organization's work. Do the same at board meetings. When bringing prospects or donors on tours, alert staff not only about the tour but about the *reason* for the tour—and then let them know the results. Share good news about gifts throughout the organization. Engage as many people as possible in understanding that they are part of the full development team. And remind them that Ken Blanchard tells us that receptionists (and anyone who meets or interacts with people from your community) are the "directors of first impressions."

In a culture of philanthropy, everyone understands that development is a process based on relationships and that they can be participants in building strong relationships that lead to increased resources.

Twenty-First-Century Tools for Stewardship

Just as the tools for database management developed in the last several decades of the twentieth century have helped us be better stewards by improving accuracy and timeliness of our record keeping, the early part of the twenty-first century has brought us new and innovative tools that will enhance the stewardship process.

E-mail is an excellent support for stewardship; frequent updates to donors via e-mail are low cost and timely. Several e-mail outreach management programs are on the market at this writing, and more are certain to follow. They work with existing donor databases.

Another tool that has been developed is an Internet software program that helps non-profit organizations increase retention and loyalty of their supporters by better recognizing and responding to their interests and motivations through more personal and relevant communications. This software, which also integrates with existing donor database management systems, leverages proven donor stewardship and engagement practices that were previously too time consuming for organizations. It focuses on donor retention and on collateral management, creation, and customization of publishing tools that support the stewardship program. The software, Papilia, completed its pilot phase in 2004 and was being released to charter customers in the early months of 2005. It should be a working tool for an increasing number of organizations over the next few years.

SUMMARY

Competition for resources in the not-for-profit sector has increased as traditional sources of funding have shrunk. Donors are more savvy and sophisticated, and seek more transparency and involvement than ever before. Donor loyalty is a known factor in successful long-term fund development, and maintaining that loyalty is the principal goal of stewardship. It is also its most powerful result.

Stewardship is the most important practice in the development process. It secures donors for the future as it honors their impact on the present. Stewardship demonstrates to donors that their thoughts, opinions, and participation are part of an involvement process that includes their gift and much more.

Budget allocation for stewardship practices, although sometimes difficult to justify in the short term, has a significant long-term impact on overall fundraising costs. If stewardship is effective, donor retention and giving levels rise. The acquisition of new donors is balanced with the nurturing of existing donors, providing healthy and vital feedback and an eventual source of renewed or increased revenues.

Because gifts are given in response to a perceived community need by funders who share the values implicit in that need, even an initial small gift may reveal a desire to become involved with the successful fulfillment of an organization's mission and goals. An increased gift is often a signal that a current donor-investor may be interested in becoming more involved.

One final example of how simple, yet meaningful, stewardship practices can be comes from the Community Idea Stations—WCVE Richmond PBS, 88.9FM WCVE, WHTJ Charlottesville PBS, and WCVW Richmond PBS. In 2003, they sent out a greeting card with a photograph on the cover of Mr. Rogers—the character so well known to children and their parents for generations on Mr. Rogers' Neighborhood (Fred Rogers died in 2003)—and this quote:

> *Through television we have the choice of encouraging others to*
> *demean this life or to cherish it in creative, imaginative ways.*
>
> Fred Rogers

Inside, the card read:

> *At the Community Idea Stations, everything we do on*
> *television and radio, in the community and classroom,*
> *reflects the philosophy of an unassuming man*
> *in a red sweater. As 2003 draws to a close, we are*
> *grateful for his wisdom, his kindness and the*
> *inspiration he continues to provide us.*
>
> *And we are grateful to have you as our neighbor.*
>
> *Best wishes for a safe and happy holiday,*
> *And for a peaceful and prosperous new year.*

Think of your own possibilities for stewardship with everything you send and say. Fundraising is not about money. It is about relationships. Let that knowledge shape your policies, budgeting, effort, and evaluation of your stewardship program.

CHAPTER 9

Maximizing Board Development and Participation

Every nonprofit organization dreams of recruiting, enlisting, and maintaining a governing or advisory board who will be wise decision makers, visionary planners, able advocates, generous investors, willing askers, informed partners, and passionate pragmatists. Those organizations whose boards are appointed by individuals outside their immediate administrative structure also share the hope that those responsible for assembling their boards will find people who meet these criteria. Putting together such a board is not an impossible dream. Organizations can influence their own board development process and move closer to this ideal board when they understand and practice some basic principles of board recruitment, enlistment, management, and retention.

BOARD DEVELOPMENT: THE KEY TO FUND DEVELOPMENT

Dynamic board development is the proven key to successful fund development. Recruitment matrices reflect this in their focus on people with connection, concern, capacity, and clout. Every organization wants people with influence and affluence, hence the presence in the nonprofit lexicon of the harsh rubric "give, get, or get off" and the three *W*'s: wealth, work, wisdom (with an implied fourth *W*: wallop).

Certain community organizations seem to attract more than their share of people with these attributes, while others struggle to recruit just one. The social cachet and prestige of the arts, education, and hospital boards are a natural magnet for high-profile community people, but this fact should not preclude human and social services agencies from attracting and retaining influential people.

To build the kind of boards that dreams are made of, we need to rebalance the recruitment equation. Traditional recruitment practices have the same flaw as traditional fundraising practices: They position the organization's needs ahead of the community or prospective board member's needs. Just as we fundraise out of desperation until we understand fund and donor development as an investment process, we frequently recruit out of desperation until we understand that board development is also an investment process. Rebalancing the equation requires us to adopt an investor attitude, based on the mutual advancement of shared values, toward board recruitment and service. Otherwise, we approach recruitment with an apologetic attitude based in a lingering notion that no one *really* wants to serve on the board (just as we may think that no one *really* wants to give).

When coupled with careless recruitment practices that put off the nomination process until the last minute, an apologetic attitude can result in the wrong people with the wrong attitude being enlisted with the wrong message. Organizations end up with new board members whose principal qualifications are that they are friends of board members. Although they may be people of goodwill and intent, they may not be the ones with the most potential for advancing the organization.

Board members who are recruited in desperation know it. Called at the last minute ("We have to get our slate of nominees in by Friday") and frequently "begged" to join the board ("I know you're busy, but please do this, even as a favor to me—we really need to get some new blood on our board"), they feel as if they are doing the organization a favor.

Unless a dramatically different story emerges at the first board meeting or during board orientation, board members recruited in this way seldom develop a level of respect for the organization that leads to commitment. The urgency conveyed to them in the recruitment process is an urgency to fill a slate of board nominees, rather than the urgency and appropriateness of their engagement in helping the organization fulfill its mission. The damage compounds when these same individuals are assured, "There is nothing much to serving on the board. Don't worry, it won't take much of your time." If this is an honest statement, then the organization has some real problems. If it is a dishonest statement, then the organization will have trouble with the new recruits when they discover what is really expected of them. In at least one instance, a recruited board member turned down the opportunity to be formally enlisted when he was told there would be few demands on him. He said it made him feel that the organization, the board, and his involvement were not very important. When he joins a board, he expects to be put to work.

Replace Your Nominating Committee with a Committee on Trustees or Board Development Committee

To do a good job at board development, dissolve your nominating committee. Create in its place a committee on trustees or a board development committee. There is an inherently flawed notion in the name "nominating" committee. It too narrowly defines the function of the committee and implies only a very occasional need to meet, perhaps once a year with an emergency meeting now and then to fill a board vacancy. The name also implies that the committee's function is over once the nomination process has been completed; it suggests that enlistment, orientation, evaluation, and retention of board members are left to some other unnamed group or to no one at all. Reformulating the committee and its functions conveys the importance of board development.

The committee charged with recruitment, enlistment, and retention of the board is the most important committee of the board. Its competency largely determines the future of the organization.

If There Is No Nominating or Board Development Committee

In very small organizations, the work of the committee on trustees is sometimes given to the executive committee of the board. As a temporary measure, until more board members are recruited, this is probably the best arrangement. Alternatively, some smaller organizations combine the board development function with the fund development function, under the aegis of a development committee. This is a less successful model. Although the two assignments are highly related, they are also highly demanding. One function usually suffers. The executive committee is a better place to assign this responsibility on a temporary basis.

Responsibilities of the Committee on Trustees

A committee on trustees, or board development committee, is responsible not only for the nomination of new board members, but also for recruitment, enlistment, and retention. *Recruitment* is the process of identifying and interviewing potential board members and then cultivating them until such time as you and they are ready for them to serve. Recruitment and enlistment are not the same functions. *Enlistment* is the process of formalizing the recruitment when it is the right time for the service to begin. It involves meeting with the board recruit and reviewing job descriptions, financial and time expectations, possible committee assignments, long-range plans, and the others aspects of board responsibilities. Enlistment culminates with a comprehensive board orientation. *Retention* is the maintenance of a stable, productive, and satisfied board. The factors that contribute to strong boards are complex, but dynamic participation by its members is one of the most important. Management of board development must include postenlistment attention to board member involvement.

The committee performs these responsibilities in the execution of its tasks:

- Meets at least quarterly to continually identify and qualify prospective board members. These meetings are staffed by the development or executive director who serves as a resource for names as well as in a support role.
- Motivates and requires board and staff to regularly supply the committee with names of potential board candidates.
- Organizes the board orientations.
- Invites other board members to assist with recruitment and enlistments.
- Checks in periodically with board members who have missed meetings.

- Arranges an annual meeting for the chief executive officer and board chair with each board member.
- Develops and maintains the summary board profile and recruitment matrix.
- Performs the nominating function in a time frame that permits the best possible recruitment.

Combining all of these board-related functions into one committee leads to greater board member involvement and satisfaction. Those recruited, enlisted, and retained in this highly professional manner are much more likely to perform their roles with responsibility and commitment.

RECRUITMENT

The board dream team is developed systematically. Good recruitment begins with the creation of a recruitment matrix. There are two principal sources of information for the matrix: the composition of the existing board and the long-range or strategic institutional plan. Existing board members are described by a number of different criteria including:

- Gender
- Age range
- Race/ethnicity
- Geography (where that is important)
- Profession
- Expertise (which may or may not be the same as profession)
- Expiration date of current board term and whether it is renewable
- Willingness to ask
- Capacity to give
- Connections in the community
- Other board affiliations

Other criteria may be pertinent to your organization; for example, an orchestra might add "love of music" to its desired prerequisites.

Using the Matrix

Most organizations put this information on a chart or grid (see Exhibit 9.1). Some organizations even weight the different criteria. The format you develop should be easy for board members to read and understand. This is the primary management tool for the recruitment and enlistment process. When the matrix is completed, make a summary profile of the current board. For example:

- *Gender:* 55% female, 45% male
- *Race/Ethnicity:* 65% white, 15% African American, 15% Asian, 5% Hispanic

- *Profession:* 5 community volunteers, 4 corporate executives, 1 teacher, 3 lawyers, 1 marketing director, 1 college administrator, 3 representatives of the client base, 1 banker, 1 physician
- *Expertise:* fundraising = 6; marketing = 2; education = 2; client services = 3; financial management = 2; personnel = 1; hospital administration = 1; legal = 3
- *Geography:* city center = 8; suburbs = 6; rural = 4; other cities = 2

Do this type of summary for all areas of the matrix. When completed, chart the expiration dates of the board terms. In this way, you can track, and not lose, vital legal, financial, or educational expertise when those members rotate off the board. Identification

---

EXHIBIT 9.1   SAMPLE BOARD MATRIX

Reading the codes: Confidential

1 = gender

2 = ethnicity, race (W = white; AA = African American; AS = Asian; H = Hispanic; N = Native American; O = other)

3 = age range: 3a, 20–30; 3b, 31–45; 3c, 46–60; 3d, 61+

4 = expertise (p = program; o = organization; d = development including fundraising, marketing, or public relations)

5 = profession (c = corporate executive; v = community volunteer; m = marketing or public relations; fr = fundraising, l = lawyer; fi = financial; r = retail; e = educator; ss = social services)

6 = expiration date of term (06 = 2006; R = renewable; N = non-renewable)

7 = experience with programs and mission (1, 2, or 3 with 1 = very experienced)

8 = time available for board work (1, 2, 3 with 1 = most)

9 = committee affiliation (t = Committee on Trustees; d = Development; m = Marketing; f = Finance; e = Executive; p = Program)

Name	1	2	3	4	5	6	7	8	9
Board A	F	W	b	O	C	07R	3	3	m
Board B	M	AA	c	P	L	06N	1	2	t, e
Board C	F	AS	c	D	FR	08N	2	3	d, m

This analysis is repeated for all board members.

When it is complete, the "profile" of expertise, ethnic/racial and gender balance, professional distribution, and so on, is matched against the needs of the organization as reflected in the institutional plan. Expiration dates are tracked to ensure that individuals providing a particular expertise are replaced as their terms expire.

Recruitment is gauged to "fill the blanks" and build strength in required areas.

The matrix should be kept current by the committee on trustees.

and recruitment of people with that same expertise should begin at least a year before the retirement of the current board member.

The next step in the analysis is to align the current board profile, changes anticipated by rotation, and the expertise that will be required by the long-range or strategic institutional plan. Base recruitment on the "gaps" revealed in this analysis, and begin designing your strategy:

Area of Current or Projected Need	Whom to Recruit
Annual fundraising	Community volunteers and others willing to spearhead events, mailings, and phone appeals, and do face-to-face solicitations
Enhanced marketing activity or planning	Marketing consultants or directors
Staff personnel expansion or reorganization	Labor lawyers, human resources professionals
Increased institutional visibility	Media representatives or those with media connections
Projected capital campaign	Potential large investors or people with connections to potential large investors; people who know city or county politics if a building project is planned
Facilities expansion	Contractors, environmental lawyers, architects

The committee on trustees should review the plan carefully with the CEO and the board chair, highlighting those short- and long-term goals and objectives that will guide board recruitment.

A Word of Caution: Ensuring Passionate Pragmatism

Recruiting for profession or expertise is essential, but requires some caution. The concept of passionate pragmatism suggests that a danger exists when board members are recruited solely for the professional expertise they can bring to an organization (see Chapter 3).[1] They must be willing to get more broadly involved in the organization. They must believe in its mission and values. The recruitment criteria need to be well defined and convincingly conveyed to the prospective board member so that all expectations are clear. Too many board members who provide only their expertise tip the board balance toward pragmatism that lacks passion and understanding for the mission and the importance of the organization. Without passion, advocacy is often minimal.

Getting Ready to Use the Matrix in Enlistment

When the committee on trustees has completed the recruitment matrix, distribute it to the board. Obviously confidential, it should be treated with the utmost discretion. To ensure clarity, allow adequate time for discussion of the matrix, particularly around sensitive areas that may strike some board members as highly personal (age range, race/ethnicity). If these criteria are too troublesome, drop from the matrix. However, some government and foundation funders are interested in how well the board composition reflects the community or the clients. Certain community foundations have increasingly stringent recommendations regarding racial and ethnic balance. They appropriately feel that the boards of the organizations they fund should reflect the racial and ethnic composition of the community. Other funders may have similar guidelines. A board matrix that reflects the importance of complying with certain funder guidelines may require some explanation to the board. This is particularly true if balanced board composition has been a neglected or difficult practice in the past.

Matrices may reflect other changes that need to be made in board composition. Many organizations evolve from early needs to build internal programs to more mature needs to reach out into the community for visibility and support. Board members with strong program expertise may resist a matrix that shows few program-related people relative to the number of corporate vice presidents, media contacts, and people with influence and affluence. This is particularly true in social and human services agencies in which the initial years of board service may have been very hands-on. The enlistment of other kinds of community leaders signals a shift in the board culture. The same kind of apprehension also occurs when private schools change from a parent-majority board to one that includes alumni and others representative of the community. Respect these protective attitudes and the concerns they reflect. The committee on trustees may need to review the institutional plan with the board to show the guidelines used in constructing the new board matrix. It is important that people feel as comfortable as possible with change.

Use the matrix as a guide. We know that few matrices are ever fulfilled 100 percent, but their existence launches the recruitment and enlistment process in a highly professional way. Distribute a written outline of the recruitment and enlistment process, including an enlistment target (number) for the next several years, to the board. Be very clear that there are steps involved in the enlistment process (see Exhibit 9.2). You do not want an enthusiastic board member to recruit someone without the committee on trustees' knowledge or involvement. This is a particular hazard when there is some pressure to fill spaces on a diminished board or to build a new or reinvented board. Assure the board that the steps will be employed with speed, but not haste. Each recruitment decision is very important to the future of the organization and therefore must be strategic. Most board members readily see that the process is crucial, and are willing to participate in lunches or other board candidate cultivation meetings organized by the committee on trustees.

With this process, as with all processes, do not become so bound to the steps that you miss opportunities. It is good to balance your committee on trustees between those who are dedicated to procedure and will keep the system on track and those with a bit bolder attitude who may stumble on an excellent candidate at lunch and realize that the match and the timing is perfect. If possible, enlist committee on trustees' co-chairs with these differing but balanced skills. Good recruitment is both strategic and opportunistic.

Getting Names into the Pipeline

From this point forward, the objective is to keep board candidate names coming into the pipeline so they can be evaluated, introduced to the organization, cultivated, and, if there is a match, asked to join the board at an appropriate time. Make the collection of potential board member names a regular part of every board meeting. Once board members are aware of the integrity of the process, they are more willing to supply names. Reach into the widest constituency possible, and involve staff, former board members, advisory board

---

EXHIBIT 9.2   PROCESS FOR BOARD RETIREMENT

1. Construct a recruitment matrix based on the "gaps" that will emerge when current board members retire.

2. Ask board and staff members, and key volunteers, to submit names of people they know who will fit into one of the "gaps."

3. Compile names; review by committee on trustees.

4. Working with the recommending board or staff member or volunteer, arrange a time for the prospective board member to meet with the CEO and the recommending board/staff/volunteer.

5. At this meeting, focus on the mission, passion, etc., of the organization and provide information for the individual. DO NOT ENLIST at this meeting. Let the individual have some time to get to know the organization (even if it is only a week). Let the process rest; see if there is consensus about inviting this person on the board now. Perhaps this person would be better on a committee at first; or perhaps this person would be good for the future (or not the right person at all for the board).

6. If the decision is made to enlist, plan a second meeting with the prospective board member at which time the board job description will be reviewed and expectations clearly related. Remember that there are talented people out there who will see this as an opportunity to make a difference. But they need to have the story straight from the outset.

7. With the approval of the committee on trustees, the board president should enlist the new board member.

8. Following enlistment, the board member will fill out the board information form, attend an orientation, receive an up-to-date trustee packet, and be assigned to a committee.

9. It is the responsibility of the committee on trustees to see that each board member lives up to his/her commitment.

10. On an annual basis, the executive director and the board chair (or chair of the committee on trustees) should meet with each board member individually for the purpose of assessing satisfaction with board service, discussing best committee placement for the coming year, and soliciting the annual gift.

11. The committee on trustees should update the matrix constantly to reflect changes in board composition.

12. Although nominations, after the initial effort to build the board, may not arise that often, the recruitment process should never stop. It is the goal of any mature organization to have a stable of recruited individuals who are just waiting to come on the board. During the waiting period, they can be involved in committees and do other volunteer service.

members, other volunteers, and funders in the identification process. An excellent and often-overlooked source of potential board members is donor, member, and subscriber lists. These people are already invested in the organization. The committee on trustees should regularly review these lists and submit selected names to the board for silent prospecting (see Chapter 4). Used more often for donor qualification, silent prospecting is also an effective tool for evaluating potential board members.

If you are having trouble building a list of potential board members, some alternative resources may be available to you. In some cities in the United States, nonprofit support organizations annually stage a board "fair" where citizens interested in serving on boards can meet and talk with representatives from organizations who are looking for board members. Community volunteer bureaus also maintain lists of people interested in board service. Some U.S. and multinational corporations, through their human resources departments, encourage employees to become involved with nonprofit organizations. Community foundations, the United Way, service clubs (e.g., Rotary, Soroptimists) are also good resources.

Whatever the source of the name, be sure to employ the same evaluation procedure.

The Evaluation Process

The committee on trustees should use this eight-step procedure for evaluating names.

1. At regular meetings, review names as they are received.
2. Telephone those who have submitted names to gather greater detail about the qualifications of the recommended individual.
3. Refer to the recruitment matrix to see what matches exist for each proposed candidate.
4. Make summary notes and place in recruitment files. Do not make any gratuitous or indiscreet comments (impending divorce, business on the brink of failure, etc.) because you never know who might see the file.
5. Review summary notes at a committee on trustees' meeting, and determine priority recruitments.
6. Make recruitment and enlistment assignments based on the priority list, and provide each member with guidelines for approaching and evaluating the potential candidate.
7. Provide regular reports of recruitment activities during meetings of the committee on trustees, and devise strategies for enlisting appropriate candidates.
8. Keep the board informed of progress.

If this sounds strikingly like the donor-investor development process, you are right. So synergistic are these two functions that the internalization of one enhances the other. Eventually, organizations are able to spread the investment attitude effortlessly throughout these two critical practices.

Making the Recruitment Phone Call

When the candidate is contacted by the committee member, it is important to use the right words. Your part of the conversation might go something like this: "This is Margaret Michaelson. I don't believe we've ever met, but we are mutually acquainted with Roger Suarez who, with me, is a board member at the City Youth Orchestra." (There may be some chat here about Roger. Then proceed.) "Roger [be sure you have his permission to use his name] thought you might be interested in joining our board at some time in the future. As you know, with the decline of public funding for music in our schools, the youth orchestra has become more and more important. Those of us who serve on the board feel as if we're helping build future audiences as well as future musicians. I realize this isn't a decision you make quickly. We don't want a yes or no now. We want to invite you to learn more about how we operate and what board member responsibilities entail. It's important for us to get to know you, too, and hear your interests and answer your questions. Roger said he thought one of your children was once involved with the orchestra. I want to invite you to have lunch with me and Mark Nakamichi, the chair of our committee on trustees, next week. We're available Thursday or Friday. Would either of those days work for you?" During the conversation, the candidate will interject and ask questions, but your "script" should include information that focuses on the importance of the organization, the community need it is meeting, why board service is important, and what the steps are in the enlistment process.

As recruitment meetings are held, be sure reports are filed by the members of the committee or by other board members assigned to candidate recruitment meetings. The matrix begins to come alive. The same kind of tiering (Chapter 4) that is done for donor-investors can be done for board candidates. Some will be enlisted immediately, and others, due to their timing or yours, will be kept informed and involved but will not be enlisted for a while. Still others will not be enlisted at all, either for their reasons or yours. Handling the latter issue is delicate, but should be addressed honestly with the person. "George, our feeling is that right now, even though we're grateful for your interest in coming on our board, your involvement as a board member with four other organizations is probably a full plate without adding us as the fifth. We'd like to keep you involved and hope that, from time to time, we can come and review marketing ideas with you. You've already been so helpful to us. We'd like to stay in touch on an ad hoc basis for now. But please let us know if you complete your service on several of the other boards, because we really enjoyed getting to know you. It's just that right now, we need someone who can give us much more time."

ENLISTMENT

A systematic recruitment process facilitates enlistment. Awkward phone calls and first meetings are out of the way. The candidate, barring unforeseen changes, is committed to serve when asked. If you have been able, over the period of a year or more, to build a stable of informed and cultivated board candidates, then bringing them onto the board is a comfortable process for them and for you. One board was so good at doing this that, by the time candidates were enlisted, they knew everyone and were somewhat informed about critical program and budget issues. It was a privilege and pleasure for board members to begin their board service with a solid basis of knowledge that would accelerate their involvement.

Materials to Use in Enlistment

At the time of the actual enlistment, the committee on trustees should meet with the candidate and review the expectations for board members. Give the new board member a tabbed binder containing information he or she will need:

- A list of current trustees with phone numbers, home and professional addresses, secretary and spouse or partner names, committee assignments, term expiration dates
- A calendar with all board and committee meeting dates and activities for the year
- Board member job description (see Exhibit 9.3)
- A list of the committees with their chairs and members and a brief description of their responsibilities
- A blank trustee information form to fill out before the board orientation and a list of committees to rank by preference for involvement
- An alphabetical list of administrative and program staff members with their phones/ extensions and the home phones and addresses of the top administrative leaders (unless there are reasons for confidentiality)
- A description of the various departments in the organization, the name of the head of each department, and a list of department staff members
- Brief profiles of each member of the administrative staff and the department heads
- A copy of the by-laws and articles of incorporation
- A brief history of the organization
- Financial information including most recent audited financial statement, budget for current year, financial statements, balance sheet
- Fundraising information including annual fund performance over a several-year period, endowment management information, and other reports of development activities
- A copy of the long-range or strategic institutional plan
- A copy of the vision and mission statements if not included in the plan
- Copies of current board policies
- A list of holidays observed by the organization
- Other pertinent material

Do not simply hand this binder to a new board member during the enlistment meeting. Show the new board member the various sections. Explain that reading the binder all the way through is very important preparation for the board orientation (and provide the date for the orientation). Review the job description and provide a verbal rundown on board members the person has not yet met. Have the person fill out the board information form at the time of the actual enlistment, and choose his or her preferred committee assignments. The purpose of giving the entire binder to the new board member at this time is so he or she can review the material before the board member orientation. Put a tight time frame on the need to read the material in the binder; otherwise it will go on a shelf.

EXHIBIT 9.3   SAMPLE BOARD MEMBER JOB DESCRIPTION

Thank you for agreeing to be a board member of [name of organization]. Your service to our organization is extremely important, a job we hope you will take very seriously yet enjoy performing.

Board members have the following responsibilities:

1. To be advocates for the organization in the community.

2. To be familiar with and willing to perform their legal and fiduciary duties, as described in the regulations for nonprofits in our [state] [country].

3. To support the organization financially at an appropriate level.

4. To be ambassadors for the organization and participate in the development of relationships with prospective and current donors that will lead to a strengthening of their support for and investment in our organization.

5. To be askers if appropriate and to participate in fundraising activities, events, and solicitations as assigned and as appropriate.

6. To work cooperatively and creatively with other board members and staff members in the advancement of the mission and vision of the organization.

7. To understand, promote, and reflect the organization's values.

8. To attend board meetings on a regular basis.

9. To attend annual [or more/less frequent] board retreats.

10. To stay connected with the organization's work between board meetings as required or requested.

11. To serve on (a) committee(s) as needed, and to attend those meetings.

12. To be loyal to the organization in time of crisis.

13. To provide honest, open, and candid feedback to staff and other board members.

14. To provide insights and perspective unique to the communities you may represent.

15. To agree to an annual meeting with the board chair and CEO to discuss your board service to let us know what is working for you and, if your board experience is not what you expected, to let us help determine ways to make it better.

Thank you again for your time and service.

Board Orientation

Orientation is really the last step in the enlistment process. Questions always arise about *when* to do the orientation. The best time is as soon as possible after the enlistment. Although it is best if there are three or four (or more) new board members for the orientation, do not put it off if there is only one. Just adjust the format and the players. A recent orientation for new trustees for an organization with a very large board was almost "textbook" in its planning and execution. It provides an excellent model.

There were six new trustees, five of whom were able to be at the orientation. Each one was greeted by a continuing board member assigned to be the new board member's "buddy" for the morning. The orientation began at 9:30 A.M. and was finished after lunch. After coffee and a little bit of socializing, the chief executive officer and the board chair of the organization welcomed the new board members, and each shared their vision for the organization. They also talked about the importance of the board and of board membership. A short (8-minute) video on the organization was shown, followed by a tour of the facility. For the next 80 minutes, the new board members were briefed on the financial situation, the institutional plan, the facilities needs, and fundraising plans. They met department heads, each of whom briefly reviewed their departmental goals and how they all worked together as a team to advance the programs of the organization. This entire group (new trustees, continuing trustees, CEO, staff) then had an informal sandwich lunch. They were joined by the committee chairs with whom new board members would work (some of whom were already there in the "buddy" group). The group was small enough (15) that a U-shaped table set up in a recreation area of the building accommodated everyone. There was lively give-and-take because each of the continuing board member "buddies" had been primed to ask and answer questions. The entire session was over by 12:45 P.M. People felt their time had been used wisely. They were impressed with the efficiency and organization of the meeting and understood the importance of their board membership.

The sixth new board member, out of town on business on the day of the orientation, did not miss out. As soon as she returned to town, an individual orientation was arranged. She met with the CEO and the financial officer, watched the video, toured the building, and then attended a department head meeting where she was introduced and encouraged to ask questions after their regular business was finished. Afterward, the CEO, one of the department heads, the chair of the committee on trustees, and the board chair took her to lunch.

There are several positive outcomes from having continuing board members pair up with new board members and attend the orientation:

- New board members get to know one continuing board member a little better.
- New board members have an ear to whisper in if they have questions they are reluctant to ask in front of the group or if they need clarification about someone's identity or what someone has said.
- Continuing board members get a "booster shot" in terms of their own knowledge, enthusiasm and commitment.

All new board members need orientation, no matter how well they may feel they already know the organization or how experienced they are at serving on other boards. It is the way in which we let them know how serious their board commitment is. If they feel they really do not have to attend, they are already showing signs of being a board member whose potential commitment may not be as deep as you had hoped.

Boards with the most stringent requirements (attendance at meetings and events, giving and asking, participation in orientation, service on committees) are often the most sought after by community-minded citizens. A county hospital formed a foundation that became the most desired community board on which to serve. The list of board requirements was very eye-opening to other local organizations that had soft-pedaled their requirements in hopes of recruiting some of the same corporate and social leaders that were eagerly signing up for this new board. Nothing lures like success. There is a strong correlation between a board management program that sets high standards and the depth of commitment that grows on a board. Motivated board members subvert mediocrity.[2]

Board Retention and Involvement

The responsibility for board development does not end with the enlistment. A well-recruited and properly enlisted board can still be dysfunctional if it is allowed to stagnate or ferment because its own dynamics are not evaluated regularly. Able, excited, visionary, and energetic new board members can become discouraged and inactive when confronted with veteran board members who are bored, cynical, or unenthusiastic. We turn "silk purses" into "sow's ears" when we allow board member malaise to dampen the enthusiasm of new members.

Attention to board health is important for these reasons:

- Self-perpetuating or stagnant boards eventually calcify their organizations.
- Unhappy or uninformed boards are poor advocates.
- "Revolving door" boards erode continuity in vision, planning, administration, and fundraising, and create a poor reputation in the community.
- Rebellious boards can do permanent damage to programs and services.

Rule of Thirds

In order to go beyond fundraising, a board must reflect this rule of thirds:

- At least one-third of the board members should place your organization as their top philanthropic priority.
- Another third should place your organization among their top three philanthropic priorities.
- The remaining third will provide expertise and be less involved, but they should be recruited with the goal of moving them into the first or second group.

Achieving this board composition is not an impossible goal. Such boards exist in hundreds of organizations that are now successfully creating the kinds of investor relationships with their board members and funders that will help guarantee their long-term ability to fulfill their mission. Analyze your board relative to the number in each third. If you are falling short in the first two-thirds, the committee on trustees will want to evaluate its recruitment and retention strategies.

The care and feeding of boards is a primary responsibility of the board itself, with leadership provided by the board chair and the committee on trustees working with the executive director/CEO and the development director. A number of factors determine a board member's feeling of investment and belonging in the organization:

- Mutual respect—by the organization, for the organization
- Understanding of the importance of the organization and of the philanthropic sector
- Value(s)—being valued, valuing the organization, sharing the organization's values and seeing them at work in the community
- A feeling of belonging within the board and the organization
- Belief that time spent in meetings and activities is worthwhile
- Experiences with the board and the organization that are not only informative and worthwhile, but enjoyable
- A sense of the future advancement of the organization and a way to play a part in that advancement
- Knowledge that the organization, and fellow board members, appreciate his or her gifts of time, talent, and "treasure"

Periodic board self-evaluation is an excellent tool for maintaining board awareness of responsibilities and potential need for strategic change. A questionnaire can be developed by the organization and administered during the annual individual meeting among the board member, CEO, and board chair (see Exhibit 9.4). For more formal instruments, contact BoardSource (formerly The National Center for Nonprofit Boards),[3] which has well-tested materials that are available for purchase by boards including a new service that is online. The results of these evaluations are reviewed by the committee on trustees and used as the basis for planning board retreats or other planning sessions.

Management of the board needs to be assigned to the committee on trustees (or the board development committee). The importance of maintaining positive board dynamics is conveyed by the committee to the entire board, whose understanding of the importance of welcoming new board members and interacting positively among themselves may need refreshing. Here is where leadership steps forward. Whoever said "It starts at the top" was right. The board chair and the CEO each have opportunities to set not only standards, but style and tone. The CEO conveys this to staff who interact with board members through committees, events, volunteer work, and fundraising; the board chair conveys it to the board most obviously by his or her own behavior and participation.

EXHIBIT 9.4   BOARD MEMBER QUESTIONNAIRE
(SAMPLE QUESTIONS)

- Have your expectations of board membership been realized?
- What changes would you suggest?
- Do you feel you're serving on the right committee(s)? Change?
- Do you feel you received adequate orientation? Change?
- Please comment on our Board Member Job Description.
- We shall all be involved in some aspect of fundraising. What can the board development committee do to prepare you for this?
- If asked, are you willing to serve another term?
- Have you reviewed our long-range plan? How do you feel about the goals and objectives? Do they work? Which ones excite or at least interest you?
- Have you suggestions for this year's board retreat? Topics? Format?
- Are there individuals you would recommend for future board membership?

There is more about board leadership in Chapter 3, but the imperative is clear. Once enlisted, board members who have the potential for being effective need to be continually listened to, nurtured, and encouraged. Capable board members are not born, they are made. The lawyer with a private practice and three small children does not come to the board meeting to be bored. The banker with a heavy schedule who is also president of Rotary does not come to meetings to be misinformed. The community volunteer who sits on other boards and sees broadly the community issues that must be met does not come to meetings to be ignored. Because board meetings are the principal place of interaction for boards, a look at what they are and what they can be is important.

BOARD OR BORED? MAKING THE MOST OF MEETINGS

Anyone who attends many board meetings quickly realizes there are certain aspects common to all of them. The players and purposes may differ, but many of the elements are remarkably similar. Some are inevitable (treasurer's report, minutes from the previous meeting, committee reports), and others are variable (special event update, capital campaign progress report). So how can a meeting, which is fairly predictable in its agenda and course, be made into something that will play a key role in sustaining board enthusiasm? By remembering, always, that the reason most of these board members are here (or should be here) is because you have an urgent mission to fulfill in the community. Give them a "product demonstration" or mission moment at each meeting so they leave having learned something new about why they are involved: testimony by a parent whose child has benefited from a learning disabilities program, enthusiastic appreciation by a student who has received a scholarship, a brief talk by a teacher who has integrated a music education program into her curriculum. These mission moments can help change the corporate culture and behavior of cliquish or social boards whose motivations may be driven less by mission than by fulfilling or seeking social connections. A presentation, tour, demonstration, or video gives board members something common to see, hear, and discuss. A dance company focused its board on the funding needed for outreach to inner-city schools by having teachers and students speak at a board meeting about the impact of the current program and its potential for growth. When asked to raise money for this program, board members had a new level of understanding and enthusiasm, which resulted in significantly more effective advocacy. For programs whose sensitivity prevents the appearance of clients at board meetings, a passionate advocate can tell the story.

The whole board meeting ritual can be very discouraging. Too often, board members do not leave feeling passionate about the mission; they leave feeling discouraged about the financial, facilities, staffing, or board recruitment situation because no solutions, except raising more money, enlisting more volunteers, or cutting an already bare-bones budget have been offered. Urged to go out and raise money before it is too late, they can only offer a tin cup message: The organization is desperate for funds and needs help. No matter how grim the financial situation may be—and full disclosure is essential if you are to retain board loyalty and investment—you have to turn it around in such a way that the urgency of the financial situation is *because* of the urgency of the community need that is being met; and if it is not—if bad management is the cause of the financial problems—then that is another issue.

Focus the board on the community need. Use one of these strategies to inspire them. There is nothing more paradoxical than to see a board wade through the cash flow, hear the discouraging report on the planned special event that may have to be canceled, see photos of the deterioration of the parking lot, learn that the lease may not be renewed, and then have the valiant development director or committee chair hand out the annual fund personal solicitation assignments, asking them all to go out and be enthusiastic and excited when they invite people to invest in the organization. Does this sound like an organization in which you could ask people to invest? Is there anyone who would want to invest in it? It will be a tough sell. Although board members may intuitively understand that the organization would not have financial needs if it were not producing results, they need to be continually reconnected with why the organization exists. Otherwise, the passion will probably be missing.

Board meetings are the most visible place where we let the organization get in the way of the mission (see Chapter 3). Unfortunately, some board members are so little involved in other activities with the organization that board meetings are their only exposure. Board meetings with a negative tone and poor focus may be the reason board members are not more involved. In one organization, a much-sought-after board member resigned after his first several meetings, citing reasons that were clearly tied to the quality of his board meeting experience. When board members stop coming to meetings, you need to find out why.

Organizations that conduct lively, mission-focused, interactive, time-sensitive, solution-oriented, and productive board meetings know how to put together meetings that inform, motivate, and inspire. They provide:

- A good agenda, developed by the CEO and the board chair with input from the committee on trustees and from other committee and staff people.

- An exciting window into the organization through the mission moment or "product demonstration." Not a report *about* something, but an informative, compelling firsthand presentation from someone who has benefited from the organization or who has worked with those who have benefited.

- An established meeting time frame that is altered only when an urgent issue demands a longer meeting. (Tabling an urgent issue in the interest of time is not in the best interests of the organization and causes the issue to slip in priority in the minds of those asked to deal with it.)

- Good attendance ensured by committee on trustee calls to those who have missed board meetings. Few things are more frustrating than not having a quorum present, thereby rendering ineffective the efforts of those members who are present.

- An atmosphere of trust, respect, consideration for each other's time, opinions, and feelings.

- A board leader who can graciously contain those board members who dominate while deliberately drawing out those who otherwise defer to their more vocal fellow members, losing their opportunity to contribute and be validated.

Board Retreats

Board retreats are a different kind of board meeting, one with great potential for elevating board commitment. When they work well, they should be called board advances, because they have a high potential for moving the organization forward. Usually based around annual or campaign planning and evaluation, and conducted at a site away from the organization's usual meeting facility, retreats offer a unique opportunity for board members to get to know each other better while addressing issues of critical future importance. Include key administrative, development, and program staff at your board retreat to ensure clarity and continuity in fulfilling retreat plans. Small organizations in which there may be much shared responsibility between board and staff often include the entire staff at the retreat. Failure to include any staff except the executive director can lead to feelings of "us versus them."

There are exceptions, of course. Some board retreats are called for the express purpose of addressing crucial staffing issues that may involve the executive director. In these cases, the retreat usually begins with an executive session where only board members are in attendance. When their business is finished, the executive director and/or other involved staff members are invited to join and to discuss the results of the board deliberations and to begin working toward implementation of changes that must be made. Needless to say, these latter kinds of retreats are tough, tense meetings. Fortunately, the vast majority of board retreats are not grim gatherings at which sensitive personnel issues are resolved. They are great opportunities for exploring issues and ideas in a more relaxed environment and for spending time getting to know each other.

The first time an organization attempts to organize a board retreat, there may be considerable resistance. This is especially true if board commitment is uneven and leadership is not convinced of the importance of an extended session. Convincing boards that it is vital for them to spend four hours (the *minimum* time for a "retreat") to three days (probably the maximum time) may be difficult. Have a solid outcomes-focused agenda to lure the committed but very busy people. Your notice, sent out after the retreat idea is introduced in a regular board meeting, might announce:

> The purpose of the board retreat is to establish financial and staffing projections for the next two years so that our grant from the Benevolent Foundation will be renewed on time. To do so, we will have to undertake an evaluation of potential growth or decline in the need for program delivery, cost centers, income fluctuations, potential government funding decreases and our other fundraising. Staff will be there to provide us with baseline data for our evaluation. At the end of the retreat, we should have the raw material for a solid proposal which will be drafted by staff, provided for our review at the November board meeting, and submitted to the Benevolent Foundation by December 31. An agenda for the meeting is attached, and the planning committee welcomes your comments and ideas about how we can make this retreat as productive as possible.

Once these outcomes have been established, and a good date and location has been identified, the retreat planners can get to work on the process and format of the retreat. Team building, while seldom explicitly mentioned in retreat announcements, is one of the primary reasons for having a board retreat. Otherwise, the materials for the Benevolent Foundation probably could be gathered through a series of committee meetings (finance, development program, personnel, executive) and pieced together for the proposal. But board commitment and cohesiveness are always enhanced in a good board retreat, and the interaction around a specific issue or project promotes teamwork.

Specific "team-building" activities, often urged by facilitators, may not be necessary if you have a solid and interesting agenda with lots of opportunity for small-group interaction. People will team-build around the work provided. An agenda that permits some "down time" (but not so much that busy people will feel their time is wasted) will stimulate informal interaction not possible within the stringent time requirements of regular board meetings or even within the small-group assignments at the retreat. So many times, however, the laughter that pours out of a small-group session struggling with a scenario gives the best witness to what happens when people come together with clarity and purpose. They have fun, and they accomplish much more than they would otherwise.

The aspects of a good board retreat are basically the same as those for good board meetings. In addition, you will want to follow the 15 steps beginning on page 179 and develop a plan (see Exhibit 9.5).

EXHIBIT 9.5 BOARD RETREAT PLANNING FORM

1. Purpose of retreat—What outcomes do you want?

2. Whom to invite—Board only, board and key staff, other volunteers? Who will plan—Staff, board, combined?

3. How to market, how to fund—What will you say to board members to get them to attend? How will you pay for the retreat?

4. What agenda—Content and format: Will it be facilitated by a professional (outsider) or handled by staff?

5. When to hold—Time of year, relationship to fiscal year and other activities?

6. Length of retreat—Half-day, full day, two days, longer?

7. Where to hold—On-site, off-site, casual or business setting?

KEEPING THE RETREAT RELEVANT: POTENTIAL TOPICS

Annual planning	Capital campaign planning
Long-range planning	Building a stronger board (recruitment, enlistment, etc.)
Mission clarification	
Vision and goal setting	Fundraising training
Program exploration and development	Management and organizational issues

KEEPING THE RETREAT LIVELY: A VARIETY OF TECHNIQUES

Role playing	Dyads, triads, small-group discussions
Case studies	Questionnaires
Problem-solving	Outside facilitator or trainer
Game simulation	Outdoor activities
Audiovisuals (overheads, videos, etc.)	"Group memory" with easel paper

KEEPING THE RETREAT PLEASANT: ESSENTIAL LOGISTICS

Comfortable setting	Include an unrushed meal
Informal attire	Ample time for introductions, getting acquainted
Attractive surroundings	
Time for unstructured interaction, conversation	"State of the Organization" remarks by executive director or equivalent

1. Start planning the retreat three to four months before it is scheduled. The board retreat should be an annual calendar date. Many organizations choose the same month each year and have the retreat in place of the regular board meeting. Include board and staff (if they are included in the retreat) on the retreat planning committee.

2. Be sure the date and place you have chosen are convenient for the majority of board and staff. Seek 100 percent attendance; be happy with 85 percent; cancel if only 70 percent sign up. If this is a new location or a first retreat, members of the committee, with the facilitator if one is being used, should visit the site to determine whether it is appropriate and has the right space and resources to support the planned activities.

3. Establish preliminary desired results and process outcomes at the beginning of your planning. Have the retreat as a board meeting agenda item at least three months before the anticipated time of the retreat. Brainstorm expectations and desired outcomes. Submit your tentative agenda to the board for feedback. Invite their comments and response.

4. Assess board member tolerance before committing to a very long board retreat. It is best to start with a short good retreat and gradually, over the years, extend the time as the need demands. In some years, a long retreat may not be desirable or necessary. Gauge the time to the tolerance and the need. One European organization, in the year after its first successful distant-site two-day retreat, opted for a half-day retreat at a closer location. It was superbly attended (88 percent) and highly productive.

5. Be clear and consistent in conveying the importance of the meeting and the anticipated outcomes. Leadership must be obviously enthusiastic and committed for others to feel that way.

6. Decide early in your planning if you will use an inside or outside facilitator. Inside facilitators come without cost, but may lack the required objectivity. The advantage to using an outside facilitator is professional skill and objectivity to move the meeting along and not get tangled up in politics or difficult relationships. The principal disadvantage is cost. In some communities, local foundations will cover the cost of a facilitator if the retreat objectives are clearly tied to long-range planning, for example. You will need time to apply for this funding.

7. If you choose to use an outside facilitator, be sure that he or she is available before you confirm the date. Have some backup facilitators in mind just in case.

8. Include the facilitator in your planning meetings to the extent possible. He or she needs to understand the dynamics and the issues. Provide the facilitator with a list of the outcomes you want. He or she should prepare a draft agenda that you can then revise and complete together. Do not bring a facilitator in "cold" to a retreat.

9. Alert the facilitator to any potentially explosive issues that could erupt in the meeting. These land mines have exploded the agenda of more than one well-planned

retreat. When the facilitator is aware of the danger spots, he or she can be much more sensitive to the issues or individuals. A skillful facilitator can sometimes surface these issues within the context of a larger discussion and in such a way that they are addressed objectively. This can help neutralize the tension so the real issues can be dealt with openly.

10. Approximately two weeks to 10 days before the retreat, reconfirm with all board and staff about their attendance. If there is dramatic fall-off in attendance, have the board chair or executive director call each board person. If that does not work, consider cancellation. If all is still on track, mail out retreat-related background materials to be read before the retreat (plans, agenda, list of participants, etc.).

11. One week before the retreat, send out a final package with directions to the site (map plus narrative directions and information regarding estimated time it will take to get there), advice about dress (casual, e.g., except for Friday dinner), information about the facility (bring your swim suit or tennis racket), final agenda/schedule (e.g., 5 P.M. check-in; 6 P.M. registration; 6:30 P.M. opening reception), and any last-minute materials needed to enhance the agenda.

12. During the retreat, stay on time and on point to the extent possible. Even if people are having lots of fun in their small-group sessions, keep the agenda moving. Be sure that people arrive on time and return from breaks promptly. Start on time regardless of who is present. If 15 minutes have been allotted for each report presentation, use a timer. It is not fair to presenters or participants to let the time get out of control. People quickly understand and appreciate a professionally run meeting. Your board and key staff members are major investors in the organization, and a well-run productive retreat is one way to honor their investment.

13. During the meeting, troubleshoot issues that get in the way of the agenda unless they are resolved. A two-day retreat for a social service agency was nearly derailed by the executive director's disclosure, during his opening remarks, that he had applied for government funding that would add a significant program area to the organization. Board members were angry. They had not been consulted, and the program implications, while exciting, were overwhelming. Used to dealing with his visionary drive and independent behavior, they at least listened while he explained. Three hours of tense but important debate significantly altered the established agenda. However, had the issue not been addressed, none of the retreat outcomes could have been accomplished. It ended well. The board was enthused about the program, which received the government funding and was a great community success.

14. Have solid closure to the retreat. Much happens during a retreat, whether it is four hours or three days. Friendships are made. Tensions arise or are resolved. Plans are made or revised. Information is given and digested. There is time for reflection and comment. Organizations miss an opportunity to further increase the intensity of board member investment when they end their retreats in a haphazard way, when people drift out with little understanding of the next steps or the purpose of their participation. Allow enough time at the end of the retreat to:

    a. Confirm the next steps, including timeline, for any planning that has been done.

    b. Have participants make their own individual commitments, written or verbally, regarding the ways they will support the plan or program, and have them turn in these commitments—which can be in the form of a checklist—to the development or executive director.

    c. Have the facilitator give his or her closing observations.

    d. Close with a short "stem-winder" (inspirational talk) from a board member, staff leader, or the facilitator.

15. Follow up the retreat with a letter to each board member, thanking them for attending, summarizing the outcomes of the retreat, recounting some of the "process" moments that were fun and memorable, outlining the next steps, restating the board member's commitment, and including complete notes from the retreat. This information should also be sent to those who could not attend the retreat, with a cover letter expressing the importance of the outcomes and the way they can participate in the implementation of the decisions.

Retreats that lack thorough planning and follow-up may be viewed as isolated and time-consuming experiences. This reaction erodes board enthusiasm and may lead to board member unrest or disinterest.

Improving the Quality and Results of Board Member Solicitations

It is a given that all board members must make a financial contribution to the organizations they serve. It is no longer an option.

The size of the gift, as with any donor-investor contribution, should be appropriate to the capacity of the individual and the current demands on his or her assets or discretionary income. We know that many community funders look for 100 percent board commitment before they will entertain a proposal. That is an external motivation for having full financial support from the board. The internal reasons are just as important.

- Philanthropy—all voluntary action for the public good—is not multiple choice; those who join, ask, and serve should also give.

- Board members cannot ask others to be donor/investors if they themselves are not.

- Board giving leverages gifts from others, including staff.

- There is a joy that comes from knowing that your financial support is helping achieve an important mission in the community.

We frequently employ solicitation language that includes words like "obligation" or "responsibility" when talking with board members about giving. This approach is increasingly ineffective, as people regard their giving as social investment. Greater gifts are realized when board members give out of a desire to make an investment based on the excitement and satisfaction they feel over their relationship with the organization. We must grow an investor attitude, first and foremost, in our leadership.

Asking Board Members for Their Gifts

The way in which many board gifts are solicited negates the spirit of investment. Countless organizations still solicit their board members by letter, phone, or (worst of all) by "group ask"—announcing at a board meeting that envelopes are being distributed so they can make their board gift before they leave. Although soliciting board gifts by letter or phone may possibly be excused in organizations that conduct all their fundraising that way, it also occurs in organizations that have graduated to personal solicitation of their larger investors. A problem arises when they ask board members who have not been solicited personally to meet face to face with others to ask for their gift. The board member who has not been solicited personally is not nearly as effective a solicitor as the board member who has.

But there are other reasons as well. The solicitation of a board member's gift is a rare annual opportunity for the CEO and the board chair to sit down one-on-one with a board member to listen as well as ask. The committee on trustees should organize a cycle of individual meetings for each board member with the executive director and the board chair (or other board leader if it is not possible for the board chair to commit to so many meetings). These can take place over a period of several months; there is no need to wait until the end of the year. At this meeting, three essential areas are covered:

1. Board members are thanked for their service and are asked to comment about their experience, including their concerns, complaints, and enthusiasms.

2. Future involvement is discussed, including appropriateness of current committee assignments, time or resources changes, or constraints of which the organization should be aware, etc.

3. An annual gift is solicited, using proper solicitation techniques (see Chapter 5) and asking for a specific amount appropriate to the individual's giving history, capacity, and constraints. Gifts traditionally made at year-end can be secured several months beforehand through a pledge. If a capital campaign is starting (see Chapter 7), this is also the time to discuss that campaign and the financial contribution the organization would like the board member to consider when the campaign gets under way.

Following Up on the Solicitation Meeting

After this meeting, the board chair sends the board member a letter, summarizing the conversation, including committee preferences for the following year, and thanking the board member for his or her gift or pledge. A copy of the letter is kept in the board member's file, maintained by the committee on trustees.

This is such a simple process, and board members like it. At first, they may say that such a meeting is not necessary. They will assure you that their satisfaction is high and they will make a gift "as usual" at the end of the year. You must convince all board members to participate in an individual meeting. They will end up appreciating the time and attention. The president of the board of a children's services organization included this summary in her report of the meetings that she and the executive director had held with board members: "Overall, the meetings produce a sense of belonging, a feeling of being valued, and a willingness to continue service to the Center, both on the part of the members being interviewed and this president. Certainly the information generated is of great value in raising Board performance levels and ensuring continued health and growth. This is a process that merits yearly repetition." That particular organization had approached each interview with a short list of questions with which to open the conversation (see Exhibit 9.4).

Carried out with candor and confidentiality, board member interviews are an essential aspect of board management, leadership, and retention. In another benefit, board member gifts will increase in size as they feel a greater sense of belonging. And, not incidentally, board member skill and comfort in asking others personally for gifts will improve dramatically. They hear the words they will want to use and watch how others make the ask. Board members are your first and closest constituents. This interview and asking process helps ensure their leadership and support.

Board Retention and Rotation

Board retention becomes less difficult as board members become more invested. Turnover is kept to a minimum, and vacancies that do arise are filled with relative ease and quickness from the stable of cultivated board candidates. The board management techniques previously described help maintain board stability, and the attention to board member health can prevent the malaise and stagnation that triggers board resignations. Leadership that keeps a watchful eye for areas of potential or growing conflict among board members or between staff and board members can move deliberately to surface and calm the tension. When board development is approached systematically, there is increased board member retention and continued motivation.

However, diligent attention to rotation is critical. Regardless of the dedication and financial support board members provide, they should regularly rotate off the board. By-laws should define board terms and the rotation process. Board recruitment and enlistment procedures should convey this information to board candidates. Many boards choose renewable terms, with a final rotation off after two or three consecutive terms. Usually by-laws provide that a former board member can be reelected after a certain period (one or two years).

An organization that was blessed with a founding board member of extraordinary knowledge and commitment still adhered to its rotation policy by naming her to the finance committee in her "year off" and keeping her very involved with fund development. Most people did not know when she was on or off the board, and she served the organization for more than 40 years until her death at nearly 90. Alert to the end, she was a formidable presence on the board and a powerful advocate in the community.

Other organizations promote longtime or high-profile board members—particularly those whose health or circumstances no longer permit active board participation—to emeritus or lifetime trustee status with full voting privileges. Whatever your by-laws say, enforce them or revise them. Organizations are too often out of compliance with their own rules.

Some major arts organizations do not apply rotation principles to their boards, and their reasons have to do with leadership, financial commitment, and community perception of the volunteer stability of the organization. Some organizations appoint board members for life. Your approach to rotation needs to reflect your culture and your needs—but infusing new ideas and people into boards still remains important.

The first board matrix an organization prepares is often revealing. One organization, which had by-law provisions calling for two consecutive three-year terms and then a year off before reelection, discovered that four of its board members had been on for 10 or more years. The new committee on trustees took charge. The board members whose term limits had passed were thanked profusely for their service and given a lasting memento and a small party at their last board meeting. They were graciously rotated, and their seats were made available for new board members. Three of the four stayed actively involved in other ways and one came back on the board; the fourth had not been to a board meeting in years.

The infusion of new ideas and new personalities on a board can do wonders for fading morale. This is particularly true in the midst of a major campaign or construction project, where it seems as if the same things have been said by the same people for so long that no one hears them anymore. New voices, new questions, and new enthusiasm change the dynamics and energize the entire board. Apprehension of change is often more draining than the actuality. Even those boards that have resisted rotation find that the presence of new people and new leadership enriches their experience.

Nonrenewal of Board Members

One issue relative to rotation that is difficult for most organizations is the nonrenewal of board members who could serve another term. We end up reenlisting board members who do not attend meetings, fail to participate in committees, are reluctant to fundraise, and make a token or no gift themselves. Because this is a voluntary commitment, we are hesitant to impose standards on our board members. When a systematic program of thoughtful recruitment, enlistment, and careful board management is working, this nonperformance, too, recedes as an issue. But there are gracious ways to deenlist when that needs to be done.

In the annual meeting with the board member, board chair, and CEO, the reasons for nonattendance or nonsupport can be raised in confidence. If there is a legitimate reason, the organization should take steps to correct the conditions or behavior responsible. Sometimes the reasons are revealed in a board meeting or retreat. For example, the anchor person for the morning and evening news programs in a small but growing town was asked to serve on the local public schools foundation. Never present for Wednesday morning board meetings, he showed up, to everyone's surprise, for a Saturday all-day board retreat nearly a year after he had been elected. During the meeting, the facilitator had used the Harold Seymour profile of volunteers in which 5 percent are described as creative, 30 percent as responsible, 35 percent as responsive, and 30 percent as "inert."[4] At the end of the meeting, board members were asked to make their commitments. Everyone was surprised when this individual said he committed to no longer "being inert." However, he said, "Can we have meetings when I can attend them?" He explained that their reason for wanting him on the board was because of his media exposure, much of which happened five mornings and noons a week. The board meetings, always scheduled for a Wednesday morning, were impossible for him to attend. So valued was his potential and so accepted was his earnest response that the board meetings were changed to late afternoon and were held at the excellent meeting facility at the station. He later became chair of the board and each year offered the station's facilities to the foundation for the preparation and editing of its annual giving informational videotape.

If you must deenlist a board member, handle the transaction carefully. You do not want angry former board members telling the community they were treated badly. Like any dismissal, this is difficult to approach. These people know they have not fulfilled their responsibilities, but they perpetually hope that they will have more time, energy, or money to give. Some standard procedures can help keep the deenlistment process objective and fair.

- Know the ways in which they have contributed work, wealth, or wisdom over the years, and thank them.
- Know the reasons why you believe they should not continue on the board, and be prepared to discuss those reasons with them.
- Offer them another role within the organization on an advisory or consulting board if they want to stay involved.
- Send only your very best emissary(ies) to do the deenlistment in person—chair of the board or committee on trustees, or other appropriate board leader(s).
- Do not delegate this task to staff. It places them in a very difficult position if, in the future, this same person is identified for a large investment.
- Try to relax. Most often, the person to whom you are delivering the "bad news" either preempts you by resigning or is visibly relieved to be done with this obligation. Be sure to keep the door open for later involvement.
- Document the conversation for the files.

Retention and rotation cannot be left to chance. They are vital aspects of effective board development and help present a highly professional profile of your organization within the board and out in the community.

The Parking Lot as Boardroom

A final word must be said about maintaining board health. Is the important business of the board taking place in the boardroom, in the parking lot after the board meeting, or on cell phones on the way home? Too many board members, unable, unwilling, or not encouraged to speak up at board meetings, speak to and confide in other board members afterward. They stand in the hallways, or linger in the parking lot, meet in a nearby coffee shop, or talk from their cars, sometimes for hours, dissecting issues that should have the benefit of full board discussion. Although some conversation may be social, much is not. These "offline" discussions make issues swell out of proportion, often resulting in an angry, frantic, or poorly timed and reasoned phone call to the board chair, CEO, or chair of the committee on trustees.

Those who initiate such offline meetings and who take time to make a series of phone calls to those they consider key players clearly have some kind of interest or issue driving them. Find out what it is, and channel this energy into a constructive activity or meeting. Confront the issues, and persuade the person that the communication structure *within* the organization can accommodate his or her grievance, concern, or idea.

Through open communication policies, in which board members are encouraged to bring even sensitive issues to board meetings or to a special meeting with the board chair, parking lot meetings of the kind just described are no longer needed. Of course, people have the right to congregate wherever they want. This is not a suggestion to start monitoring parking lot or cell phone conversations. It is merely a warning based on experience: These gatherings can be the early warning signal of failing board health. The information in this chapter will help organizations create an environment in which the only meetings in the parking lot are social.

Summary

Board members are an organization's major investors, regardless of the size of the gift they make. The time, effort, and advocacy they give, in addition to their gifts, have a huge impact on the overall health and community perception of the organization. When recruited and enlisted appropriately, and drawn into a working partnership that encourages them to use their expertise and energy in activities that are productive, satisfying, and fun, board members can flourish. And so can the organizations they serve.

Notes

1. Kay Sprinkel Grace, "Towards Passionate Pragmatism: Building and Sustaining Board Commitment," pp. 109–120 in Richard C. Turner, ed., *Taking Trusteeship Seriously* (Indiana University Center on Philanthropy [550 West North Street, Suite 301, Indianapolis, IN 46202], 1995).
2. Kay Sprinkel Grace, *The Ultimate Board Member's Book* (Emerson & Church, 2003), p. 59.
3. Board Source, Suite 900, 1828 L Street NW, Washington, DC 20036-5114; *www.boardsource.org;* (202) 452-6262.
4. Harold J. Seymour, *Designs for Fund-Raising,* 2nd edition (Fund Raising Institute/The Taft Organization [12300 Twin Brook Parkway, Suite 450, Rockville, MD 20852; 1-800-877-8238], 1988).

CHAPTER 10

The Power of Planning

The nonprofit sector is in the eye of tremendous change. Demands for accountability, transparency, and disclosure from institutional and individual funders have increased, and donor-investor expectations regarding return on social investment are on the rise. Expected to behave in a more businesslike way, we are required to implement sound practices in planning, accounting, data management, and reporting. These demands come at a time when there is increasing need for our services and in many organizations less money to meet these service demands. Although opportunities to make a lasting impact have never been better, the expectations for sound management and systematic fund development programs have never been greater.

We find ourselves juggling huge challenges as we attempt to respond to community needs while strengthening our own infrastructure. The dramatic changes in levels of government support for essential arts, environmental, human, social, medical, and other services in the United States and around the world, coupled with a residue of "psychic poverty" that has been created by the economic volatility and global unrest, have stretched our resources and imposed new requirements on our management practices.

As we recalibrate for the twenty-first century, we have to give deliberate and careful consideration to the community need for our programs and services. We must organize more effectively to ensure our own continuing vitality and visibility. Donor-investors are looking for organizations in whose future they can participate. Although the fast-paced changes in our funding and social environment make it difficult to plan, funders need to see a plan in order to see the future. Both the planning process and the resulting document are critical internal tools for maintaining stability in a time of rapid change and important external tools for attracting funders and volunteers. This chapter focuses on the institutional plan, three levels of operation and how they are contained in the plan, and one of the plan's most important components, development and fundraising.

WHY ORGANIZATIONS NEED TO PLAN

You need to have an institutional plan if you want to run your organization more effectively and invite donor-investors to become long-term supporters. Just as investors in the for-profit sector require a business plan, nonprofit donor-investors need to see where we are going and how their investments will be used. A smart donor-investor will need and want to see your long-range plan, understand your vision, and know how you will be implementing and evaluating your goals and objectives.

The lens for the plan is the marketplace. Your programs exist to serve the community; your organizational and development/fundraising structures ensure effective program administration and support. The community need for your services and the potential for financial and volunteer support are the two key external factors in institutional planning. They drive staffing, program growth, and board and volunteer expansion. Too many organizations develop plans that have no relationship to the world outside their windows. They focus on what *they* want and need, rather than on what the *community* wants and needs. Successful plans begin with an assessment of marketplace needs, continue with an evaluation of internal resources required to meet those needs, and then develop strategies to fill the gap between current and needed programs and to generate the needed resources.

There are two basic reasons for planning:

1. To create an internal management tool for board and staff to help them implement and evaluate general organizational activities, specific programs or campaigns, and financial performance
2. To provide an external document—usually an executive summary of the institutional plan—for use when meeting with potential donor/investors or when recruiting board members

In both cases, the quality of the product is largely determined by the integrity of the process. The degree of ownership of a plan by a staff and board, established by the process used in its preparation, will determine the success of the plan. Success is measured by the commitment to implement and evaluate the plan internally and the impact of the plan as a donor development and board recruitment tool.

Why Organizations Resist Planning

Organizations resist institutional and development planning for one or more of seven reasons:

1. There are too many urgent needs to be met and time cannot be taken for the planning process.
2. Staff leadership may be concerned about being held accountable.
3. Board leadership may be impatient with the planning process.
4. Previous plans have gathered dust on the shelf, and the organization feels it was a wasted effort.

5. The organization seems to be functioning well without one.

6. The board may subconsciously feel that the organization is so fragile that planning would be fruitless.

7. The organization does not know how to approach the task.

The following story illustrates the fallacy of the first five points listed and hints at the sixth. The seventh point inspires this chapter.

CASE STUDY

Years ago, an educational and cultural organization with long history of community service and great potential for community investment nearly had to close its doors because the executive director did not believe in institutional planning. He ignored an early plan that was in place when he was hired. He squelched all board and staff attempts to revive or renew it. Because the chief executive officer seemed visionary and was charismatic, he enjoyed some early fundraising and programmatic successes that worked to negate any sense of urgency about formulating a new plan. The busy board, with few exceptions, did not push for a plan because members did not want to spend time in the process. The CEO, when questioned by the new development director about the lack of a plan, expressed his belief that a plan would inhibit the organization's capacity to be flexible and responsive.

In the absence of a strategic plan, and needing to raise a great deal of money in a relatively short period of time, the development director and the development committee prepared a two-year plan for development and fundraising. Because there was no overarching design for the organization, the development plan was more tactical than strategic.

Although the fundraising plan provided a departmental and volunteer road map for action, the absence of an institutional plan made it extremely difficult to approach funders for general program support. The board lacked reasons and results on which to base community development and fundraising. Although the organization had been established many years before, it had a long and chaotic history of staff and board leadership problems, poor fundraising and financial management, and lackluster marketing. Much of the case for support was based on the urgent need for funds to keep the organization running rather than on the realities of the marketplace need for its services. Community interest in general programming had diminished due to poor market analysis of what educational and cultural programs were needed and wanted. The CEO was superb at project funding (publishing, exhibitions), the funds for which were restricted and could not be used for general support.

Repeated funding crises plunged the organization into management and financial crisis. Staffing cuts were made and programs were reduced. The open hours for the primary service area for members and the community were drastically cut. General fundraising dwindled, and with it the financial stability of the organization. Not only did the board fail to demand a plan from the executive director, it also decided it would not develop one in the absence of administrative endorsement. After several years, the board saw the problem and did not renew the CEO's contract. This move came too late; the damage had

(continues)

been done. The organization was in disarray, and its image in the community was extensively damaged. Although the absence of an institutional plan was not the only problem leading to the organization's decline, it had profound impact on its inability to recover. It also had an impact on potential external funding that might have restored the organization's financial and program stability.

A potentially very large donor had been brought, through his friendship and respect for a long-time board member, into a growing relationship with the organization. Seeing both the problems and the promise of the organization, he was ready to make a very large gift—in effect, a financial "bailout"—because of his passion for the mission and regard for the highly esteemed board member (who was also a major donor to the organization). Despite earnest cultivation and numerous meetings with the development director and several board members, the prospect ultimately refused to make a gift because the institution did not have a plan. As a retired president of a multinational corporation, he valued planning, even in a fast-changing world. He has since died, leaving millions to other organizations.

The organization without the plan drifted into near obscurity and failure before new visionary leadership and financial necessity combined to force a planning process that has completely repositioned it.

The lessons derived from this case study are striking. No organization can afford to ignore the necessity of a solid institutional plan. A plan is not an option in today's philanthropic environment; it is a necessity.

ORGANIZATIONAL AND DEVELOPMENT PLANS

Organizational and development/fundraising plans come in several types, can be comprehensive or specific, and are produced through a variety of processes. Budgets, the financial plans for organizations, are included in this overview of planning. A plan without a complete budget for the first year and budget projections for subsequent years has little value for management or fundraising, and will be insufficient for the needs of funders.[1]

Types of Plans

Plans can be long range, strategic, or specific.

- *Long Range:* Vision and goals span three to five years; specific, measurable objectives may be limited to one to two years; others are included but are less precise or an annual continuation of the same objective. A three- to five-year long-range plan should have a "rolling base." The plan should be updated annually, the year just completed evaluated and retired from the plan, and a new final year added. A plan should never expire. Every three to five years, a "deep dive" or zero-based process should be used to evaluate the environment, the organization, and the vision.

- *Strategic:* An annual plan; goals may be long term, but they are a framework for a tightly focused set of objectives encompassing the strategy of the organization. An annual strategic plan may be part of the long-range plan.

- *Specific:* For a specific department or activity (e.g., annual fund, membership, board development, capital campaign, special event).

Scope of Plans

Plans may relate to the institution as a whole, to a department, and/or to finances.

- *Institutional:* The plan covers the entire organization and is shaped by the institutional vision. It is inclusive of all administrative and program departments and is supported by the organization's budget.

- *Departmental:* Within the institutional plan, there may exist discrete plans for each administrative and service area that guide their specific activities. Accompanying budgets are limited to that administrative area.

- *Financial:* All plans have to have a budget component. Although it is difficult to project precise budget figures beyond one year, educated guesses for the three- to five-year period of a long-range plan provide benchmarks for evaluation. Program budgets are recommended. In this format, the line item budget (staffing, benefits, other expenses) is further broken out by assignment of expenses to each department or project. This format makes it easier to prepare funding proposals because assignment of costs and sources of revenue for each program have already been determined. Zero-based budgeting, also recommended at least every two years, is a further aid to accurate planning.

The budgeting process is developed in more detail later in the chapter.

Types of Planning Processes

Planning may be either top down or participatory.

- *Top-down:* Principal energy and control of the process is provided by the CEO and other administrators, working with a few key board members. They develop the plan and the budget and then present them to the rest of the staff and the board for review and approval. The entire process can be done within several weeks if intensive time can be allocated. The CEO may work alone on the plan and budget and then involve others to review and react to the preliminary draft. Some CEOs take a few of their key people away for two or three days to hammer out a budget and plan for the following year. In very small organizations, this latter process can include all staff as well as board leadership.

- *Participatory:* Wide participation is sought through a process in which staff and board engage in a several-month process of performance analysis, needs assessment, market evaluation, resources requirements, and position appraisal before coming together as a complete or representative group in a retreat or other setting. The overall plan and budget is developed from this basic information, usually by a smaller task force. When completed in draft form, the material is presented at board and staff meetings for review and revision. The process takes several months for annual revision; the first time such a process is done, it may take as long as a year to complete.

Ownership of the plan is a critical success factor in implementation, and can result from either procedure. It is more apt to result with the second. However, if the outcomes of the first process are widely shared, and if feedback is honestly sought and respected, the result can be nearly the same.

There are variations and compromises to both of these processes. The method selected is dependent on the tradition, organizational culture, time constraints, attitude about planning, external urgency to develop a plan (e.g., a potential funder has demanded one), and knowledge of the process.

Time required for the process and the resulting document will vary according to the process used. Some organizations devote nearly a year every three to five years to do a very thorough zero-based process. Although this is a sound approach, the rate of change within our sector may not permit that amount of time. If the plan is kept current on a rolling base, with evaluation and revision done annually to retire the previous year and add a new year, even the zero-based process probably will not require more than a few months. By looking annually at shifts in the marketplace and changes in internal resources and circumstances, the plan maintains its relevance and vitality.

Gaining Support for the Planning Process

Planning for the kind of changes nonprofits are anticipating is very challenging. Funding resources are uncertain. The environment for development and fundraising continues to fluctuate. The position of an organization may change in the community as other similar service organizations thrive or wither. An organization's capacity to fulfill its mission may be dramatically diminished by the loss of a single funding source.

Yet organizations must plan. Some believe it is pointless to plan in a time of rapid change because circumstances shift dramatically and quickly. Plans, when developed through a participatory process and structured to accommodate change, are fluid, dynamic, and owned. A plan is meant to be evaluated, altered, and modified. A plan's validity is in large part determined by the way in which it is used, challenged, and revised.

Involving Board and Staff in Planning

To engage your board and staff in planning, be sensitive to the objections they may have. Such objections are usually drawn from experience at other organizations or yours, or from what has been heard from others about plans and planning. Use the process that is most appropriate for your organization's size, resources, and commitment to the process. The first plan developed by an organization may be done by the executive director with very little assistance, or with full participation by the board or a committee. To emphasize the importance of the plan, be positive about the impact it will have on internal management and external support and understanding. Most important, once the plan is developed, use it. We add fuel to the fire of those who scorn plans when, after considerable effort by 1, 5, or 15 people, the plan is relegated to the shelf, never to be looked at again until it is time to revise it for the following year.

Developing a Plan That Will Work

The planning *process* begins with evaluation of existing plans and budgets and a thorough analysis of the current position and resources of your organization. It also requires a sharp analysis of the marketplace: demand for your services, changes that will have an impact on that demand, and opportunities to which you can respond.

It engages key volunteers and staff and is strengthened by their involvement in review and response sessions or meeting. The goal of the process is to attain ownership by the broadest possible constituency for the plan. The degree to which ownership of the plan is secured is the degree to which commitment to the plan will be gained. Ownership is intensified when the structure of the plan is well presented at the outset of the process and when outcomes and purpose are clear.

Three Levels of Planning and Operation

Plans, and the practices they inform, consist of three different levels of analysis, preparation, and implementation: philosophical, strategic, and tactical.

Vision and mission are the obvious philosophical ingredients of a plan, but do not neglect other beliefs that help form the philosophy of your organization: the importance of volunteerism as the connection between your organization and the community; the value of the nonprofit sector and how it affects the well-being of your community; your understanding of why people give (through your organization to help meet community needs); a commitment to collaboration with other organizations through a belief in the need to fulfill a larger mission in the community; and an understanding of and respect for ethics of the sector and in the organization.

Planning itself is a strategic function, and the parts of a plan that are called "Goals" or "Strategies" are really the strategic heart of the plan. When organizations drill down on the priorities and frame them as goals and strategies, they are identifying what they need to do to act on their philosophical beliefs. Aligned with strategies are systems (communication, management, data tracking, etc.). Systems liberate, and allow organizations to focus on the important, not just the urgent. Systems are also an anchor against mission drift (Chapter 3), providing a clearly defined and understood framework for standardizing routine activities and allowing more time for creative initiative and response.

The tactical level of planning and operation is where the action happens. In the philanthropic arena where results and impact are increasingly demanded by investors, productive and powerful tactics have to be part of every strategic plan. These tactics are described in a plan's objectives and action plans, which are measurable: their success metrics are the principal way that managers and funders evaluate the performance of an organization.

Given these three levels, the ingredients of a completed plan should include:

- Vision
- Mission
- Goals
- Objectives
- Action steps

These components are often confusing, and definitions of each may vary.

There is a difference between mission and vision and a difference between goals and objectives. Action steps are usually not confused with any other part of the plan, and are frequently incorporated into a quarterly timeline produced on a computer program.

The following workable and appropriate definitions for not-for-profit planning are based on experience with many plans and many planning exercises.

Vision

Vision describes the organization's aspiration and the difference it will make in the community. That time may be 5 or 10 years hence. A vision is guided by dreams, not constraints. It is what an organization hopes will happen if its dreams are realized. The founder of an organization that was created to fill in where Head Start was not able to reach in a large Southern city in the United States offered this vision to a large crowd at an awards event: "Our vision is that every child in the greater New Orleans area will be ready when it is time to start school."

Jane Lathrop Stanford, who, with her husband, Leland, founded Stanford University in California in memory of their son, had a very long-term vision for the university that looked beyond the financial hardship and regionalism of the early years: "I could see a hundred years ahead, when all the present trials were forgotten. . . . The children's children's children coming here from the east, the west, the north and the south." She was right. Her inspiring vision has guided the university and was a centerpiece in literature celebrating the university's centennial.

Steve Jobs, cofounder of Apple Computer, had a vision to "reinvent the future." In many ways, he did.

A vision may change with time and circumstances. It is a little-noticed fact that the word "revision"—which is used casually to describe the process for altering or updating plans or policy documents—is re*vision,* which implies that a new vision may be required.

Someone once said that a person with vision is a visionary, but a person who can share a vision is a leader. Similarly, my years of experience have resulted in a belief that there is a fine line between a vision and an obsession—the former can be shared, the latter seldom is. Vision inspires and directs fundraising and development. It is the force that will result in the long-term engagement of donor-investors.

Mission

Mission has two elements: the philosophical expression of the values-based need the orga-nization is meeting in the community (why the organization exists) *and* a brief summary of what the organization is doing to meet that need. The first element is critical for expressing why the organization exists and the vital values to which donor-investors will respond; the second is important as a succinct statement of what the organization is doing to meet the community need. The mission is seldom revised, and it should not go into great detail. Chapter 1 looks more closely at mission and provides several examples.

Goals

Goals summarize the principal program, development, administrative, or other major accomplishments the organization hopes to achieve in order to realize its vision and ful-fill its mission. Goals come from and are validated by the vision. They are very general, not quantified, can be short or long term, and are evaluated annually. Most often, the majority of plan goals carry over for several years with only modest revision. A typical goal for an organization providing meals to the elderly might be: "To provide education and training in proper nutrition to clients receiving in-home meals."

Objectives

Objectives support the goals and provide more details. They are "SMART." This acronym stands for:

Specific: They pertain to a certain task or program.

Measurable: Unlike goals, which are general, objectives are quantifiable (completion date, outcomes, person[s] responsible).

Attainable: They are doable within existing constraints using available human and financial resources.

Results-oriented: They are focused on short-term activities to attain the longer-term goals.

Time-determinate: They include a date by which the task must be completed (or revised)

Objectives should also answer the question: *Who* will do *what* by *when?* An *objective* for the previously stated goal for the elderly would be: "By (month), (year), educational staff to develop a 30-minute nutrition education program, using audiovisual materials and lec-ture format, for pilot delivery at the Washington Street Senior Center site."

Action Steps

Action steps outline what needs to be done so the 30-minute audiovisual and lecture pro-gram will be ready by September. Action steps can be set up as a spreadsheet of tasks and timelines on the computer, or by using special timeline program software available through commercial software outlets. The steps also can be laid out in a simple word-processed timeline that states task, person(s) responsible, date due, and allows for comments (see

Exhibit 10.1). Whatever format is selected, it is important for all people concerned with achieving the objective to know the tasks of the others involved and the dates against which they should work to keep the project on schedule. Action plans should be reproduced, when they are completed, and distributed to each person whose name appears on the plan. It is helpful to highlight the name of each person to whom the plan is being distributed, so each participant can easily see where he or she fits into the total project.

PREPLANNING ANALYSIS

The long-term validity of the planning process and the resulting institutional or development plan will be in large part determined by the comprehensiveness of the preplanning analysis. Just as zero-based budgeting offers organizations opportunities to rethink cost allocations and income from programs and services, there is great value to analysis of the overall organization.

The questions in Exhibit 10.2 are offered as a sample of the kinds of inquiry that may be conducted as part of a planning meeting. They may also be used as "homework" and assigned to task forces of board and staff to prepare for presentation at the first planning meeting. They apply equally well to general institutional and development/fundraising planning.

EXHIBIT 10.1   ACTION PLAN

ACTION PLAN

Date _____ Project _____

Page _____

Task or Responsibility	Responsible Person(s)	Date Due	Date Done	Comments

Results of this analysis, if conducted prior to the planning session, may be written and distributed to those who have a stake in the planning process and the eventual enactment of the plan. The analysis then forms the basis for the planning session. If analysis prior to the planning session is not possible, these questions can be discussed in small groups during the session itself. Each small group reports its findings, and the findings then become a source of guidance and evaluation for goal and objective setting. A planning task force, often appointed at the end of a planning session to take the material from the session and craft it into a first-draft plan, also benefits from revisiting these questions as it pulls the plan into shape.

EXHIBIT 10.2   PREPLANNING ANALYSIS—QUESTIONS AND CONSIDERATIONS

1. Position Analysis

   Evaluate the effectiveness of the current organization. Issues to be considered:
   — What are the most effective programs and activities?
   — Is there any evidence this effectiveness is changing?
   — Do we focus on the areas of most current community need and program potential?
   — What are our major strengths? Weaknesses?
   — How well are we using all of our current resources, especially board, other volunteers, staff?
   — What is our most limiting constraint?
   — How is our overall performance compared to other similar nonprofits?
   — How are we positioned relative to other not-for-profits?
   — Are we well organized and staffed to accomplish our job?
   — Do we adequately involve new volunteers?

2. Marketplace Analysis

   Identify the significant changes we can anticipate in the marketplace, and assess their potential impact on the organization. Issues to be considered:
   — How will our client (or audience) base change in size during the next few years?
   — How will demographics affect our client (or audience) composition?
   — How might the trends and changes in the economy affect our efforts?
   — Are political and social attitudes likely to require modification in our approaches?
   — What new opportunities can we identify?
   — What can we learn from other similar organizations? How can we work more effectively with them?
   — Can we anticipate changes in our major sources of clients/audience?
   — Are there major changes anticipated in sources of earned or contributed revenue?

3. Organizational Development

   Evaluate the adequacy of current activities within the anticipated environment. Assess the need to develop new activities, services, and programs. Issues to be considered:

   (continues)

EXHIBIT 10.2   PREPLANNING ANALYSIS—QUESTIONS AND
CONSIDERATIONS *(Continued)*

— What is the current growth rate of our constituency, and is this rate likely to remain constant? (Note: Constituency includes all those who are currently involved, or have a potential for involvement, as volunteers, participants, donors, clients, etc.)

— How can we achieve greater participation by our constituents in programs and activities?

— What should be done to ensure maximum long-term commitment from present constituents?

— Do we have a well-managed contact process for current constituents?

— Are there better ways to identify and approach constituents than we have been using?

— What are we doing to overcome the weaknesses identified previously?

— What information is needed to help assess the potential of new programs?

— Do we need to test certain program elements before full implementation?

— What new systems for coordination and communication are required by these new programs?

4. Distribution of Resources

Describe the resources (staff, volunteers, funds) required to develop and implement the existing and anticipated programs and activities. Issues to be considered:

— What existing resources are underutilized? Are we using board members effectively and in the area(s) of their expertise that will lead to fulfilling involvement for them?

— Do we have any excess resources (e.g., more volunteers in a certain program than are currently required, funding restricted or assigned to an area that is overfunded)?

— What resource trade-offs can be made to increase and strengthen program and volunteer and staff involvement and satisfaction?

— How should the organization be changed, if at all? What new and different strategies are required to most appropriately manage our resources?

— Do we need some new skills and expertise? Is our board structured to help us meet our long-term goals?

— Can we form specific task forces to address special projects?

— Are our resource requirements comparable to those of other similar organizations?

Putting the Ingredients Together: TRI-POD Planning Process

The TRI-POD process has been used successfully with countless organizations. It takes its name from its three (TRI) elements, which are Program, Organization, and Development. All not-for-profit organizational goals and objectives fall under one of these headings.

- **Program** includes programs and the facilities/equipment used or needed for those programs.

- **Organization** includes staff and board development.

- **Development** includes donor development, fundraising, public relations, and marketing.

Each of these plan components requires goals, objectives, and action plans. All three components will be driven by the vision and mission of the organization and include not only that philosophy or belief framework but also the strategic and tactical approaches that ensure implementation and measurement. The process begins with an exercise or discussion that generates or validates the vision, and goals are drawn from that vision.

The process works best with a representative group of board and staff. For a small organization, it can include all board and all staff; for very large organizations, it can include the board and key leadership staff. For example, a library involved its board and all development staff and department heads. A small community-based organization included not only board and staff, but also clients, auxiliary volunteers, and former board members. At an independent school, faculty, administration, and board were involved. If one of these configurations is not possible for your organization, modify the list of participants to suit your needs and resources.

Resources permitting, an experienced outside facilitator is brought in to guide the planning day. This outsider provides an objective approach, which enables organizations to more easily get through difficult or controversial planning areas. This individual may also work with the organization throughout the entire planning process.

Timing of the Meeting

The planning meeting must be timed to serve the optimum role in the planning process. Three options for the purpose of these meetings are:

1. *To* **initiate the planning process** *with the organization,* particularly if the board and/or staff are new to planning. The meeting is then followed by assignment of task forces to work on the analysis questions and/or refine goals and objectives based on the visioning and goal-generating work completed at the meeting.

2. *To provide an opportunity for some* **group process** *at a point in the overall process* at which internal and market analyses (see above questions) have been completed. Following the meeting, the plan is refined based on the vision and goals.

3. *For some organizations, whose culture or urgency does not permit a lengthy process, the planning day may be the only* **opportunity for consideration of these issues.** Responsibility to prepare the plan is given to the executive director, the process facilitator, or other designated individual(s). When completed, usually on a very short timeline, the plan is presented to the board in draft form for review and approval.

Generating a Vision That Inspires Institutional and Development Planning

All planning should begin with a shared vision. Getting people to discuss vision is not easy. This is particularly true of board and staff members who are very busy, quite task oriented, and perhaps stuck at the tactical level of operation. Because this is a philosophical exercise with strategic implications, some creative work with potentially resistant groups usually overcomes the hurdle and gets them thinking about vision. Organizations that are developing or revising their plans must express or revisit the vision. Asking groups that have been consumed with the day-to-day operations of an organization to suddenly think about a time five or more years hence may require an innovative approach. One of the easiest ways to do this is an exercise that takes about an hour and a half and is fun and productive for everyone. Never has this experience failed to engage even the most skeptical participant.

Participants are provided with a simple scenario. They are asked to work in small groups and to imagine it is the same day and month, but five (or longer) years later. On that date in the future, the local newspaper (or a national or international newspaper or professional journal) has just published an article about the accomplishments of the organization, detailing community impact, outstanding results, principal accomplishments during the time between the present and the future date chosen, board involvement, staff leadership, and so on. The instructions (see Exhibit 10.3) can be open-ended or prescriptive. If too prescriptive, they stifle imaginations. If too open-ended, some participants do not know how to get started. Adapt the model to suit the temper and talent of the participants.

The small groups may be random or designed. It is best to have at least one staff member in each group to provide program information for the board. You may also want to provide the groups with certain facts about the organization. Or the groups can brainstorm from their existing base of knowledge.

Each small group is provided with at least three sheets of easel paper and two colors of pens. Each group chooses a facilitator, who may also be the recorder or may appoint a recorder. The groups are instructed to be creative, to work together as a team, and to bring back to the larger group, after about an hour's brainstorming, their "newspaper article." Invariably, some of the stories will verge on fantasy, and others will lean to the mundane. Some will be illustrated, although not always with publishable art. With all, however, there will be recurring accomplishments, issues, market observations, and headlines. The exercise never fails to involve all participants in developing strong future scenarios for the organization that then become the basis for development and fundraising plans.

Critical Outcomes

Each group presents its vision. Invariably, the common threads among the stories are so remarkable that the organization begins to see the shared dream even through it may not have been voiced in a long while or may never have been expressed. After each group has presented its story, the facilitator reviews all the stories for the recurring visionary ideas.

Participants are asked to identify the "common themes" and the "uncommon ideas," which the facilitator then lists. The scope of each of the planning areas—program, organization, and development—is explained to the participants, and the themes and ideas are then identified as possible goal areas in either "P," "O," or "D." Usually these are easily

THE INSTITUTIONAL VISION

A vision statement summarizes the future that you imagine is possible if your organization achieves its goals. A vision needs to be present and shared if the organization is to move to the next level.

The vision must be shared to be effective. A person with vision is a visionary; one who can share the vision is a leader. Sharing the vision is a daily commitment you make to yourself, your volunteers, and your staff. The vision, like an organization's mission, can inspire and motivate those who work on your behalf. It is also very important in drawing people into a closer relationship with you. People will want to be part of your future. Its focus is on the institution and what it hopes to accomplish.

This example from Stanford University was written by Jane Stanford in 1904 when she and the university were facing financial ruin. It was used extensively in the materials celebrating the centennial of the university.

"I could see a hundred years ahead, when all the present trials were forgotten. . . . The children's children's children, coming here from the East, the West, the North and the South."

ENVISIONING THE FUTURE

It is February 24, 2010. Today's edition of the *New York Times* has an article about [name of organization] and its accomplishments over the past five years. The article begins on page one of the "Lively Arts" section and continues to a second page complete with photographs and sidebar features.

What is the headline? What is the major story the article covers?

What are the accomplishments the story reports? What photographs will be included?

What will the article say about [the organization's] impact? Importance? Artistic accomplishments? Programming emphasis? Its governance? Financial condition? Staff? Community awareness and involvement? Fundraising activities and accomplishments? National recognition?

What will be newsworthy about [the organization's] growth, importance, or activities? What kind of recognition will [the organization] have received from its communities? What new constituencies will have become involved with [the organization]?

These questions are just the beginning for your small-group discussions and are advisory only. Be imaginative, creative, innovative—and stay focused!

Logistics

You will have 45 minutes to prepare your presentation. You should have ready, in that time, a headline, lead for your story, and bullet points covering the principal ideas in the story and the sidebars (features), To ensure accomplishment of your task in the time allotted, be sure to:

1. Appoint a facilitator.
2. Appoint a recorder.
3. Find a reliable timekeeper.

At the end of 45 minutes, each group will have 5 minutes to present its story.

Enjoy!

identified; some of the themes and ideas may receive more than one identifier. Many of the development and fundraising goal areas are implied in the vision (new headquarters, scholarship programs, endowment strength); the program goal areas are usually obvious; and the board and staff organization goal areas may be either implied or stated directly.

The strongest outcomes are the vision and goal areas for development and fundraising. With few exceptions, all program vision requires additional or expanded funding, as does staff development.

From this visioning session, the planning process grows. This early process does not create a "vision statement." Instead, it provides essential baseline information from which program, organization, and development goals will be derived. If your organization desires a vision statement, wait until the end of the planning process and have the chief executive crystallize the dream and the realities into a compelling statement. It will have more validity than trying to generate one through "group think."

Starting the Plan

Having generated some initial goal areas in the visioning process, you may also need to look at the mission statement. Although it is risky to start the planning session by *revising* the mission statement, an affirmation of the statement helps guide the planning process. If participants feel there need to be extensive revisions, identify the areas in question and assign a task force to work with the mission statement and come back to a future board or planning meeting with some draft statements. Entire planning sessions have been derailed by lengthy arguments over the validity, syntax, and meaning of the mission statement. However, at some point, the mission statement has to be reviewed and related to the vision ideas and goal areas that have emerged.

Translating the Vision Ideas into Development and Fundraising Goals

The next step in the exercise moves the vision and initial goal areas into more concrete statements. Depending on the time constraints and number of people involved, evaluation of goals for each of these areas can be done as a full group or in small groups. Or you may wish to focus only on development and fundraising.

Using the vision ideas and preliminary identification of goal areas as a base, but expanding on that material to include other potential areas for growth or accomplishment, generate tentative goals. The purpose of this exercise is to generate as many goals as possible or practical. Prioritization and reduction comes later. If the three areas (program, organization, and development) are discussed and assigned to three separate groups, much overlapping occurs, which will reduce the final number of potential goals. One instruction is essential: Participants should not get tangled up in trying to phrase the goals perfectly. Plan writing comes later. What is more important is to get the ideas down on paper.

The facilitator records the goals if the group works as a whole; if small groups are formed, each group is responsible for recording its proposed goals. These proposed goals are then presented to the entire group. Overlaps are noted and combined (e.g., both program and development may call for the creation of a marketing plan). A relatively simple process can be used once the array of possible goals has been combined and discussed and is ready for prioritization: Each person asked to "vote" for the 5 (or more or less) goals they feel are most important. The fastest way to have people vote is to give each person the correct number of colored dots—5 if they have 5 votes. They vote for the goals they feel are the most important by putting their dots next to the number of the goal. When they are out of dots, they have used all their votes. If you do not like the dot process, you can supply each person with a marking pen, and everyone can vote in the same fashion but by making the standard tick mark next to the goal. People can be limited to using one vote per goal or, in a variation on the process, people can use all their votes on one goal if they want or to apportion them in the way that reflects their priorities for the plan.

When the voting is finished, the votes are counted and goals are put in priority order. Keep the goals in their planning area (e.g., program, organization, development) so the balance in the number of goals can be assessed. If one area seems "short"—or if an important goal has been knocked to a lower order—discuss adding others or raising one or more in priority. Many organizations try to limit themselves in their goals in order to keep the plan manageable and the objectives, which will grow out of the goals, attainable.

Building Objectives from Goals

The agreed-on and prioritized goals are strategic, but they need tactical objectives to come to life. If goals are the "what," objectives are the "how." The language for objectives is often complex, and there is no need for the whole group to be constrained by proper phrasing. Instead, use the "SMART" and "Who will do what by when?" frameworks and have people generate a list of the activities that need to be done to reach the goal. Participants can work together as a whole or in small groups. If working in small groups, engage the same people for the objectives as were involved for the goal-setting.

After these lists of activities or objectives have been generated, the whole group should review them and prioritize them using the same method employed for the goal prioritization. Or the group may decide it has done enough and that a smaller task force can handle the remainder of the exercise.

If these activities cannot be completed in a single planning day, assign the unfinished tasks to appropriate working groups, keep them on a schedule, and have them bring their preliminary plan back to the board when it is ready for review.

Aligning the Budget and Planning Processes

It is difficult and unwise to separate the budgeting and planning processes. The kind of analysis and process that generates a strong plan also inspires a healthy budgeting process. Too often, budgets are created at the last minute by the chief executive with little buy-in from program or administrative staff. Budgets prepared in this way are often viewed as a threat or constraint, rather than as a vital management tool. Budgets that are developed concurrently with an extensive planning process or with an annual plan review and update are seen as requisite companions to the fulfillment of the plan. At a minimum, if not done within a larger institutional planning process, the budget analysis, preparation, and approval sequence should take three to four months, involve both board and staff, and have sufficient opportunities for review and adjustment. Boards and staffs resent budgets that are pushed through against a deadline without time for adequate preparation and review.

A declining but unfortunately still occurring problem regarding budgeting in the not-for-profit sector is the failure to involve the development and fundraising staff sufficiently in the process. When this happens, development offices are informed, after the budget is completed, about how much money they must raise in order to meet the budget. In one instance, the development director for the local branch of a national organization was informed, after the budget was approved, that she would have to raise a figure that represented a 20 percent increase over the previous year. In addition, she was also told that certain major donors on whom she counted for substantial support would not be available to her for solicitation because they were being reserved for a national endowment campaign. Frustrated and feeling out of the management communication loop, she battled for an adjustment on her goal or leniency on the policy relative to the major donors. Both efforts failed, and she resigned.

Involvement of Development Staff in Budget Planning

A realistic assessment of the capacity to fundraise, as part of a deliberate development effort, must play a critical part in the budgeting process. Staff and board volunteers should engage the development director and others responsible for fundraising in the overall analysis for budgeting and planning. The fundraising and development effort should mirror the excitement and vitality of the program vision and goals.

The premise and importance of going beyond fundraising is lodged solidly in the planning process: The development office must stretch, innovate, and work tirelessly to see to it that the programming planned to meet marketplace needs is funded. However, to place unrealistic demands on an office or an individual is to set an organization up for failure. This is why involvement of development staff in the planning and budgeting process is essential. One development director burned herself out and ending up leaving the not-for-profit field for more than a year, after she nearly single-handedly had to mobilize herself, her staff, and the few board members willing to fundraise to increase their fundraising 73 percent over the previous year. This daunting goal was handed to her by the budget committee, and included not only funds for current program support but also over $300,000 in funds for deficit reduction. At no time was she asked whether the staff and volunteer resources could take on this challenge. New to the job, she was determined to meet the goal. She did, but at high personal cost.

Setting Up a Successful Budgeting Process

The best budgeting processes are those that provide broad involvement of staff and volunteers and ample time for program, resources, and marketplace analysis. The preplanning

analysis questions that apply to the larger planning issues (see Exhibit 10.2) may be effectively applied to budgeting as well.

Approaches to Budget Preparation

Zero-Based Budgeting

The most thorough budgeting process is *zero-based budgeting*. In this process the entire
budget is rebuilt periodically to reflect a deep analysis of marketplace needs and the organization's existing and potential resources to meet those needs. It assumes, for the purpose of analysis only, that no funding is assigned to any programs or services in the
organization. The budget is a blank slate. Program directors and staff are required to look
exactingly at their costs, needs, and impact, and to make budget requests based not only
on past practices, but on future requirements.

Program staffs may respond defensively the first time this process is introduced: It is
helpful to have outside consultation to ensure support and understanding of the process.
One organization successfully implemented a zero-based process, after initial resistance,
by bringing in an alumni team from the business school at a local university. This
volunteer team worked capably and correctly with the program staff to assure them that
this process had the same benefit as proper pruning of trees or roses: Building on the same
root stock, the resulting growth would be healthier and fuller than ever before.

When the extensive analysis has been completed for each program, there are meetings
to compare, combine, and adjust the needs from the various departments and programs.
Then, based on earned and contributed revenue projections, the budget begins to evolve.
Revenue and expenses are thoughtfully assessed and assigned to program and administrative areas that have been solidly evaluated through the planning process.

The resulting budget is owned, accurate, and an effective companion to the long-range
or strategic plan. This process does not have to be repeated *in its entirety* every year; every
two or three years is usually often enough, provided there is modest yet careful evaluation annually. This approach to budgeting is far preferable to the approach too often taken
by organizations in which an increment (or decrease) is uniformly applied across the
budget to reflect an increase (or decline) in available or anticipated funding. To require
all programs to reduce expenditures by 5 percent, for example, may be punitive to programs that need to grow to serve clients or audiences. Zero-based budgeting, in conjunction with a planning or plan evaluation process, helps ensure that the organization
will allocate its resources in the area where the market need is greatest. Although zero-
based budgeting may seem to be a threat initially, it is most often respected as a more fair
approach in the long run.

Program Budgeting

A companion to zero-based budgeting in its effectiveness in assigning costs is *program
budgeting*. A line item expense budget is the *framework* for program budgeting. However,
rather than having a lump-sum line for salary, benefits, printing, fundraising, and so on,
for example, each of those expenses is broken out by program and distributed across the
various cost centers of the organization (see Exhibit 10.4). Thus, a children's services

EXHIBIT 10.4 EXAMPLE OF PROGRAM BUDGET EXPENSES

	Administration and/or Development	Child Psychiatry	Counseling	Parenting	Speech Therapy	Occupational Therapy
1. Salaries						
2. Benefits						
3. Travel						
4. Office • phones • postage • etc.						
5. Program, etc.						
Total budet for each program						
Total budget for agency						

agency assigns its various expense lines into child psychiatry, social work, occupational therapy, speech and language therapy, or other program areas. The resulting budget, which has been approached from a zero-based or modified zero-based process, clearly assigns costs to the appropriate program. This benefits the organization in two ways:

1. It is a more effective management tool for monitoring expenses.
2. It is easier to prepare proposals and other program-related information for funders, staff, and volunteers.

Program budgeting permits certain administrative costs to be assigned to program areas, enabling the organization to approach willing funders with proposals that include a certain amount of essential support costs for a particular program.

The budget process integrates with the planning process. Both should be fluid, accessible, and participatory. The resulting budget should fit into and support the plan and be an excellent financial translation of the plan. When the plan is completed and ready to be used to guide internal management and attract external constituents, the budget should also be completed.

Getting the Plan Done

Long-range planning committees are ad hoc committees appointed by the board chair for the purpose of fulfilling a time-determinate task and/or for continued monitoring of the plan. An organization may choose to dissolve the long-range planning committee after the completion of the plan and assign the monitoring function to the executive or finance committee. Continual evaluation is essential to the vitality and usefulness of the plan, so be sure some existing or specially appointed group within the organization accepts that responsibility.

The written plan documents the planning and budgeting process. Final plans vary considerably. Some organizations produce very extensive and complex plans that may run to 100 or more pages with charts, action plans, and other support materials. Other organizations prefer a slender plan in which timelines and even goals and objectives are done in chart form. The style of the plan should reflect the culture and needs of the organization. If an outside consultant has been guiding the process and continues to be involved through the writing of the document, the product may be in a format standard to that consultant.

Whatever the length or complexity of the document, it must have these six elements to be effective:

1. An executive summary, which introduces the document and can be shared with potential donor-investors or volunteers
2. A summary budget as well as the detailed budget
3. A list of the goals for the plan, organized by program (including facilities and equipment), organization (board and staff), and development (donor development, fundraising, marketing, public relations);

4. Measurable objectives, keyed to each of the goals, stating task, person(s) responsible, and date by which the task will be completed

5. Action plans keyed to each of the objectives, giving details about how the particular objective will be accomplished

6. A statement describing the plan evaluation process that will be used (e.g., quarterly reviews, who is involved, who is responsible)

SUMMARY

Although it seems difficult to plan in chaotic times like those we are experiencing, planning has never been more critical. As expectations for accountability, transparency, and disclosure have mounted, a solid institutional plan that includes a strategic development plan is no longer an option; it is a requirement. From a practical management standpoint, it is impossible to be effective in development and fundraising today without an institutional plan to inspire and justify the reasons for inviting community support. When a plan includes a budget that has been developed in a concurrent or companion process of analysis, preparation, and validation, the plan both stabilizes and stretches an organization. Plans that are developed using the TRI-POD method, described in this chapter, are inclusive of program, organization, and development goals and objectives, all of which are based on a careful assessment of marketplace needs and institutional capacity.

Ultimately, the planning process and the resulting document must engage the organization in a way that results in the highest levels of ownership and commitment.

Development is more than a component of the plan. It can be both a driver for its success and a beneficiary of its vision. Success in development and fundraising will ensure the achievement of the organization's long range plan. Likewise, the vision and wisdom of the long range plan will ensure the success of development and fundraising.

NOTE

1. Further information on comprehensive budgeting processes can be found in other Wiley publications. See Jody Blazek, *Financial Planning for Nonprofit Organizations* (1996); Blazek, *Tax Planning and Compliance for Tax-Exempt Organizations,* Fourth Edition (2004); Thomas A. McLaughlin, *Street Smart Financial Basics for Nonprofit Managers,* Second Edition (2002); Edward J. McMillan, *Not-for-Profit Accounting, Tax, and Reporting Requirements* (2003); McMillan, *Model Policies and Procedures for Not-for-Profit Organizations* (2003); and McMillan, *Not-for-Profit Budgeting and Financial Management* (2003).

CHAPTER 11

Beyond Fundraising:
Implementing the Principles

Life "beyond fundraising" is a tantalizing proposition. Those who succeed in transforming their organizations understand both the requirements and the benefits of moving away from an array of isolated and often urgent fundraising activities to an integrated cycle of fundraising that is the natural outgrowth of an effective development process.

Organizations whose volunteers and staff members have mastered the theories and strategies advanced in this book find that fundraising is easier and more rewarding. They understand the interrelationship of philanthropy, development, and fundraising (see Chapter 1). The volunteer and staff leadership of these organizations view fundraising as the process of providing people with opportunities to act on their values. They end up *wanting* to ask for the investment because they see it as the most appropriate way to continually renew the relationship between the donor-investor and the organization.

These leaders also readily confess that there are basic steps to implementing a development program. To a large degree, those steps are dependent on many of the institutional behaviors and resources described in this book.

This chapter describes the proven behaviors and required resources, offers 10 steps that will take organizations "beyond fundraising," presents two organizations that have begun their journey, and concludes with a review of emerging trends in the nonprofit sector that will affect development and fundraising.

IMPLEMENTING THE PRINCIPLES OF THIS BOOK IN YOUR ORGANIZATION

Certain behaviors and resources are needed if your organization wants to go beyond fundraising. Earlier chapters on the philanthropy/development/fundraising relationship, development of the investor attitude (putting away the tin cup), institutional planning for development, the strategic role of stewardship, and the urgency of adherence to mission traced the critical paths organizations must follow to achieve vigorous development practices. There were other requirements as well: commitment to building and maintaining relationships, sound governance practices including board self-assessment and rotation, honest evaluation of systems and personnel, partnerships between board and staff and throughout the organization, a solid business approach to budget preparation and financial management, and an integrated approach to annual and capital fundraising.

The purpose here is not to elaborate on these strategies or requirements, but to restate and underscore their importance and provide some tips to get things started. The intent of this book has been to persuade organizations that they can attain the power and capacity to fulfill their mission and engage their communities when they are committed to developing the behaviors and resources they need to go beyond fundraising.

FIVE BEHAVIORS REQUIRED TO MOVE BEYOND FUNDRAISING

Organizations striving to implement development practices have to consistently encourage five behaviors among board, staff, and committee members and in all education or training about donor and fund development:

1. Acceptance of the values basis of philanthropy, development, and fundraising.
2. Adoption of an investor/investment attitude and retirement of the tin cup in fundraising.
3. Willingness to operate at three levels: philosophical, strategic, and tactical.
4. Belief in donor-centered development and fundraising.
5. Commitment to mission.

1. Acceptance of the Values Basis of Philanthropy, Development, and Fundraising

Healthy nonprofit organizations know, believe in, and manifest their core values. Often affirmed in published mission-vision-values declarations, these statements have an impact on employees and volunteers as well as on prospects, donors, and other community partners.

They are the context for institutional pride and for community relationship building and frame the case for inviting and retaining investment. Volunteer and staff partners in a successful development process take those statements one step further: They master the ability to tell the story of the organization and its impact and tie those stories back into the core values of the organization. In telling the story of one child who benefits from a therapeutic day care program for emotionally disturbed youngsters, they suggest the impact those benefits have on all 600 children and their families served by the organization. They also convey the organization's belief in children and their potential for growth. In describing the long-term impact of a scholarship program on one student whose life was changed, the core educational values of an independent school are understood in the implicit understanding of the transformation of all scholarship students. Translation of core values into actual program benefits is a key behavior. Organizations must continually articulate and reinforce those values through these activities:

- Annually, at the board retreat, reaffirm the core values of the organization through brainstorming and discussion.

- Reflect those values in all written materials to the extent possible and appropriate.

- Coach board members and other volunteers in how to tell the story of the impact the organization is having on the lives of those they serve.

- Express the values as the foundation of all practices.

- Prevent the erosion of values practices into hollow statements not reinforced by practices.

- Reflect the accomplishments of the organization within a values context that reinforces the donor-investor's motivation.

Belief in the importance of core values in donor-investor motivation leads to an increased respect for each contributor. Donor-investors are understood to be acting on their values when they make a gift. The gift, the giver, and the process of inviting investment are approached with more appropriate phrases and attitudes. Phrases like "arm twisting," "hitting him up," and others that imply an aggressive organization and an unwilling donor disappear from the development vocabulary of the organization. Instead, it is remembered that each gift reflects the donor's values and is a piece of the giver's self. Each gift is a symbol of the relationship, and renewal of an investment is really renewal of the relationship. These realizations create and maintain a higher level of respect that is a catalyst for solidifying the relationship.

2. Adoption of an Investor/Investment Attitude and Retirement of the Tin Cup in Fundraising

As an outcome of values-based development and fundraising, the investor/investment attitude (see Chapter 2) influences all interaction with donor-investors. It is also extended to volunteers who participate in program and development activities. When regarded and treated like investors, donors and volunteers view themselves increasingly as critical partners in the long-term capacity of the organization to provide and perform.

Fund, donor, and volunteer development are most effective when the invitation to give or join is extended without apology or desperation. Unfortunately, the posture of organizations that still conduct an array of unrelated fundraising activities *without* the larger context of development and philanthropy is one of "urgency": not the urgency of the need that is being met (children's services, school scholarships), but the organization's compelling need for money or volunteers. This latter philosophy leads to a tin cup approach and an implicit apology for "needing" money or volunteers. Nonprofit organizations need both, but only because of the community needs they are meeting. Nonprofits provide donor-investors with a vehicle for investing in community programs. Gifts come *through* an organization into the community. Our accountability is multilayered: how well we manage gifts, how well we manage programs, and how well we manage results. Retirement of the tin cup requires a reversal in traditional attitudes about fundraising and volunteer involvement.

There is every reason to believe that the tin cup has been retired by nearly all successful nonprofits. Where pockets of resistance remain—in some public broadcasting membership appeals on-air and via mail, with some social service agencies hard hit by government cutbacks, with arts organizations that have seen their funding and audiences erode, and with international agencies dealing with critical issues of terror, natural disasters, hunger, and war—the hope remains that expectations of donors to be treated and talked to like social investors eventually will mean that the begging language and focus on organizational needs will disappear from our vocabulary and practices.

3. Willingness to Operate at Three Levels: Philosophical, Strategic, and Tactical

This behavior can boost the organization's capacity to go beyond fundraising because it requires volunteers and staff to examine nonprofit planning, governance, and development as complex and interrelated processes. The philosophical level, too often ignored by organizations rushing to raise a dollar, provides the values analysis needed to create a solid platform for board and fund development and a compelling case for support and is the basis for strategic planning. It is the platform for creating a vision that embraces the community as well as the organization. Thoughtful evaluation of the organization's beliefs isolates core values and assists organizations in presenting their case to potential donors. This is the level at which we evaluate and communicate mission and use it as the ultimate decision maker at critical junctures. Philosophical commitment to volunteerism and stewardship are translated into strategic goals and tactical plans that build the organization's capacity to implement strong development practices.

Strategic planning, conducted in an environment where philosophical issues have been clarified, is more productive. The strategies that emerge are solidly grounded in shared beliefs, and the common understanding of volunteers and staff members leads to ownership and implementation. Finally, at the tactical level, there is energy and commitment to get the job done. Action plans, derived from strategies based in philosophical consensus, are inspired and driven by a sense of commitment to mutual goals.

This trilevel framework, applied to crucial management areas of the organization, helps create an integrated and powerful plan that leads to better management and attracts more investors.

4. Belief in Donor-Centered Development and Fundraising

If there is one thing we have learned during the last decade, it is that the donor, not the institution, is the center of all development transactions. Development and fundraising practices should be developed with this in mind, especially cultivation, solicitation, and stewardship. This belief is reflected in every transaction we have with prospects and donors beginning with the initial personal contact. However, even direct mail, if properly segmented to target specific constituencies for acquisition or renewal, can show a donor-centered focus. It is in the establishment of personal relationships with donors and volunteers that this emphasis on the donor becomes so important. The definition of "donor" extends to volunteers as well. They are major donors of time, even when their gifts may be at a lower than major level.

As an institutional philosophy, the view of the donor-investor as the center of all development transactions is one of the most important. As an institutional strategy, it is vital. And, at the tactical level, it is constantly evaluated by the best test market of all, the donors themselves. Their excitement and commitment increase as their sense of partnership and importance grows. Cultivation, solicitation, and stewardship of donors are most effective when the focus is on them.

5. Commitment to Mission

This behavior influences the first four. Commitment to mission has to be a given in the nonprofit sector. We often speak of our sector as "mission-based." We discuss programs in the context of "consistency with the mission," and we applaud organizations that are able to raise the funds to "fulfill their mission."

The mission statement is the expression of the organization's mission, and the initial creation and occasional revision of the statement is a priority task for board and staff leadership. Mission statements may be agreed to or quarreled about, and sometimes remain unfinished due to lack of consensus and highly charged emotions. What is ultimately more important than the statement itself is a commitment to the institution's *understood* mission by the board and staff and its integration into practices. For development to flourish, the understood mission should reflect the institution's core values and clearly state what needs the organization is meeting in the community.

Keeping the commitment to mission fresh is the true challenge in going beyond fundraising. We meet this challenge by:

- Planning a time at every board meeting for recipients or beneficiaries of services to give a 10-minute presentation (mission moment) about the impact of those services on their lives and/or on the community
- Reaching agreement on a statement of mission that is clear, crisp, and compelling
- Ensuring that all printed materials for general or fundraising purposes reflect the core values and mission of the organization
- Engaging board and staff leadership in strategic discussions at least annually about consistency of mission and program and how well the two are aligned
- Using the understood or written statement of mission as the basis for making key new program decisions

- Informing constituents through publications, electronic communications, and personal interaction about the mission and core values, and how their support enables the organization to advance the mission

- Keeping key decision makers in the community, including civic leaders and funders, informed about the importance of the mission to the community and why investment in the organization is an investment in a better community

These five key behaviors are the foundation for a strong development program. When complemented by three additional resources, discussed next, organizations are better able to go beyond fundraising and establish an effective development program.

Three Resources Required to Go Beyond Fundraising

The resources required for a successful development program are:

1. People (internal and external)
2. Budget
3. Plan

Seemingly simple, these three resources are broadly inclusive.

People

Ours is a people business. People are an essential component in the development equation and include board and other volunteers, staff at all levels and in all departments, prospects, donors, community members, and all those who have a stake in your mission or organization. Chapter 4 explores the development partnership and its inclusiveness.

For development programs to work effectively, people have to be involved. Getting and maintaining their involvement, and growing their commitment, depends largely on the degree to which the behaviors discussed in the last section are manifested in the organization. The commitment of people both inside an organization and in the community grows when they perceive:

- The institution's core values and the role these values play in decision making
- An investor/investment attitude toward donors and volunteers, and the partnership that attitude implies
- A comprehensive approach to planning and to the analysis and resolution of issues
- A sincere focus on donors or volunteers in all development transactions
- A commitment to mission that influences all program and development decisions

Budget

Organizations cannot implement a true development program without adequate resources to fund long-term prospect, donor, and volunteer relations. As observed in Chapters 1 and 10, budgeting for development is always more difficult than budgeting for fundraising.

Fundraising activities (annual and major gifts, capital campaigns, fundraising events) are easily tracked by revenue, expense, and net gain analyses. Development activities (cultivation, stewardship, recognition, and acknowledgment) are often not quantifiable. The causes and effects are more difficult to relate. When budgets are trimmed, the dollars assigned to activities without immediate measurable impact are the first to be cut. To ensure the most successful fundraising, organizations must invest in development. It is the function that sustains the organization over time. More important, development is the function that builds lasting relationships with people whose time and financial resources ensure the future of the organization.

Plan

Development planning can be effective only if there is a comprehensive long range strategic institutional plan in place. Chapter 10 focused on institutional planning. Not enough can be said about the importance of having a solid plan in place. Funders are not nearly as interested in an organization's development plan as they are in the institutional vision, goals, and objectives. Fundraising and development do not drive programs; programs drive fundraising and development. A development plan without an institutional plan guiding its priorities may have internal tactical value, but its strategic and philosophical structure will be frail. Funders invest in organizations because they see ways to partner in the solution of a problem or in providing a service or enhancement to the community. Only the institutional plan can convey that bigger picture.

Volunteers and staff responsible for the development function in an organization must persuade reluctant administrative or board leadership of the importance of institutional planning, and ensure that the document that emerges is owned by the staff and volunteer leadership. Sometimes getting a plan done where there is initial or lingering opposition takes a fair dose of courage (see Chapter 3). The quandary often distills to questions that are both troublesome and enlightening: Is it more important to keep a job, or do a job? Is our behavior more mission-oriented or job-oriented? There are several known instances of development staff and volunteers who eventually separated from an organization because of staff executives or board leaders who simply refused to plan.

The process of planning is a healthy catalyst for organizations as they resolve institutional priorities and goals. However, it is the plan itself that provides concrete guidance for staff, volunteers, and funders about how their investments of time and money will advance the organization's mission and meet the community's needs.

These behaviors and resources are the tools for creating a high-impact development program. They are the foundation for successful implementation of the 10 steps organizations must take to go beyond fundraising.

PREPARING TO TAKE AN ORGANIZATION BEYOND FUNDRAISING

Engagement of key internal and external constituents is the key to successful implementation of the steps that will take your organization beyond fundraising. There is a need to market the development function internally to staff and board and to market the impact of your nonprofit among your community constituencies.

Internal marketing of the development function should be a primary task for all development professionals and board leaders. Organizations benefit greatly when internal education through presentations at meetings, "good newsletters" e-mailed or circulated to staff, special mailings or e-mails to board members and other volunteers, and diligent reporting of progress and results leads to these levels of understanding and advocacy for development and moves organizations toward a culture of philanthropy:

- Program staff who understand the impact of development and fundraising, and their role in it

- Board members who realize there is a role for them to play in development even if they are still reluctant to make a face-to-face ask

- Nonprofit executives and administrators who honor the development process by guaranteeing budget allocations for cultivation and stewardship activities whose impact may be impossible to measure until long after that budget has been retired, and who convey to all staff that development is an institutional priority

- Nonboard volunteers who view development as a highly rewarding activity in which they can play many supportive roles

- Major donors who feel like participants and investors, and who readily see and can explain their "return on investment"

External marketing of the impact of your nonprofit in the community is also an essential step in going beyond fundraising.[1] Until potential and actual donor-investors realize they are investing in results, not needs, and that their investment in your organization is really an investment in the community, they cannot know fully the power of partnering with an institution to act on common values. We must be consistent in our messages. We must be relentless in letting people know the impact of what we do, how their time and gifts have made those accomplishments possible, and why their continued role as donor-investors is the one sure way to guarantee the continued value of their involvement.

On the strong foundation of an educated internal and external constituency, nonprofits can build organizations that go beyond fundraising to achieve new levels of impact and effectiveness.

10 STEPS TO TAKE AN ORGANIZATION BEYOND FUNDRAISING

The following 10 steps are provided with an implicit understanding that the previously described behaviors and resources must be present. The responsibility for carrying them out falls to the partnership of volunteers and staff that is the basis of all successful development endeavors.

The 10 steps that will take organizations beyond fundraising are:

1. Assess
2. Evaluate
3. Plan
4. Recruit
5. Inspire
6. Persuade
7. Engage
8. Involve
9. Retain
10. Renew

1. Assess

A perceived need for change must exist before a commitment to evaluate and possibly redesign systems for fundraising and development can occur. Assess board composition, communication, function, practices, and understanding of fundraising and development. Excellent self-assessment instruments are available through BoardSource (formerly the National Center for Nonprofit Boards) in Washington, D.C. Their board self-assessment sets the standard in the field.

Assess materials and community image. Conduct client, donor, and community surveys to obtain feedback about programs and messages. Surveys and focus groups are valuable tools for gaining this information. Thankathons and phone appeals also provide opportunities to ask donors and prospects a few key questions. Volunteers who make personal calls to enlist or solicit community members often receive feedback that should be passed along to the organization. A form or other mechanism for easily transmitting that information helps ensure that it is conveyed.

2. Evaluate

When the assessment is complete, evaluate it. Figure out what it means. What are the implications for board recruitment? Board training? Capacity of the organization to convey the investor attitude? How inclined is the board to move into a development program? If there is reluctance to fundraise, what will the organization do to overcome that? Assessment without evaluation of the results is virtually meaningless: It is the assessment that provides the data for the plan, but it is evaluation that makes those data useful.

Use information obtained from focus groups or surveys to enhance programs, materials, client services, or outreach. Are our donors satisfied? Is our stewardship working? Are our programs meeting critical needs? Do our publications convey our mission and values? Are our fundraising letters and materials free of apology, and do they project accomplishment and results? Does our mission statement really convey our mission?

Evaluation feedback is less threatening to staff and volunteers when both the content and methodology of assessment and reporting is explained beforehand and when the use of the data is made clear.

When setting out to gather information, be sure to have a system developed prior to the assessment that will guide the evaluation of the feedback. If the data are to be computerized, set up the program before the data start coming in. If there is to be a board, committee, or staff report with manually prepared data presentation, familiarize people with the format and purpose of the presentation before it is made.

3. Plan

Chapter 10 addresses the process of institutional planning as well as its relationship to the development and fundraising process. Planning is vital to successful organizations. Funders demand it and internal management practices require it. Vision, goals, objectives, and action planning depend on strong assessment and evaluation for their development. The institutional plan is a tool for building community support and investment. It inspires the plan for development and fundraising, a largely internal document that focuses on ways to bring the community into partnership with the institution's vision and goals.

4. Recruit

With assessment and evaluation informing a solid institutional plan, the recruitment of the board, other volunteers, and staff is conducted with much more knowledge of the community, the organization, and the needs of both. Recruitment of volunteers and staff needs a well-understood framework. Policies and procedures for recruitment, job descriptions that convey desired behaviors as well as responsibilities, and the capacity to clearly communicate expectations are the three key aspects of successful recruitment (see Chapter 3).

Recruitment is the first step in building a development team. It involves mutual exploration on the part of the organization and the potential employee or volunteer. It is a time of inquiry and investigation that may or may not result in a hire or an enlistment. Recruitment—or cultivation—of prospective donors is a similar function. To the degree that it can be systematized with solid policies and procedures, it will be more effective. Recruitment should never feel rushed. Decisions should not be made in haste, nor should procedures be set aside for fear of losing a candidate. The old adage about acting in haste and repenting at leisure is particularly true in nonprofit organizations that find themselves with board members or staff managers whose organizational fit or commitment is lacking, or with donors who were solicited prematurely. Too many organizations end up having to deenlist—or endure—board members, buy out contracts of key staff people who were hired in haste because of a sense of urgency, or know disappointment from a solicitation that missed the mark because they felt pressured to enlist, hire, or ask. Be patient with the recruitment (and cultivation) process, and be sure your criteria for the process are not compromised by internal or external pressure.

5. Inspire

Expose recruited board and staff candidates, and potential donors, to the inspirational aspects of your organization. Arrange tours. Let them observe programs, if appropriate, or see a video that describes the programs. Introduce them to staff people. Set up meetings with those who have benefited from the services of the organization. If candidates are equally inspired by financial stability (and if you are financially stable), schedule a time for meeting with the business manager or investment consultant. Bring them to board meetings. If your board meetings are not inspiring, alter the format and emphasis so they become more interesting not only to recruits, but to those already enlisted or hired. With potential donors, involve them on committees that have a mission-related purpose (marketing, program, development). Be prepared to answer tough questions, but make the mission manifest through opportunities to intersect with inspirational people and programs.

6. Persuade

Once recruited and inspired, excellent donor, volunteer, and staff candidates need to be persuaded. Nonprofits cannot assume that their mission, integrity, or values are obvious. Those involved in donor, board, and staff development must explain, listen, present, respond to objections and be well equipped with compelling evidence of the organization's impact. Board members and other volunteers involved in enlistment and solicitation must be able to tell the story of the organization in a way that relates to the perceived needs of the potential staff member, volunteer, or donor. Persuasion is not manipulation. It is based on a real connection between values and opportunities. Persuasion is not deliberately forceful. It becomes powerful when like minds link around shared values and goals. Strong boards, energized staffs, and solid ranks of donor-investors share one principal motivation: They are persuaded of the value and impact of the organization to which they offer their time, careers, and money.

7. Engage

A more powerful function than enlistment, *engagement* implies a deeper involvement. When organizations truly engage a volunteer, employee, or donor, they are adding another partner to the development process. Informed, inspired, and aware of the role they can play in advancing the organization, people enter into the engagement with standards that are taken seriously. Expectations are clearly stated. Implications for sustained involvement are conveyed. This is a powerful moment for the individual and for the organization.

8. Involve

Once engaged, the involvement deepens. Engagement is the "click," or connection, and may be emotional in its root. Involvement allows people to strengthen that sense of engagement. Although some involvement is the natural result of increased exposure to the organization, there needs to be deliberate involvement as well. Continual matching of skills and interests with opportunities leads to a growing sense of involvement with an organization. Understanding the motivation of staff, volunteers, and donors is a key component in successful deployment for development. Listening is the key strategy for identifying motivation and increasing involvement. Find out what ignites a person's enthusiasm. Connect people with other people and programs that will encourage their motivation. Get people involved in projects and programs that provide satisfaction. The benefits will astound you.

9. Retain

Carefully recruited, properly persuaded, strongly engaged, and appropriately involved people will stay with your organization. They will continue their employment, serve their board or committee terms, and keep renewing their gifts. The formula is simple; its implementation is sometimes difficult. Changes in leadership, problems within the organization deriving from shifts in external or internal priorities, and the impact of major campaigns or programs on organizational stability can interfere with even the best-intentioned desire to retain the people who are key to the organization. One way to head off devastating loss of employees, volunteers, or donors in times of change is to maintain open, honest, and direct communication. Talk about the issues as they arise. Meet with employees, board members, and donors. Hear their ideas about strategies for getting through difficult times. Listen to their concerns. Mobilize their energy toward positive solutions. Be willing to implement their suggestions. Honor their efforts to resolve the problem even if their ideas are not used. Give feedback on progress toward solving the problem. Be accessible. Trust is a crucial element in retention of employees, volunteers, and donors. Trust them, and be trustworthy. Organizations that survive crises are those that take time and effort to maintain relationships with their partners and investors. They are also the organizations that sustain development practices even in times of perceived urgency.

10. Renew

We focus a lot of energy on renewing gifts; our real efforts, however, need to be on renewing *relationships.* The gift is the symbol of the relationship. Development is the process of uncovering shared values and of growing relationships. These relationships must continually be renewed through outreach, recognition, stewardship, and appropriate involvement. In the quest to renew gifts and relationships, volunteers and staff should not forget the importance of self-renewal. Taking time to attend a conference, meet with other volunteers or staff, observe a program at a similar organization, read a relevant book, or just revisit the programs at your own organization can be very renewing. Combined with enough exercise and sleep (often neglected during busy times), these renewing activities can help ensure that the other kinds of renewal stay on track.

These 10 steps will set your organization solidly on the path toward development. Two short case studies illustrate the mechanism and benefits of implementing a development program.

TWO CASE STUDIES: GOING BEYOND FUNDRAISING

The first case involves a social service organization that successfully completed an ambitious capital campaign in spite of the fact that, at the outset, it had few volunteers, little board involvement, a largely undeveloped donor base, no major donors, and a very small staff.

The second involves a state-licensed public telecommunications station that has recently begun its major giving program. It is doing a great many things right, things that will eventually take it beyond fundraising.

CASE STUDY

THE SAN FRANCISCO FOOD BANK

In 1993, a venerable but largely unknown organization, the San Francisco Food Bank, a supplier of food to more than 300 meal-providing agencies in San Francisco, wanted a new warehouse. The first significant behavioral shift by board and staff was the realization, with coaching, that the *food bank* did not need a new warehouse: The *community* needed a new warehouse to help solve the problem of hunger in San Francisco. The food bank was the vehicle for meeting this community need. The existing warehouse could no longer adequately supply the 300+ meal-providing agencies. Further, available food was going to waste because of the inadequacy of freezer, refrigeration, and shelf-storage space. Although 7 million pounds of food were processed each year, a larger warehouse would permit the storage and distribution of 13 million pounds a year.

Principal visibility for the food bank was among corporations whose employees participated in seasonal food drives. Several prominent professional athletes had also lent their names and endorsement for food drives. The barrels for collecting food were visible at major grocery stores and events, particularly at holiday times. An excellent newsletter, "Give and Take," related stories of the impact of the food bank on agencies and individuals.

Financially, the organization was stable. Fiscal management was prudent, drawing admiration and support from corporations and individuals. It was the rigorous financial management that drew the initial investor in the campaign, and it was the integrity of the staff leadership that drew the volunteer who leveraged several very large gifts. An executive director and a development director, with lean staffs, worked with a dedicated program staff and array of volunteers, many of whom were beneficiaries of feeding programs supplied by the food bank.

The board experienced high turnover during the planning and early phases of the campaign. It was a time of sorting out priorities, and many felt a campaign for $5 million would be too significant a drain on their time and financial resources. For a period of time, board membership was low. Care was exercised in the recruitment of new board members, and the board was slowly rebuilt, using policies and procedures based on a recruitment matrix.

(continues)

The campaign steering committee, comprised principally of board leaders with key staff, other community volunteers, and the consultant, planned the campaign. A feasibility study, funded at great sacrifice by the organization, was a good investment. It identified potential funding sources, provided information for building the case statement, marketed the program for the first time to several corporate, foundation, and individual constituency groups, and provided the basis for initial discussions with the eventual lead funders. The lead funder had been identified prior to the feasibility study: a corporation that provided its chief executive officer as co-chair of the community committee for the campaign, an outright six-figure gift, and in-kind services in site identification, preparation, and project management.

The campaign got off to a slow start. Difficulty in identifying the right site was finally resolved through the donation of a suitable piece of land, perfectly located. The donation was nearly a year in coming, during which time groundwork for soliciting other gifts was prepared. A community committee was enlisted, and an informational (and inspirational) meeting of the committee was held at the food bank on a rainy day that revealed clearly the leaky roof and the generally inadequate facility.

Significantly, in support of the principles of development, was the connection of the agency with an individual in the community who had no previous knowledge of or involvement with the food bank. Identified early in their planning as someone who might be interested or helpful, he was persuaded, engaged, and became involved. His efforts resulted in the leveraging of more than $1.2 million from corporations and foundations, and he and his wife also made a significant personal gift to the campaign. The relationship was based on mutual respect, on the expertise the volunteer could provide in several areas, on the volunteer's respect for the integrity and impact of the organization, and on the enthusiasm of the steering committee leadership. They sought the volunteer's advice long before they asked for his assistance in raising money, and they listened to his cautions.

Once the land was secured and the community committee was in place, the campaign got under way. At that time a campaign manager was added, who worked under the direction of the development director and monitored aspects of training, stewardship, cultivation, donor relations, and fundraising. Large gifts from corporations, local government, and foundations and an anonymous gift from an individual rocketed the total from under $500,000 to nearly $4.5 million in one year. The remaining funds were generated with the help of two challenge grants, and involved many more individual and smaller donors, including the regular donors to the food bank's annual giving programs.

Elapsed time for the campaign was more than three years, with the highest activity during the last 18 months. The campaign had, as its goals, the successful accomplishment of the financial target *but also* increased visibility and an expanded donor base. All the goals will be met.

A campaign is not necessarily the best vehicle for going beyond fundraising. Usually the pieces must be in place before a campaign begins. In this case, the food bank successfully assembled the bicycle while riding it and integrated the behaviors and resources while taking the steps. It followed all 10 steps in the development process (Chapter 5) and was successful in involving people internally and externally in the project. One of the major gifts was brought in through the connection of a program staff person, who felt like a part of the development team and wanted to see the project succeed. The co-chair of the community committee leveraged the donation of the site. The co-chairs also solicited numerous corporate gifts. An accounting firm in San Francisco "adopted" the food bank and vowed to leverage its $25,000 gift into $250,000 by soliciting other companies and individuals.

Budget for the campaign, while kept modest, was well placed. The consultant's pre-campaign study led to her continued involvement on an ad hoc basis. Materials were kept to "desktop" format until the campaign went public. At that time, an advertising agency provided pro bono services for theme and materials development. The theme was based on an assessment done by the food bank, known as the hunger study. The study showed that the biggest problem in resolving hunger was food distribution: having a warehouse that was adequate for processing. Materials for the campaign had this enticing opening: "People are hungry. There's plenty of food. So, what's the problem?"

Volunteers and funders alike perceived the core values of the organization. An investor/investment attitude characterized all transactions with volunteers and donors, and any sense of tin cup fundraising was dispelled when they found the eager acceptance of the impact they were having in the community. They could speak with conviction about their results and invite investment in a future that would address the issue of hunger even more powerfully.

In the process of designing and implementing the campaign, they wrestled with philosophical issues around the involvement of volunteers, the necessity of training and planning, and the allocation of resources to this fundraising effort. Resolved, these were the backbone of the eventual campaign plan, the public announcement of the campaign, and the kinds of stewardship and recognition provided. The needs, expertise, and involvement of potential and actual donors became the focus of planning strategies and events. And, in all, the commitment to mission was the motivator.

The campaign was a success, but the people of San Francisco were the true winners. Now, nearly nine years since the new food bank was completed, they are processing nearly 18 million pounds of food a year and distributing to more than 400 agencies. The need for food distribution in San Francisco has continued to increase, and the San Francisco Food Bank is facing new decisions regarding expansion. The facility is straining to keep up with the demands, and discussions are under way about how to address the continued need. The executive director, who continues to inspire his staff and the community with his leadership, will go forward with an expansion if that is the decision, and rely on the same principles that guided the success of the first campaign.

NEBRASKA EDUCATIONAL TELECOMMUNICATIONS—NET

In the spring of 2004, an initial group of 80 public television licensees signed up to participate in a major giving initiative funded by the Corporation for Public Broadcasting (CPB). A second group of licensees enrolled in the autumn of 2004, bringing the total number enrolled to 114. Built on the recommendations of a study conducted by McKinsey and Company, management consultants, the program involved stations in curriculum and site-based visits from consultants and had multiple goals:

- To increase the percentage of station revenue coming from major gifts (defined in most stations as gifts greater than the highest membership level of $1,000)
- To increase the median gift size
- To develop consistency in messaging across all programs and platforms in the station's development and community marketing
- To position stations as "more than broadcasters"—that broadcasting (or other means of sending out programs and information) is not *what* public television does, but is *how* public television does what it does
- To create resources that would allow public television to produce more local programming and create more local partnerships
- To develop an integrated development plan focusing on "pipeline" programs (pledge, membership at all levels, special events) as the avenue for creating the relationships with donors that would lead to major giving
- To refocus public television on a case for support that inspires investors through its focus on mission (why), vision (for the community) and values

Another key aspect of this program was to encourage stations to build relationships with their members. Research conducted by TRAC Media, a firm widely relied on by public broadcasting, had yielded an anecdote that became a challenge for all stations. A lapsed public television member was asked by TRAC interviewers to say what it would take for her to become a member again. Her answer was, They would have to show me that they know me. With that as a call to action, here is the story of how one public television station is building the base for a new era in its fundraising.

Nebraska Educational Telecommunications had developed a major giving program prior to participating in the Major Giving Initiative but joined the CPB-sponsored program to gain additional training, resources, and support. For all public television stations, the shift away from traditional heavy reliance on transactional giving (pledge, membership, events) to development of relationship-based transformational giving (major and planned gifts) has required key changes in resource allocations (staffing and budget) and approach to the overall development process. For Nebraska, the changes had already begun, but participation in the program allowed the station to refine its practices and develop a new vocabulary based on these beyond fundraising principles:

- Gifts to NET were really gifts to the community, given through NET.
- Meeting community needs, not its own needs, was the real reason to invite investment.
- Development is about the investor, not about the organization.

Operating on these key principles, NET launched several programs that have proven the validity of these ideas and have led to a commitment by the station to increase its emphasis on major giving and on the integration of its other development programs into a seamless donor-focused process.

History of NET

What is now known as Nebraska Educational Telecommunications (NET) is one of the oldest public broadcasting networks in America, celebrating 50 years of "service to Nebraska" in 2004. Earnest beginnings in the mid-50s produced immediate results. By 1960, NET was producing instructional television in six Nebraska school districts which had incorporated as the Nebraska Council for Educational Television (NCET). By the 1980s, the School Telelearning Service (STS) offered more than 150 instructional television programs to teachers across Nebraska, and by the 90s the educational programming reflected a changing community and the opportunities presented by new technology.

But this was only one side of the picture. In the 1970s, NET launched what would become one of Public Broadcasting Service's (PBS) most respected public television (and later public radio, with the development in the late 1970s of a statewide NPR network) resources. Proud of being the source for national public broadcasting programming, yet equally determined to produce local/statewide programs of distinction, they have done both. An early NET production, "Anyone for Tennyson" premiered on PBS in 1976. Today, NET is a network of public television and radio stations serving all of Nebraska, as well as the permanent site for Native American Public Telecommunications, a consortium funded by the Corporation for Public Broadcasting.

Fundraising at NET

Fundraising was the usual mix of pubic broadcasting strategies: on-air pledge drives, direct mail, special events. Friends' groups were formed (Nebraskans for Public Television, Inc. (NPTV) and Public Radio Nebraska Foundation, Inc (PRNF) and giving levels established. The Jack G. McBride Society is comprised of approximately 220 individuals and organizations that give $1,000 or more to the Jack G. McBride Funds for Excellence providing vital annual support for programming and educational services that enrich the lives of Nebraskans. In addition, there is also a Friends of the Future Society, recognizing approximately 60 donors who have established bequests and other planned gifts to an endowment through Nebraskans for Public Television and/or Public Radio Nebraska Foundation.

On their own, several years before the implementation of the Major Giving Initiative by CPB, they began to look seriously at what it would take to build a more engaged constituency and more depth in their major giving. When the opportunity to join the CPB Major Giving Initiative came along, they felt it would provide them with the resources they would need to keep what they had begun moving forward. It has.

While their early efforts at major and planned giving were significant, the President and General Manager of NET felt more and more that they were not reaching out into the

(continues)

community sufficiently to build a base of increasingly engaged members and friends who would perhaps make ever larger gifts. With that realization came the knowledge that to do so he would have to do some internal rebalancing of staff and budget, cutting back on some of the more traditional funding programs to focus limited resources on relationship building and major giving. That in itself would be a challenge, but there was a deeper issue as well—one that tied production and fundraising together in a very traditional way. Production practices were very "internal"—concept, funding, and actual production were generated by people inside the station and then revealed to the viewing public as a fait accompli. There was little community involvement in productions, except as viewers who provided feedback after the production was done. This realization, coupled with the recognized need to engage more people with the station in ways that would build strong relationships, laid the platform for a hugely successful project that has been the tipping point for NET in its community outreach and focus on relationship building.

The Canteen Spirit

During World War II, millions of men and women in the armed services criss-crossed the United States by train. On their way to be deployed, or furloughed or go home, their journey was "dull, lonely, dirty." On December 17, 1941, just 10 days after the attack on Pearl Harbor and the declaration of war, a train was due to arrive at the Union Pacific railroad depot in North Platte, Nebraska, filled with men from Company D of Nebraska National Guard. Showing their support for these men and the war, more than 500 residents of North Platte showed up at the train station, bringing gifts, cakes and other food. But it was a case of mistaken identity: the train had a load of servicemen and women from Kansas. Initially disappointed and thinking they would take the food and gifts home, the residents of North Platte instead gave what they had brought to the people on the train, and thus began a "canteen" that would, between that date and April 1, 1946, serve more than 6 million service people with cake, coffee, hospitality and encouragement.

The North Platte Canteen story is about America's heartland extending its heart. It is one of leadership, humanity, superb organization by a dauntless group of women, fundraising ($30,000—they think it would take $1.3 million to do the same thing today) and sheer will to keep the canteen going "24/7" for nearly five years. It is the story of 20 birthday cakes a day (600 a month!) and of 40,161 cookies, 30,000 hardboiled eggs and 6,000 donuts in the month of March, 1945 alone. It is the story of meeting 23 trains and 3,000 to 5,000 personnel each day for 10 minutes, during which time the travelers received food, big band music and admiration. It is also the story of 55,000 volunteers who never missed a train from east or west. The women created a board, got organized, and called it their "war council" and their "army of volunteers."

By the summer of 1942, they were completely organized, with women serving as "Platform Girls" and being admonished about not fraternizing. Occasionally, volunteers would put their names and addresses into popcorn balls that the men took on the train, but only one romance led to a wedding as far as anyone knows.

Chronicled by archivists and historians, good records were kept. A wrecking ball took down the Union Pacific Depot on November 21, 1973—demolishing the canteen and the memories overnight. As the distance between the time of the canteen and the present time grew to nearly 60 years, NET decided it was time to produce a documentary. "The Canteen Spirit" is a great documentary—but it is the impact of an involved community that is the real story.

The documentary is the story of the canteen, told by those who were the canteen. Women who served people, and men and women who were served, are together in this extraordinary work. The process of engaging these men and women to tell their story involved reaching out to many others—and in so doing, the interest, enthusiasm and engagement in the project grew. The documentary production and preview were done within full view and with wide participation by the community. More than 400 donors contributed $30,000 toward the project—with leadership gifts from the North Platte Lincoln County Convention and Visitors' Bureau, the North Platte Chamber of Commerce, and the Mid-Nebraska Community Foundation. At the time of the preview, July 23, 2004, more than 100 survivors—and 200 "Canteen girls"—attended a ceremony at the North Platte Canteen Memorial Park followed by a big band dance.

At that ceremony, Rod Bates, President and General Manager of NET, gave NET Partner Awards to the lead funders, citing their role in making "The Canteen Spirit" a reality. In his remarks, Bates affirmed the beginning of a new era in NET's outreach to the community: "This film truly belongs to each one of you, and your families and this generous community. The idea for the film was conceived here—by people like Keith Blackledge and other community leaders who championed the need to remember what was done here over sixty years ago. The funds to make the film were raised here, under the leadership and cooperative efforts of the Mid-Nebraska Community Foundation, the Lincoln County Convention and Visitors Bureau and the North Platte Area Chamber of Commerce. And most importantly, this film was made possible by each one of you, who have given your time, your money and your hearts to once again welcome strangers into your community to celebrate North Platte's enduring Canteen Spirit.

"Elaine Wolf, one of Nebraska pubic broadcasting's great friends, recently made this point more eloquently than I ever could. Elaine said, 'All of us need to begin giving within our own communities, Because great institutions and communities don't just come out of the blue. They are built. And it's people's desire to give and to serve that builds them.'

"We at NET value service to others above all else. When people contribute money in support of our services, we want them to believe that it's not just a gift they're making, but an investment—an investment that returns its value many times to the communities we are proud to serve. On behalf of all of the community partners and all of my colleagues at NET, thank you for sharing this extraordinary experience."

NET is now poised to go beyond fundraising.

These case studies are the tip of the iceberg. Other stories could be told about countless organizations across the United States and around the world whose programs and practices have achieved deeper, greater and lasting community impact.

TRENDS TO ANTICIPATE IN NONPROFIT DEVELOPMENT AND FUNDRAISING

As we have seen, the nonprofit or public benefit sector is growing in its impact in the United States and around the globe. Human, social, medical, educational, environmental, cultural, and other needs have increased as the traditional sources of support have diminished. Fortunately, the awareness of philanthropy has increased along with these needs, and the willingness of those with wealth and influence to make social investments in our sector is growing. More on this in Chapter 12, the Afterword.

As we trend spot for the early twenty-first century, we can anticipate these nine pressures and opportunities among others that are sure to arise:

1. *There will be increased emphasis on responsible regulation and legislation of nonprofit activities.*

The corporate scandals of the late twentieth and early twenty-first century were not limited to for-profit organizations; problems with United Way of America and United Ways in several communities, financial issues with the Baptist Health Foundation, and personnel compensation and contract challenges among nonprofits that ended up on the front pages of national and local newspapers have led to a tightening of requirements and regulations. In California, Senate Bill 1262, passed in October 2004 for implementation in January 2005, is changing the way nonprofits in the state organize their boards, review their finances, and conduct their fundraising. Sarbanes-Oxley, federal legislation aimed at for-profit corporations and boards, is seeping into the nonprofit sector. Calls for greater nonprofit accountability are coming not only from government, but also from the press, the public, and nonprofits themselves. According to Evelyn Brody, in a paper prepared for the State of America's Nonprofit Sector Project, a joint undertaking of the Nonprofit Sector and Philanthropy Program of the Aspen Institute, and Les Salamon, of Johns Hopkins University, this increasing burden of responsibility is a positive sign of the sector's development. Brody submits that nonprofits must now devote more "care and resources to earning the trust of their constituents and the public."[2] A study conducted by Brody in 2002 explored models and strategies for nonprofit accountability and discussed the impact of key stakeholder groups, including government, the nonprofit sector itself, and nonprofit boards.[3]

2. *Communities will expect nonprofits to play an increasingly important role as community builders, filling in for important government functions that will be unfunded. Nonprofits also will be expected to build strong and financially solvent coalitions of mission-directed organizations that are worthy of community investment.*

Government support of community causes will probably never return to the levels once available. Federal priorities have shifted; many states, counties, and communities are struggling to avoid bankruptcy; and nonprofits are called on to provide the safety net when programs are severely cut. This requires reorganization, a new approach to social investment, and new messages. Our communities are looking to us to join forces as similar organizations addressing the same mission. But these mergers and coalitions are not occurring rapidly enough. Although we can point to some success stories—two muse-ums in southern California that merged, a few independent schools that combined in the Northeast, and two Catholic universities in Minnesota that are sharing facilities, cur-riculum, and essential student services—for the most part nonprofits continue to be very territorial and unwilling to look at the broader purpose of our organizations: to meet the community needs that are implicit in our mission. Striking among recent positive col-laborations was the 2004 merger of WNET and WLIW, two public television stations serving New York City and Long Island. Their unique approach to resource and market sharing is a model. Community issues have to be addressed, and the sector has to find the best ways to organize to solve problems and provide services. We are change agents, and yet we resist change. We need to create a community vision for children, the aging, the arts, the environment, and other pressing aspects of a healthy society that transcends indi-vidual organizations. Coming together around that vision will increase our impact and potential for social investment. Our current fragmentation and competition is not the way to solve the overwhelming needs that many communities now face. Consider ways to become a catalyst for change, even if that means merging or collaborating with other sim-ilar organizations.

3. Donors will continue to focus on fewer organizations but make larger gifts.

Predicted in the first edition of this book, this statement was remarkably accurate. From universities to grassroots agencies, we have seen that donors want to perceive the impact of their giving and so are concentrating their investments. In spite of economic downturns and unstable national and international conditions, we are still seeing mega-gifts directed toward a single or few institutions. These transformational investments are funded by donors who buy into the mission of particular organizations and want to see them thrive. It will become increasingly important to practice excellent stewardship to retain donors.

4. Nonprofits will not only have to provide services and be accountable to their communities, they also will need to continually educate new potential investors about the joy of giving and the impact they can have on their communities.

Nonprofits will have to define philanthropy and the role organizations play in sup-porting philanthropic investment. As we have effectively repositioned the sector as a vital partner in meeting community needs and affecting our community's vitality, we now must educate people about our impact. We speak comfortably of "reach" (number of families treated, number of elderly served, the geography of our outreach); now we must also speak clearly about impact: what is different for those families, how these elderly citizens responded, how communities across the state or region are bettered by what we have done. Story-telling and statistics combine into a powerful educational tool, one that can shape suc-ceeding generations of investors. This educational effort will require new paradigms for communication—tapping into the vast electronic resources that provide new opportuni-ties for fast and segmented information—and new commitments on the part of organi-zations to gather information about their impact and promote it in the community.

5. Combined fundraising campaigns in corporations and communities will continue to be questioned and their results will decline.

Donors want more participation in the allocation of their contributions and a stronger relationship with organizations they fund. United Way and other combined funding programs will face continued challenges. Community foundations, with their donor-designated funds, will be an increasingly attractive option for those who still want to give funds as a block for distribution by an organization. The lower administration costs at community foundations ensure that more of the donor's money goes to the designated agencies. The astronomical growth of family foundations (more than double in the last decade, from 20,000 to 40,000) and in donor-advised funds reflects the growing social-investor attitude among donors.

6. Organizations must be more and more issue and mission focused, with a high results orientation.

Donors are increasingly seeing themselves as investors in organizations that are addressing the issues they care about and want to see substantial return on their investment by understanding what their dollars are doing. The Bill and Melinda Gates Foundation is very clear about its priorities (global health and education), as are others, such as Cate Muther's Three Guineas Fund (women and girls). Annual reports, solicitation materials, and all outreach must be based on the issues being addressed and impact of gifts on the long-term resolution of the needs surrounding those issues.

7. Volunteerism will continue to change, but will remain a major force in the success of major gifts programs in spite of increasingly professional staff.

Emphasis in volunteering will be on partnerships between board and staff to increase the amount of personal contact with donors. As more demands are placed on volunteers in their own work and lives, and as more professional skills are available to nonprofits through those volunteers, nonprofits need to be savvy about making the best use of volunteered time. Whether on a volunteer-to-volunteer level or staff-volunteer level, all respect for commitments of time and energy need to be based in mutual respect for the other demands on people's lives. Volunteers want a return on their time investment—an affirmation of their values, a sense of satisfaction, the feeling of a job well done, the visibility of results. Appropriate reinforcement and rewards will keep volunteers interested and loyal, but the best tool for forging a long-lasting relationship is respecting a volunteer's time. Be clear about your expectations, generous in your materials and other support, and accommodating of unanticipated changes in a volunteer's life or schedule.

8. Donors will increasingly feel and express a need to belong: not only through their gifts but by offering their opinions, ideas, and counsel.

Organizations must be prepared to embrace the donor not only as a source of money, but as a source of guidance. Social investors, eager for return on their investment, are making accountability demands as indicated elsewhere. However, let us not forget that gifts are symbols of a deeper desire for a relationship with organizations that help social investors fulfill their dreams for their communities. We have to provide adequate information and be honest evaluators, but we also need to "encourage the heart" at the same time.[4] Giving is both a rational and an emotional process; in our zeal to comply with accountability and transparency demands, we cannot forget to feed the passion.

9. We have seen only the initial impact of technology in improving our capacity to communicate with potential and continuing investors; the role will increase as technology continues to grow.

Since the outpouring of Web-based giving that occurred after the 9/11 terrorist attacks in the United States and more recently after the Tsunami of December 2004, the growth in comfort and confidence levels for online giving has accelerated. The shopper-to-buyer conversion has broken through a barrier as people have responded with urgency to the need to relieve devastation and grief. As a giving tool, online is growing; however, most online donors still say a personal contact is important to them in making and renewing online gifts. Although online solicitation for very large gifts is relatively new and not widely used, there is a growing use of Web sites and e-mail in the awareness building and information dissemination about planned giving. Astonishing things are still ahead, and we will watch and wait as a new generation of philanthropists, raised with the Internet and comfortable with surfing the Web, look for ways to participate in philanthropy. For continued relationship building, as a stewardship tool, Web sites and e-mail communications will grow in importance. Technology has also affected our ability to learn more about our donors quickly. As described elsewhere in this book, more sophisticated methods for prospect research will continue to raise ethical questions. Organizations need to be very mindful of the issues of ethics and the potential for technology to invade privacy.

10. Countries in western and eastern Europe and throughout the world will increasingly emphasize the philanthropic responsibility of their citizens.

Eastern Europe and Hungary in particular have focused in the last decade on developing a civil society with philanthropy as the catalyst. Seeded by funding in several instances by American philanthropist George Soros, these efforts are now taking flight. Decline of government support in most parts of the world and the dismantling of decades-old infrastructure in eastern Europe and parts of South America, Africa, and Asia have created an awareness of the need for education about philanthropy. Annually, more than 700 representatives of over 50 countries gather in The Netherlands for the International Fundraising Congress. Over the past five years, the progress these organizations are making to provide state-of-the-art opportunities for social investment, more emphasis on transformational gifts,[5] and increased involvement of citizens in philanthropy is a great sign of hope. Combating AIDS, poverty, hunger, oppression, violence, lack of education, and lack of health services is no easy job, but the tools for success are now available.

SUMMARY

Going beyond fundraising requires new commitments and new paradigms. We are reminded by sages to dream no small dreams and to hitch our wagons to stars. Ultimately we are confronted with the reality of the needs we are meeting and our capacity to meet them. It is the gap between the desire and the reality that we strive to close.

There are two bottom lines in all of fundraising: the money raised and the values secured. And there are two more key benefits as well: the joy of asking and the joy of giving. Both are essential emotions in the advancement of our sector. When people are moved to ask and give in the context of investment and results, they know they have made a difference. They have touched lives. They have made it possible for the hungry to be fed, the religious to be served, children to be educated, seniors to be comforted. When people give in that knowledge, they give part of themselves.

We must be stewards of the gifts we receive: the gifts of money and the gifts of heart. Build those relationships. Curry your passion so it is inspiring to others, remembering that commitment is sustained passion.

You will then travel beyond fundraising and know the value and results of development.

NOTES

1. Kay Sprinkel Grace and Alan L. Wendroff, *High Impact Philanthropy: How Donors, Boards, and Nonprofit Organizations Can Transform Communities* (John Wiley & Sons, 2000).
2. Evelyn Brody, "Accountability, Effectiveness, and Public Trust," in Lester M. Salamon, ed., *The State of Nonprofit America* (Brookings Institution in collaboration with the Aspen Institute, 2002).
3. *Ibid.*
4. James Kouzes and Barry Posner, *The Leadership Challenge,* 3rd edition (Jossey-Bass, 2003).
5. Grace and Wendroff, *op cit.*

CHAPTER 12

Afterword

Beyond Fundraising: Philanthropy and Social Entrepreneurship in the Twenty-First Century

Increasingly, philanthropy is back in the news. Pushed into the background temporarily during the depths of the economic downturn at the turn of the twenty-first century and by the focus on combating global terrorism, philanthropy is once again capturing the interest, energy, and resources of those who are concerned with the need for social change and improvement of the quality of life. There has been a great deal of publicity and broad fascination with the intergenerational transfer of wealth under way and anticipated, including an estimated $8 trillion that will be available for philanthropic purposes. We have seen and read the results of philanthropic investment (George Soros's Open Society efforts in Hungary have been so successful that a number of organizations in that country are now successfully on their own; the Gates Foundation's commitment to global health and education is revealing the impact of private investment in areas previously left to government attention) and gained renewed respect for what is possible. And, in the midst of all this, and encouraged by it, we have seen the robust initiation of a new kind of philanthropic approach, social entrepreneurship. The power of philanthropy is ours to develop.

The philosophy, principles, and strategies in this book can and have moved organizations into realizing that power. Since the first edition was published in 1997, staff members, students, and board leaders around the world have embraced the concepts and implemented new practices that have raised the perception and success of their organizations in their communities. Awareness of the importance of nonprofits in meeting critical needs, balancing service delivery, and providing outreach is increasing, and the subsequent willingness by individuals and institutions to invest in our work is rising.

In communities around the world, philanthropic principles incubated for centuries in the United States are flourishing thanks to the growth of professional organizations and the impact of globalization. In spite of the jarring economic, social, global, and health changes we experienced in the last decade of the twentieth century and the first few years of this century, philanthropy, as a solution to the chronic and emerging issues of our time, is thriving. Although giving was down in 2002 in the United States, it is showing signs of steady recovery. However, at the end of 2004, it was more than the money being given that was drawing attention to philanthropy: The greatest impact was the passion philanthropy was creating, the people it was engaging, and its potential for growing impact around the globe. As an issues-driven, values-based, and mission-focused phenomenon that has the capacity to be the single strongest influence on our society in the early twenty-first century, philanthropy is in a new era that will be characterized increasingly by social entrepreneurship.

SOCIAL ENTREPRENEURSHIP

Concurrent with the growth in business entrepreneurship that marked the astonishing economic achievements of the late twentieth century, many of the same individuals who were generating phenomenal ideas, products, and wealth began to turn their attention to the chronic problems of our local, national, and global communities. Founders and employees of companies, financially enriched by their own success, sought ways not only to give back money to the causes they cared about but also to effect change.

Books have been written on the topic of social entrepreneurship, and Web sites abound.[1] Centers at Stanford, Harvard, and Duke universities and elsewhere in the United States and abroad have drawn thinkers and practitioners to develop scholarship and strategies for extending the impact of social entrepreneurship. One of the leaders in the social entrepreneurship movement is the Skoll Foundation. Founded by Jeff Skoll, first employee and president of eBay, the mission of the foundation is "to advance positive social change by investing in social entrepreneurs." The Skoll Foundation made a $7.5 million gift to the Said Business School at Oxford University in 2003 to create the Skoll Centre of Social Entrepreneurship. Its online community for the social sector is called Social Edge (*www.socialedge.org*). Social Edge regularly sponsors open dialogue on pressing social issues. In an open dialogue on September 22, 2003, Sally Osberg, president of the Skoll Foundation, wrote:

> *Like business entrepreneurs, social entrepreneurs see and act upon what others miss: opportunities to improve systems, create solutions, invent new approaches. Like business entrepreneurs, they are also intensely focused and hard-driving, even relentless in their pursuit of their visions. Unlike business entrepreneurs, however, they operate within a social rather than a purely economic context, which means they have limited access to capital and traditional market support systems. As a result, social entrepreneurs must be exceptionally skilled at mustering resources—human, financial and political. Ultimately, social entrepreneurs produce significant returns. The results of their efforts transform existing realities, open up new pathways for the marginalized and disadvantaged, and unlock society's potential to effect positive change.*

Although early descriptions of social entrepreneurship focused on the generation of earned income to reduce reliance on contributed income, most of the operating centers in the United States and abroad take a broader look at the concept. Duke University's Fuqua School of Business, home of the Center for the Advancement of Social Entrepreneurship (CASE), states that social entrepreneurship is "an approach to creating social value that embraces the fundamental principles of entrepreneurship" (*www.fuqua.duke.edu*).

Ashoka (*www.ashoka.org*) was an early entry into the social entrepreneurship field. Pioneering both in the United States and abroad, it is now operating globally through stipends offered to 1,400 fellows in 48 countries who work on pressing issues of social change and are "transforming the lives of millions." Their approach is summarized by Richard Steckel, whom Ashoka quotes: "Remember, 'nonprofit' is an IRS classification. . . . It's not a management style."[2] Ashoka describes the work of a social entrepreneur in this way. Social entrepreneurs:

- Change the system
- Spread the solution
- Persuade entire societies to take new leaps
- Are not content just to give a fish or teach how to fish—they will not rest until they have revolutionized the fishing industry

Related areas to social entrepreneurship include social enterprise (greater focus on sources of earned income) and social innovation (often synonymous with social entrepreneurship).

So, what does all this have to do with going beyond fundraising? Plenty.

WHAT WE FACE, WHAT WE MUST DO

We are facing a time of unprecedented expectations: service delivery, program accountability, unprecedented requirements for collaboration, strategic partnerships, financial stability, and measurable impact. There are two critical approaches to meeting these expectations. One is internal, the other is external.

The first approach is to make the commitment to go beyond fundraising. Grow relationships; expand the commitment to development; be more mission, vision, and values focused; engage your board in new ways; implement systems that will give you the time and freedom to innovate; approach all donors as investors; and communicate the return on investment. Put away the tin cup, position your organization as a vital change agent meeting needs in your community, and be creative in the ways you raise and earn money for your organization. Doing this will position you for the future: It will brand you as a social entrepreneur and innovator, and the interest in your work and your vision will increase at first steadily but later with astonishing acceleration.

The second approach is to collaborate, cooperate, and mesh your mission with those of organizations that are doing like or similar activities in your community. Sacrifice territory and ego and embrace, instead, the larger mission: the need you are meeting in the community. The more you can work together with other organizations that are meeting the same need to ensure the greatest possible impact in the arts, culture, education, health, environment, social, or other needs, the stronger your community will be come. This is not a time for silos or costly competition. In the maelstrom of the dramatic changes we have already experienced in this new century, the more our sector pulls together, the greater impact it will have. Social entrepreneurship, characterized by these behaviors, invites investment in ways you have never dreamed were possible. Finding partners in the community—those with wealth, vision, energy, and excitement—will leverage your resources in innovative ways. Get familiar with what the social entrepreneurship movement is about, and become connected. Join Social Edge or other forum and exchange ideas with others, and subscribe to journals such as the *Stanford Social Innovation Review* (*www.ssireview.com*).

Traditional philanthropy will remain at the core of our principles, but our actions must be geared to this century and to the host of new investors who have come out of the entrepreneurial explosion of the late twentieth century and expect our organizations to be more entrepreneurial, nimble, swift, and accessible. Although after the "dot-bomb" economic downturn and the terrorist attacks on the United States, we worried that the passion of those new to wealth and philanthropy had faded, what we are finding is that it did not go away, it was just on hold. All that has been written about the "new philanthropists" remains true.[3] It is now our task to engage them and delight them with our vision and responsiveness and our willingness to be change agents.

Beyond fundraising is a foundation: On it you can build an organization that will be more successful in generating funds and engaging volunteers. But let it also be a launch pad for a future that is not only brighter for you but for your community.

We have a distance to go. For many of the newer philanthropists, in the time of their greatest wealth and social awareness, the existing nonprofit sector did not present itself as a capable outcomes-oriented solution to the human, health, educational, social, cultural, environmental, or other needs in which they wanted to invest their money and their time. It was a frustrating experience for many of them, and some created their own operating foundations to address problems directly without going through already-established organizations. This is not to paint the entire sector with the same brush. Those who have worked in the sector and those who are its observers and funders know that many public benefit corporations have and continue to meet community needs with great skill and accountability. Although some nonprofits (please, let us stop calling them charities) may not have been as responsive as they should have been, and others failed the transparency test, there were and are many doing an incredible job against sharp odds and with measurable, significant results.

Now, the good news is that through an increasing awareness of the principles of social entrepreneurship and the pressure of increased demands, diminished resources, and competition, we are moving closer to our investors' expectations.

It is our charge, then, to embrace the principles of social entrepreneurship that are appropriate to our mission and organizations and to educate this new generation (whatever their age) of philanthropists. We must inform them of our goals and outcomes in measurable terms, and we must enroll them in our vision. We must develop opportunities to participate for those impatient for a better world. We must help them understand the tremendous economic and societal impact of the "third sector" and let them know that we are a good investment.

We are so very fortunate in the United States and in the world to have an engaged philanthropic sector and the financial resources to make a difference in lives and communities. At the annual conference of the the Resource Alliance (formerly the International Fundraising Group) in October 2004, more than 700 delegates from 55 countries met with a mutuality of passion, conscience, and commitment that portends well for the future of nongovernmental agencies and nonprofits worldwide. Their stories of increasing interest among global investors and the impact they are beginning to have in their regions and countries are more than hopeful; they are brilliant.

It would be a pity to lose this moment because we are unable or unwilling to change the way we do things, or are too slow to adapt our systems and structure to the more nimble and measurable practices of the twenty-first century. The pressure is already on the sector. The transfer of wealth that is under way and the generation of wealth that has occurred in the past two decades point to new opportunities for nonprofits, but new responsibilities as well. Increased expectations must result in increased performance; and increased community needs can only ratchet up many already-strained systems. We cannot stop the tide; we need to build better boats and navigation systems to ride it to the best harbors.

WHAT DONOR-INVESTORS MUST DO

Those with the capacity to change lives and communities through their philanthropy need to learn more about the existing vehicles in which they can invest. Too often, the entire sector suffers because of the poor performance or one or a few nonprofits. There are already nearly 1.5 million nonprofits in the United States, and the number throughout the rest of the world is growing, too. Creating a new organization to implement a funder's vision may not always be the best way to solve a problem; some of the more successful investments have been made not only in the *program* of a particular organization, but in the *people* who are delivering that program. Management and technical assistance and other capacity-building grants strengthen both the people and the program, and ultimately ensure a strong and measurable impact in the community. Donor-investors should consider this opportunity before walking away from an existing organization whose mission is strong but whose infrastructure is immature or weak.

Donor-investors must continue to set standards, ask for results, and carefully assess where they put their investments. Greater knowledge of and comfort with the sector will ease some of the difficulties eager investors have in trying to find an organization with which they feel comfortable pursuing a shared vision.

In the midst of imposed regulations, such as Sarbanes-Oxley and California's Senate Bill 1262, there is also increased self-monitoring of the sector. More and more organizations are imposing sterner standards on themselves. Strategic planning, budgeting, annual reports, and other goal-setting and measuring strategies are becoming routine in responsible organizations. This book provides some basic suggestions for planning and budgeting, but thoughtful organizations will seek more detailed information or counsel. Donor-investors need to ask for evidence of sound fiscal and program management, but there is more. Although nonprofit organizations are increasingly and appropriately run more like businesses, certain aspects of these organizations fall outside the business model. Donor-investors need to understand the strong values basis and the immense human and social capital involved in nonprofits and embrace those differences as the distinguishing and powerful characteristics that identify the third sector. Making a site visit, meeting with clients, sitting in the lunch room (not just at the boardroom table) are experiences that can go a long way in exciting donor-investors about the uniqueness and importance of the nonprofit sector.

The breadth of potential philanthropy—and the wealth of mutual pleasure and benefit to both organizations and their donor-investors—has been barely tapped. Much has been written about the end of checkbook philanthropy and the beginning of hands-on philanthropy, a shift we applaud. The more donor-investors understand about the sector, and the more nonprofit organizations move toward management and delivery models that reflect an understanding of social entrepreneurship and guarantee measurable results in the community, the greater will be the impact of philanthropy.

What Communities Must Do

Communities must define the needs of their citizens and translate those needs for nonprofits and for donor-investors so there is a three-way partnership for social entrepreneurship and high-impact philanthropy.[4] A partnership that welcomes all participants as equals will help invigorate the nonprofit sector, giving it responsibility for meeting community needs by engaging and nurturing donor-investors.

Mending and strengthening social, human, and health causes or issues specific to geographical communities is not the only way social entrepreneurship can make a difference.

In 2000, John W. Kluge, billionaire chairman of the Metromedia International telecommunications and entertainment company, gave $60 million to the Library of Congress in Washington, D.C., to create the John W. Kluge Center. Its goal is to assemble the finest minds characterized by broad historical or philosophical vision and capable of providing dispassionate wisdom and intelligent mediation of the knowledge in the library's collections and of the information streaming into the library via the Internet. Fellows and scholars have the opportunity through their residence both to distill wisdom from the rich resources of the library and to stimulate, through informal conversations and meetings, members of Congress, their support staffs, and the broader public policy community. The Center's scholars and fellows will help bridge the divide between knowledge and power.

The Kluge Center seeks to be catalytic rather than bureaucratic and to deepen rather than merely recycle the work of the many other fine institutions and individuals in the Washington, D.C., area who also seek to narrow the gap between thinkers and doers. The center encourages its resident scholars to make wide-ranging use of the print and electronic multilingual, multimedial, multidisciplinary resources of the library and to bring their inquiries and rich learning into the intellectual life of the library, the Congress, and the nation.

Resident in the Kluge Center are senior distinguished scholars, occupying the Kluge chairs, postdoctoral fellows, and such other appropriate categories as the librarian may designate.

The impetus for this gift was the belief that American self-government was created by a small group of people who were thinkers as well as doers, engaged in the world of affairs and the world of ideas. The Library of Congress, at the beginning of its third century, now has an unprecedented opportunity to help revive this traditional American interaction through the insight and benefaction of John W. Kluge. In an age where power and influence depend increasingly on knowledge, citizens and their leaders must rely more on wits than weapons to sustain global progress. Leaders need to tap the wisdom of mature scholars whose judgment and objectivity will bring fresh perspectives to government.

The John W. Kluge Center at the Library of Congress is fostering this mutually enriching relationship between scholars and political leaders. It is also witness to this new kind of entrepreneurial philanthropic investment.

Kluge, 85, helped the library raise about $160 million during the 10-year period preceding his gift. At the time of the gift, Dr James H. Billington, the librarian, remarked to the *New York Times* about the potential for bringing government and scholarship into a new dialogue. "These two worlds just kind of fell apart in the 60's and haven't really come back together again," Dr. Billington said as he explained his new program for the "ultimate mix in political town and academic gown." The potential impact of this gift is vast; much has already been accomplished and is reported on the Web site of the Kluge Center (*www.loc.gov/loc/kluge/kluge-about.html*). The Library of Congress had built a relationship with this social investor, through his volunteering, that helped Kluge know that his investment was needed and would have an impact. Defying our usual image of governmental lack of entrepreneurship, the Library of Congress positioned this investment well for Kluge. Engagement of volunteers and investors and precise definition of needs that need to be met can combine with very happy results.

THE LAST WORD

Build the base for social entrepreneurship and full participation in the exciting vision of twenty-first century philanthropy by taking the steps to go beyond fundraising. Visionary communities working with well-marketed and managed nonprofits and inspired donor-investors can ensure a much better future for our communities. Communities may be geographical, social, intellectual, cultural, or any other grouping of people, issues, and ideas. They can cross all global boundaries or exist in one town. What is essential is the commitment to development, engagement, investment, and results that focus on the impact of what fulfilled vision can produce.

Although education and health continue to dominate giving, it is also important to note that gifts like John Kluge's to the Library of Congress are igniting the intellectual capital of our increasingly connected world. And investment in the world's artistic and educational institutions, heritage, and future is also being made. From Cambodian temples painstakingly restored through entrepreneurial partnerships forged with the United Nations and private investors, to National Public Radio (NPR), whose entrepreneurial we-can-do-it attitude attracted and secured a $200 million bequest from the late Joan B. Kroc, we know that development works and that mere fundraising is simply not enough. Relationship building, visioning, outreach, and accountability need to mingle in an entrepreneurial approach that will inform and change the future not only of philanthropy, but perhaps our world.

It is an inspiring thought. The moment is now, and the time and the challenge are ours. Let us work together to go beyond fundraising and to transform our communities through philanthropy.

NOTES

1. J. Gregory Dees, Jed Emerson, and Peter Economy, *Strategic Tools for Social Entrepreneurs: Enhancing the Performance of Your Enterprising Nonprofit* (John Wiley & Sons, 2002); J. Gregory Dees, Jed Emerson, and Peter Economy, *Enterprising Nonprofits: A Toolkit for Social Entrepreneurs* (John Wiley & Sons, 2001).

2. Richard Steckel, Robin Simons, and Peter Lengsfelder, *Filthy Rich and Other Nonprofit Fantasies: Changing the Way Nonprofits Do Business in the 90s* (Ten Speed Press, 1989).

3. Kay Sprinkel Grace and Alan L. Wendroff, *High Impact Philanthropy: How Donors, Boards, and Nonprofit Organizations Can Transform Communities* (John Wiley & Sons, 2000).

4. *Ibid.*

Index